D1552592

Jerome Schneider's Complete Guide to Offshore Money Havens

by Jerome Schneider

Second edition ISBN 0-933560-04-4

Published by
WFI Corporation
357 S. Robertson Blvd.
Beverly Hills, CA 90211
Telephone: (800) 421-4177

Trade discounts available on 25 or more copies

Jerome Schneider's Complete Guide to Offshore Money Havens

Author's Acknowledgments

This book was written with the encouragement and constructive comments of many people. I owe a debt of gratitude to the many business associates and colleagues who suggested that it be written. The members of my personal staff have earned a special thanks. In particular, I wish to express my appreciation to Max Benavidez and Kate Vozoff for their editorial guidance. I must also thank Howard Fisher for his legal insights into matters both taxing and complex. The helpful staff at Mead Data in Los Angeles also deserve a thank you. Finally, but perhaps most importantly, I wish to thank Jaycee Cooper for her continued support and patience.

TABLE OF CONTENTS

CHAPTER ONE   11
The Coming Apocalypse

CHAPTER TWO   35
The Offshore Solution

CHAPTER THREE   57
The Open Door: Doing Business Offshore

CHAPTER FOUR   81
The Profit Incentive

CHAPTER FIVE   107
In Pursuit Of True Financial Privacy

CHAPTER SIX   131
Offshore Tax Protection

CHAPTER SEVEN   155
Protecting Your Assets

CHAPTER EIGHT   179
Eight Steps To Offshore Success

CHAPTER NINE   201
Offshore Money Havens: Where To Go

CHAPTER TEN   225
Investors On File

CHAPTER ELEVEN   251
Getting Started The Easy Way

APPENDIX   273
How to Open A Foreign Bank Account

INDEX   331

Introduction

Introduction

Bankruptcies. Foreclosures. Defaults. These frightening words are now commonplace from New York to California. Times are tough and they're going to get tougher. I recently heard about one super-successful investor whose net worth had as many digits as his Social Security number. That was before the current economic disaster hit him. Now he lives off his Social Security check.

We are headed toward a financial disaster. I predict that over the next few years, we will experience the decisive economic shakeout of this century. It will be one of the worst downturns in history, and it will test the guts of every investor from Hong Kong to Vienna.

I also predict that, even in these worst of times, some of us will survive financially. In fact, some of us will flourish. And the critical factor in determining whether you win or lose is internationalization of assets. In other words, taking your assets into the offshore arena.

By offshore investment I mean banking, borrowing and investing in those countries that have laws and regulations that are more favorable to you than those of the country you are operating in now. It makes little difference whether you live in the United States, Europe or Asia. Offshore simply means doing business where the laws are most conducive to your financial goals.

Unless you're willing to be brutally swept away by the coming economic storms, you must protect what you have, and that simply cannot be done with an onshore perspective. The U.S. and other affiliated economies are too shaky, too tenuous, too vulnerable. Money maintained in such environments is nothing more than playboard currency in a financial Disneyland.

If you own a viable business or have accumulated valuable assets, then you have a lot to lose in the coming economic wreakage that will soon be all that's left of the

U.S. and affiliated economies. To outlast the odds, you must operate from a position that compensates for your weaknesses and leverages your strengths. And that is a question of perspective.

It's for you and thousands of other investors like you that I've written this book. In the pages that follow, I think you will find the outlines of a realistic and exciting asset protection strategy that can see you through the coming years of crisis. This is a recipe book, you might say, because it will teach you that a bunch of lemons really can be turned into lemonade.

It's also a how-to book. In my sixteen years as a financial consultant, I've found that people are only somewhat interested in any economist's philosophical perspectives on market upswings and downturns. What they really want is a step-by-step plan for protecting what they have and adding to it. So every chapter of this book tries to tell you exactly what you need to do and how you need to do it.

Hand-in-hand with protecting your assets, however, is maintaining the value of those assets. A million dollars is only worth a million dollars in a prospering market. When the market evaporates, that money loses value like water running through a sieve. With that in mind, I have tried to offer advice on how you can make sure that assets retain (and actually increase) their value — even as we sit on the brink of an economic apocalypse.

This revised edition also adds to the last version a number of new and very specific suggestions for sound portfolio management. The international marketplace is constantly changing and expanding. That means there are new opportunities available that should be capitalized upon now. One of the important new recommendations is the foreign asset protection trust. I have devoted an entire chapter to this concept: what it is, why it works, and how it can be established.

I have also added material on how to start your own offshore investment fund. Again, the message is simple: if you want to be successful, you must remain alert to the profitable opportunities available to you in the offshore market. The offshore investment fund is proving to be a unique and timely means to raise capital, increase returns on various investment instruments, decrease tax liabilities and obtain a significant level of financial and personal privacy. With the collapse of the credit markets, there is an additionnal and clear benefit to the investment: the ability to raise capital. I try to emphasize the mechanics of obtaining and operating an investment fund because I believe that this is the wave of the future.

Apart from these few important developments, I'm happy to report that the offshore investment market still operates by the same rules and offers the same advantages that it did when I first started out as a financial consultant in the 1970s. Of course, I have adapted them to the changing economic currents and financial tradewinds. But my advice to my clients and readers then was based on certain financial principles, and I still follow those same principles today because they continue to constitute the backbone of financial protection and success.

Slowly, the economic establishment of this country seems to be coming around to my side. Not long ago, many of this country's three-piece-suit consultants and bankers viewed the offshore concept as "way ahead of its time," and only for hardened risk-takers. Today, that's changed. Offshore financial involvements are now accepted by everyone as a part of big league economics. Today, all the smartest and most prudent investors have a good portion of their assets offshore.

Researchers are also getting in on the act. A study recently released by Columbia University's business school shows that investors who mix their holdings between domestic and offshore do much better than those who invest only within the borders of their home country.

All this strikes me as incredibly funny, really, because the offshore option has always proved itself to be the one sure-fire route to financial profits, privacy and tax protection. It's just that now, as the domestic tide turns from bad to worse, even the stuffiest Manhattan investment advisors are being forced to see the offshore solution as the best way out of a giant mess.

That's what it takes sometimes: being forced. I remember one investor, John "Buzz" McNally, who came into my office in early 1981 for a free private consultation — just before the last major recession. John was, as the expression goes, a mountain of a man. Big and ruddy-faced, he was a larger-than-life businessman. (The way they grow in Texas, where he was from.) With his cowboy suits, snakeskin boots and huge turquoise-laden belt buckles, he was a sight to behold.

But even big guys like Buzz can quake with fear.

When he stepped into my office that day, I could see that he was upset. He was beside himself with uncertainty. A venture capitalist, John's business was down. His sources of capital were drying up. Profits were off. He was beginning to lay off employees. An all-American, dyed-in-the-wool patriot, John had come to me as a last resort. And he had only one question: what can I do to save my assets?

After getting all the details from John, I sat down with my staff for a brainstorming session. I knew we had to come up with an answer — not just for Buzz McNally and his company but for all the clients that would probably be calling during the next few months. As I recall, things did work out fine. I remember reading about John years later in a trade publication and seeing that he had become financially secure.

What I recommended then is still sound advice: protect yourself by going offshore now, into the international market. Why? Because the U.S. economy is shattered due to the multi-trillion dollar debt and it will take years for all the pieces to be put back together.

In the last edition of this book, I made certain predictions. Among them, I foresaw the collapse of the junk bond market and the beginning of the S&L crisis. These were just early indicators of the economic chaos we are now facing. In such an environment, there is only one thing to keep uppermost in your mind: financial survival. It's a time to play it safe. That's why this revised edition of my book focuses on practical asset-saving advice.

I can tell you that by following my advice you can survive and prosper during the coming dark years. But time is of the essence. Of course, I could be wrong. The questions becomes: are you willing to risk everything on the chance that I am wrong? If your answer is no, then read on as fast as you can.

Jerome Schneider
Beverly Hills, California
June 1991

CHAPTER ONE

The Coming Apocalypse

"...the nation is about to face its toughest challenge since the Second World War. Right now is the time to prepare yourself for any eventuality. You should hope for the best, but prepare for the worst. Believe me, if current trends persist, the worst will indeed occur."

—Dr. Ravi Batra
Economist

There's a time bomb ticking in this country. Experts differ as to who set it, and the precise moment of explosion has not been determined. The initial blast is expected to hit New York City but, within hours, deadly explosions will be reported in every metropolitan center.

It will happen on some otherwise normal day, while we all go about the ordinary business of living our lives: showing up to work, fulfilling family responsibilities, enjoying a few hard-earned leisure pursuits. We'll hear the news and, oddly enough, many of us will react with indifference. The trouble isn't in our hometown, we'll think to ourselves. And with a fleeting sense of pity for those directly affected, we'll go to sleep that night without fear.

Unfortunately, that will probably be our last carefree slumber because, if the predictions are correct, this time bomb will have the destructive capability of a nuclear warhead. What's more, it will ultimately blow up in all our faces.

The time bomb to which I refer is, of course, our national economy. On the verge of literal collapse, it already threatens to destroy some of the oldest and most respected financial houses in the United States. Also among the captives in its undeclared war against America are a slew of internationally acknowledged money moguls, ingenious business giants who operate from one end of this country to the other. Together, these institutions and individuals make up the bulwarks of our domestic marketplace. When they do down, they'll take everybody with them.

Everybody but you, I hope, and a relatively small number of other forward-thinking investors who stop to see the writing on the wall.

You don't have to be financially destroyed by the 1990s. In fact, if you are careful, you can actually beat the odds and exit this century wealthier than you are today. But you have to make one essential move: you have to internationalize. Every reliable indicator points this country toward the most severe financial downturn since the 1930s. Many economists even go so far as to argue that the coming decade will bring harder times than the Great Depression. So if you confine yourself to the domestic market, you're on a sure course for disaster.

If, on the other hand, you take a rational look at investment opportunities available outside the bounds of your home country, you free yourself to operate globally. Granted, the coming crisis here at home will have a significant impact all around the world. But unlike Wall Street, foreign markets will continue to function and grow.

With your money strategically put to work for you in specific finacial centers abroad, you can avoid the worst of what lies ahead. You can protect what you already have, and aim for handsome (if not startling) economic gains. In truth, you may not reap the fortune you might have earned in better economic times, but you will stand to amass a sizable profit. Most important, you will position yourself to enter the next century comfortable and confident. That's a fate far better than the overnight bankruptcy that will befall a lot of Americans.

■A SLOW COUNTDOWN TO DISASTER

This economic crisis did not come about suddenly. Just the opposite, in fact. It has been building for a long time. It is rooted in bad financial decisions that have been made for the past fifty years — personally, on the corporate level and, most importantly, within government.

Actually, the beginning of our economic ailments goes back to the period immediately after the Second World War. In a manner that can only be described as "frenzied," Americans moved from the 1940s and into the 50s and 60s with money popping out of every pore. As a nation, we spent incredible sums on everything from suburban housing to space projects. Without a second thought, we used our tax dollars to educate poor youngsters, send adults to the moon, and support less-affluent governments all around the world.

At that time, we could afford it all, too. Extravagance and conspicuous consumption were possible because we had the revenue to support them. Now, all that has changed. In the last decade and a half, we have borrowed our way into deep debt and financial chaos. As the Gulf War showed quite clearly, we can't even pay for our own armed forces. We must ask other countries to help pay for the war.

When President Jimmy Carter left office in 1980, the United States was saddled with a higher rate of unemployment than most Americans could remember, a prime lending rate that exceeded 20 percent, double-digit inflation, and an international hostage crisis that nobody seemed able to solve. Put simply, this country was well on its way to internal fracture. Nevertheless, we had one good thing going for us: we were the most financially powerful nation on earth. Individuals and governments from every continent turned to us for money and got it.

By 1987, as President Ronald Reagan prepared to leave the White House, things were very different. On the positive side, many of the burdens brought about by Carter's Administration had been lifted. (Apparently.) And, as an added bonus, the U.S. stock market was soaring. What only a few of us seemed terribly concerned about back then was a U.S. foreign debt that just kept growing and the largest budget deficit in our national history!

During the Reagan Administration — in a span of just

eight years — this country went from being the world's biggest creditor to it biggest debtor. In 1981, we had net overseas assets of nearly $141 billion. By 1986, we had accumulated a foreign debt of just under $264 billion. That represents a total loss of more than $404 billion. Some countries did still owe us money, but we owed others much more.

The economic picture was equally worrisome on the domestic front. Despite all the campaign promises, America's median family income was no better in 1983 than it had been in 1973. Upper income families still constituted only 10 percent of the national population, and even among this top segment, prosperity was more an illusion than a reality. The average "wealthy" family income went up 24 percent — from $70,000 to almost $90,000. But it didn't matter much because the rate of personal debt was simultaneously reaching an all-time high. Most upper-income Americans found that their economic edge was swallowed up by the escalating cost of car loans, home mortgages, and insurance premiums.

It was only the top one percent of Americans who really benefited from the economic policies of the 1980s! Their annual family income in 1977 was "only" $301,000. By 1988, it had leaped more than 50 percent, to $452,000. Research done by *Financial Report* found that of the hundred highest salaries on Wall Street, the top annual pay was $250 million and the lowest was $3 million. The ultra-rich were doing very, very well.

Meanwhile, their effective federal tax rate dropped by 5.5 percent. With two years still to go in his Administration, Reagan had managed to ensure that the creme-de-la-creme of all U.S. households controlled 68 percent of our national wealth. Our wealth: yours and mine.

By reviving virtually the same economic policies as President Herbert Hoover (who, by the way, positioned us perfectly for the Great Depression), Ronald Reagan and his supply-side economic advisors tried to improve upon a financial experiment that had failed once before. They tried to make workers work harder and capitalists invest more — believing all along that unprecedented prosperity would follow. For its part, Congress played along by rewarding the nation's wealthiest with generous tax cuts.

Too bad for all of us: the experiment seems to have failed a second time.

Every reliable measuring stick indicates economic reversal from one end of the country to the other.

When President George Bush took the oath of office in 1988, our foreign debt had grown even beyond what Reaganomics could publically justify. We owed $500 billion — nearly double what we had outstanding just two years earlier. We were in debt to just about everyone: wealthy Japanese, Germans, Englishmen, Canadians, Arabs, Dutchmen, Taiwanese, and Koreans. What's more, the federal government showed no signs of reversing its course. Uncle Sam still borrows around $350 billion dollars a year just to stay afloat. Not to be left out, consumers and corporations were also eager to borrow and spend. They were $8 trillion in debt.

Yet, despite this apparent glut of available revenue, it was hard to find anybody anywhere who could find anything at all to tuck away in a savings account.

And so began to die the myth of Ronald Reagan. He had presented himself and his policies as the champion of the hard-working and productive American. Based on that message, the majority of wealthy entrepeneurs and investors supported him. Ultimately, though, they were given the short end of his stick. While the best perks went to the tiniest and most elite segment of this society, affluent men and women could only stand back and watch as their real income was dwarfed by their increasing burden of debt.

■TICK, TICK TICK...

During such times — times like this — consumers and investors look for signs that the people in charge are doing things right. But it's hard to take comfort from anything coming out of Washington these days. True, President Bush and Congress regularly scurry around, doing their best to get a dangerous situation under control. Their efforts, however, seem more of a gesture than anything else. It's all too little, and too late.

The struggle toward a balanced budget, toward any semblance of fiscal equilibrium, is waged in baby steps. In theory, everyone agrees that federal spending should be reduced and our total debt overcome. Just how we can accomplish that magical feat, however, remains unclear. Taxes will have to go up, that much is certain. (Whenever government fails to manage money properly, it's the already over-burdened taxpayer who suffers.) But who should be taxed how much to pay for all that Uncle Sam buys? And what should be eliminated from his ever-expanding shopping list? These are matters of endless political fighting and backroom negotiation.

The final outcome of the in-fighting over the 1991 budget was a joke! Even after all the cuts were made, only one budget area — defense — was actually reduced from the prior year's spending. (Now, with the success of the Patriot intercept system, that too will change.) Every other area received more money than ever before. Even more significant, despite the bitter political animosity that it took to trim the budget shortfall, experts estimate that we will be left with triple-digit deficits through (at least) the rest of the 1990s.

In the meantime, of course, we'll have to look for capital to keep operating. And with our current credit image — a foreign debt that may well reach $1 trillion by the time you read this — it's anyone's guess what will happen when other nations stop lending us money.

As this book goes to press, the United States is well into a recession. Technically, that means we've experienced two consecutive quarters of decline in final sales of all goods and services after adjusting for inflation. In everyday language, it just means we've lived through six straight months of a pervasive, persistent decline in economic activity. Employment is down, production has slowed and profits are meager, investment has tapered off, and consumer confidence is almost non-existent.

In the effort to stay solvent, major American companies have sliced costs to the bone and announced sweeping layoffs. Chase Manhattan, the second largest U.S. bank, had to let go 5,000 employees. That's 12 percent of its total work force. McDonnell Douglas, the number one defense contractor has slashed its payroll by 17,000 workers, or 13 percent of its work force.

Aggravating the slump is a worldwide credit crunch that affects everyone from individual auto shoppers to mom and pop businesses and multi-national corporations. Even the richest are feeling the pinch — banks and big-time developers who over-extended themselves a few years ago and now must try to flip the bill for past excesses. Developers who once could walk into any major bank and get almost 100 percent of a project's cost up front now can't get the time of day. Major lenders who were burned by bad loans in the 1980s are now prudent to a fault. They're pushing the panic button.

They don't care about the particulars of any situation. They just want their money, and they want it today.

At the same time, the big cash exporters of the 1980s now have little to spare. Japan, which was a net buyer of $26 billion in U.S. bonds in 1989, dumped them to the tune of $9 billion in mid-1990. Their interest is obviously on the skids. And since its unification, the German government has announced plans to spend upwards of $700 billion over the next ten years on rebuilding its eastern area. So there won't be much leftover cash to secure from them.

Many economists fear that the sharp downturn could have a snowballing effect because of the high levels of debt we have accumulated, and because of the shakiness of the overall financial system. Leveraged by buyouts and other takeover deals, many companies are already hard pressed to make their payments. At the same time, banks and insurance firms are tottering beneath huge portfolios of bad real estate mortgages.

One of the big problems is that the federal government stands behind these institutions like a pillar of Jell-O. After all, it's committed to an S&L bailout that could ultimately cost $1 trillion and carries a total national debt of $3 trillion. If more bailouts are necessary, Uncle Sam would have to borrow so much money from the credit markets that interest rates would be pushed well beyond anything we've ever experienced before.

"We're skating on thin ice," says Harvard political economist Robert Reich. "It is thinning rapidly, and we really don't know how thin it is."

Recession is no laughing matter. It takes billionaires like Donald Trump and chews them up in a matter of months. It was only a few years ago that Trump appeared on the cover of every big magazine in this country, the crowned prince of the 1980s' fast-profit market. By early 1991, just a few months into the recession, his $3 billion real estate and gambling empire had started to tumble down around him. He was forced to put one of his biggest casino hotels into bankruptcy and had to give half interest in the complex to his creditors. Why? Because he didn't have enough cash to make the interest payment on the junk bonds used to finance the project.

And Trump is a smart guy.

So is John Portman, the architect and developer who literally reshaped several American cities. From the hulking Marriott Marquis Hotel in Manhattan to the sprawling Embarcadero Center office complex in San Francisco, Portman has left an imposing mark on our urban skylines. Still, the Atlanta-based billionaire recently surrendered to creditors control of Atlanta's 13-block Peachtree Center, the cornerstone of his worldwide empire. Why? Because he was burdened by more than $2 billion in debt and hurt by low occupancy rates in many of the buildings he built during the real estate boom of the last decade.

Jeffrey Cohen is a smart guy, too. He is a Washington tycoon who also filed for bankruptcy after defaulting on more than $11 million in loans.

These are only a few examples of the fortunes that are being destroyed by the ongoing economic crisis. In dozens of U.S. cities, the commercial-property market is reeling. Dozens of overleveraged developers are being forced into bankruptcy or into an only slightly less painful alternative: renegotiating their loans in excruciating "workout" marathons that leave them with far less control over their holdings.

For most of us, of course, the scale of such profit and loss is almost inconceivable. Very few of us have ever tried to structure multi-billion dollar development deals.

So very few of us can relate to what it must be like to see the corresponding fortunes evaporate. But, beware. The size of an investor's loss is directly proportionate to the size of his portfolio. The average American investor doesn't have a billion dollar portfolio. But what he does have is about to be lost if it is foolishly trapped within a drowning U.S. economy. The current recession could shrink it down to pint-size. A true depression would unquestionably destroy it altogether.

■LOOKING FOR THE BOGYMAN

Who do you blame for this tragic absurdity? It depends a lot upon your political leanings and (more to the point) your overall portfolio profits. People who did well during the 80s — and there were many of us who did — are typically hesitant to blame President Reagan. Whatever can be said of his overall economic policies, we fared well and made money. So, sometimes, we are usually willing to overlook the big picture.

During the heyday of Reaganomics, people with significant wealth cleaned up. The top individual tax rate was reduced from 70 percent to only 28 percent. The number of millionaires more than doubled and billionares increased ten-fold. Nothing like that had happened in this country since the era of the Vanderbilts, Rockefellers and Morgans.

Unfortunately, however, the opulence of the 80s has given way to much leaner times. And as the economy gets worse, new criticism gets levied against the economic theorists of "trickle down." As even the shrewdest investors begin to grapple with the unpleasant consequences of their orgy with unproductive private investments — everything from leveraged buyouts to junk bond financings and merger mania — a lot of people are coming to question the wisdom of everybody involved in running the economy during the 1980s.

Classic liberals, naturally enough, have found a great scapegoat in Reagan. Among his transgressions, they say, are short-sightedness and an offensive bias in favor of the ultra-rich. By trying to decrease taxes while simultaneously increasing defense spending, they judge him to be the architect of our collective demise.

Conservatives, on the other hand, like to point the finger at a largely Democratic Congress which, they say, has nothing less than a passion for throwing good money after bad. They argue that by continuously taxing productive Americans to fund inefficient and often useless government programs, Congress has left American business with too little capital to invest and hindered its ability to successfully compete overseas. They also point out that because it dithered so long on the savings and loan bailout crisis, Congress continues to cost the American public $150 million a day.

The White House has its own villain: the Federal Reserve, which President Bush maintains is over-zealous in its efforts to keep inflation at bay. By holding too tight a rein on credit and money growth, the Reserve and its Chairman, Alan Greenspan, have stifled economic expansion.

In my opinion, all these arguments side-step the main problem. Too many critics of the national economy continue to blame this party or that president for the economic woes that besiege us because, in their hearts, they truly believe that there's an omnipotent somebody somewhere who has the power to change the situation. That's like still believing in Santa Claus.

I think we need to begin seeing our economy as a self-propelling and out-of-control force to be reckoned with. A Frankenstein monster, if you will, capable of destroying anything that stands in his path, anything that plays along and, in the process, makes itself his victim. Frankly, it doesn't matter who created him. It's the monster himself that must be avoided.

Unfortunately, for a great many Americans, the monster is quickly gaining from behind. And he's carrying a sledge hammer in his hand. As he gets closer, they can almost hear him raise it high above his head, ready to bring it down, full-force, on top of their heads. Everyone from the bottom to the top of this country's economic ladder is already beginning to feel his power and his malevolence.

Everyone except for the privileged few.

Remember the stock market crash of 1987? The market plummeted 508 points and lost $1 trillon in just one day. Who lost their shirts in that sudden crash? Not the true economic elite. I remember getting a call from a client of mine just a few days after that October plunge. He was understandably shaken, but relieved to know that his offshore investments were virtually unscathed by the U.S. crisis. We talked at length and he mentioned to me that his father, one of the wealthiest self-made men in this country, was not at all upset by the economic downturn. Despite the fact that his father lost more in one day than he had made in the first 60 years of his life, he referred to the Dow Jones shake-up as "just a readjustment in the market."

Easy for him to say. My client's father is part of the almost infinitesimal percentage of the American public that controls almost all the wealth in this country. He is part of the richest 1 percent of this nation that Reagan truly served, the 1 percent that owns and controls more than one-quarter of the net worth of all adults. Within that 1 percent there are even finer lines of distinction. The top .5 percent of all families, for instance, control more than 30 percent of all commercial real estate in this country, half the corporate stock and even more of the bonds and trusts. Along with others from the super-rich, they own 67 cents of every dollar's worth of everything owned by every family in America.

From the comfortable cushion upon which these lucky individuals sit, everything probably looks fine. They can afford a recession. In fact, if they've internationalized their assets (and, believe me, all of them have), they may even be able to afford a depression. Why? Because they can afford to lose a few million dollars overnight and still take it in stride.

Beware. The size of an investor's loss is directly proportional to the size of his portfolio.

That's not true for most American investors. The majority of wealthy U.S. citizens have worked hard for what they have and as the economic crisis gains momentum, they worry about what will become of what they've managed to accumulate. Unlike the poor and middle class, they have something substantial to protect. And they worry about how to protect it.

■ A CASE IN POINT

All you have to do to better understand the real effects of the escalating U.S. economic downturn, is peel back the thin coating of urban affluence that covers almost any metropolitan center in this country. Boston, for example.

Driving into work each morning, the city's executives fight their way, just as they always have, through bumper-to-bumper expressways. Every other car has another well-dressed businessman or women sitting behind the wheel, apparently in route to a well-paying job. The downtown skyline is dotted with lots of new high-rise office buildings. Stores and restaurants teem with consumers. Old warehouses and factories now house chic boutiques and innovative service companies.

If newspaper headlines are any indication, then things still seem fairly good for Boston. Reports indicate that local unemployment is no worse here than it is anywhere else in the country. Per capita income is actually higher than in most parts of the nation. Home prices are two to four times what they were a decade ago.

So what's the problem, you wonder. For a recession, things sure look good in Massachusetts.

On the surface, yes, they do. But scratch away that surface, examine the cornerstones to Boston's real economic life, and you'll see a much starker picture. For example, official statistics indicate that tax collections in the city fell 3.3 percent in 1989 and another 4.4 percent in 1990. That put the city's overall tax take at 1987's level. What's more, there are some revenue collections that are even lower. Excise taxes on commercial bank profits, for instance, have plunged to 1982's level, and on savings and loans profits, they've fallen to the lowest level since 1979.

Meanwhile, the city's jobless rate, at 6.3 percent, is 250 percent higher than it was just three years ago. Over the last year, the entire state of Massachusetts lost 63,000 jobs. That's one out of every fifty of its workers. The bulk of the losses came from small businesses that, faced with an ever-tighening credit crunch, have no where to turn for necessary infusions of capital. Big employers are paring their payrolls, too. Boston boomed during the 1980s largely on the growth of its home-grown computer companies and financial-services firms. Both sectors, their profits shrinking, are now downsizing.

While the unemployment rate is rising, home values and real estate transactions are falling in Boston (and, for that matter, all across the Northeast). The median value of a single-family home has declined from a peak of $186,000 to $175,900 in one year.

Local banks are also hurting. Consider the Bank of Boston, the largest financial institution in the Northeast, which lost $208 million dollars in just the first three quarters of 1990. There, customers need constant reassurance that their money is safe. And prospective borrowers are being put through a virtual obstacle course on their way to even mid-size loans.

"Someone who typically buys a new car every year always completes an application," explains one of the bank's branch managers. "Part of that application asks for how much was in their most recent paycheck." At one time, that line was pro-forma for preferred customers. "This year," she admits, "even when I know in my heart that there's been no change, I have to ask to see that paycheck."

"Usually, the customer comments about the fact that I've never before asked for check stub validation. But, as I tell them, things can change in a year."

And how! They've certainly changed for the 206-year-old Bank of Boston. It has 750,000 customers and $37 billion worth of assets. Yet in the third quarter of 1990, it felt the need to set aside $200 million to cover anticipated loan losses. It actually wrote off $91 million in lost loans on real estate and $84 million in various other loans. It has $608 million worth of domestic real estate loans classified as "non-performing" — that means in default or no longer paying interest — and another $665 million worth of real estate that it has been taken from borrowers who have defaulted on their loans.

Just to put all this in perspective, you might want to

think about it this way: in just one quarter of one fiscal year, the Bank of Boston put so much money aside to cover possible loan losses that it took $50 billion in available credit out of the state! That's unprecedented.

For the average Boston resident this translates into leaner and meaner times. Fewer new cars, fewer new business ventures, indefinitely-postponed new house purchases, and, frequently, reduced lines of credit. Even if their credit history is impeccable. I recently read that 27 different Massachusetts companies, none of which had ever missed a single loan payment, were unable to get credit. One executive had a home loan and a revolving line of credit both pulled out from under him. And he had been a valued customer of his bank for more than 20 years!

The point is, all that glistens is not gold. In fact, despite its still attractive veneer, Boston is in some serious trouble. There's rust below the city's economic surface, and every local resident stands to get tarnished if things don't change for the better fairly soon.

■ IT'S ALL IN YOUR MIND

Of course, Boston is just one example. We could just as easily have looked at a dozen other big American cities because every reliable measuring stick indicates economic reversal from one end of this nation to the other: more bankruptcies, higher unemployment, fewer (and less profitable) homes sales, burgeoning foreclosures, dwindling tax receipts, plummeting retail spending, and slipping salaries and wages.

Look around you. Chances are, if you're like the majority of upper-income Americans, you're seeing your financial safety net getting smaller and smaller. You're making over $100,000 a year, but after you get done paying your taxes to the absolutely ravenous federal and state governments, financing your kid's education, and servicing your credit card debts, you wonder where the "rest" is — the money you had hoped to put into investment savings.

I bet you can also look around you and see your hometown collapsing before your very eyes. Physically and economically. You don't need an official research study to tell you that cities have never faced the kind of infra-structure problems they do today. Our downtown streets and neighborhoods are, literally, falling apart.

Experts also tell us that even within the pristine world of uptown business districts, there are big problems. For instance, so much rental space is left over from the high rise development bonanza of the last decade that, even if all new construction were cut off today, it would take eight years to fill the spaces we already have. The average American city, they tell us, has a 20 percent office vacancy rate. And some places (like Phoenix, Dallas and San Antonio) are closer to 30 percent.

Business is shrinking, not expanding. So no matter what industry you work in, regardless of your profession, things are probably getting tighter. There are fewer opportunities for expansion available. Promotions are harder to land than they were even a few years ago. Fewer than half of all new business started this year will survive into the year 2000. During the 1950s and 60s, Americans could look forward to earning one-third more than their fathers. Today, they should expect — at best — to earn one-sixth less.

Throughout the 80s, smart money flowed not into productive investment but into corporate takeovers. Raiders and financiers made fortunes while America's basic industries rotted. A handful of companies now dominate our economic life. In manufacturing, for instance, the top 20 corporations control more than 40 percent of the profits. Among the nation's 14,000 or so commercial banks, the top 100 hold roughly half of all deposits. The largest 14 of those institutions hold one-quarter of the desposits.

The bottom line is sobering. The net worth of more than a quarter of all American families is less than $5,000. Another 6.5 percent have under $10,000. And still another 12.5 percent have under $25,000. Summed up, nearly half of all families in this country have less than $25,000 to their name, counting everything they own, minus debts.

Stacked up against these kind of facts and figures, it's difficult to swallow the trendiest new argument: that our current economic problems are largely a psychological phenomenon. There is a cynicism at work within this country, the argument maintains, and it is not rationally based. American consumers constitute a hefty two-thirds of the national economy. According to the principles of this psycho-economic theory, their inexplicable bitter-ness and disgruntled thriftiness are to blame for our slip-ping economy. It's a kind of financial Puritanism, we're told. Deeply rooted in our national psyche is the belief that good times must be followed by bad. Excess must lead to retribution.

They must be kidding! Americans are bitter, alright. But for very good reason. Recent figures from the Con-ference Board — a group of the nation's top corporate leaders — and the widely respected University of Michigan survey of consumer sentiment show that the average American is turning darkly pessimistic about the national economy. As the 1990 elections made per-fectly clear, they don't want to vote for much of any-thing. They especially don't want to vote for anything that's going to cost them any money. Balanced against their fears of a coming depression, conservationist argu-ments didn't make much headway. Neither did social service needs, prison reform packages, or urban renovation proposals.

Americans have had it! They're frustrated, jaded and legitimately concerned about waking up broke some morning soon because of mismanagement within government.

In my opinion, that's a good first step. I hope you're one of those pessimistic, disgruntled, jaded Americans. I think that you'd better get mad. And after you've become good and angry, I think you'd be smart to do something about it. You need to accept that the domestic economy is shot for everyone except a smaller than small, inner circle of multi-billionaires. Now, it's true that financial miracles can still happen. If you really think that for all the bureaucratic redtape and recession difficulties that stands in your way, you can work your way into that inner circle, then far be it for me to interfere with your game plan.

If you take a rational look at investment opportunities available outside the bounds of your home country, you free yourself to operate globally.

But experience has shown me that most investors and businessmen, when faced with the reality of the situation, want an escape valve. They want to stop beating their heads against the brick wall of a crumbling U.S. economy. They want out. They want to explore the full range of money-making opportunities that exist not within the blur of only semi-legal U.S. financial dealings, but within the various foreign markets that operate just a mental perspective away.

That's all that internationalizing really requires: a fresh perspective.

▮THE BOTTOM LINE

No matter how you figure it, things don't look good.

The United States has already sunk into a recession and may well be on its way into a bonafide depression. It that happens, experts tell us that the financial picture will get worse and last longer than it did during the 1930s. Millions will be lost while frightened investors scramble to claim a few cents on every dollar that they have buried in the sinking ship of the domestic market.

You don't have to be one of them. As an international financial consultant for nearly twenty years, I've seen many economic cycles begin and end. None of them brought the extreme circumstances that are likely to arise during the next few years. They did, however, teach me that nothing lasts forever. During the 80s, many of us feasted at the banquet table of financial opulence. Those with a nest egg to work with were able to invest creatively and watch those investments earn fast and fat profits.

But the 80s are behind us. We're well into the 90s and into a new cycle. Whether we like it or not, the economic environment has changed. The quick money has disappeared. Financial hocus pocus is both out of fashion and dangerous.

Of course, this phase, too, will pass. But for the time being, my advice is simple and straightforward: if you have your assets tied up within the U.S. economy, get them out. If you have already begun the process of internationalizing your portfolio, increase your efforts. It's the one sure way of ensuring that you and your children are not among those who pay the price for past fiscal mismanagement.

As a global player, you'll be free to observe the crisis in this country with enviable nonchalance. While most Americans see their investments evaporate, you'll be free to move your money into highly-liquid and limited partnerships all around the world. You may decide on a Tokyo real estate project in February. By May, you might choose to transfer funds into a very short-term money market account in Luxembourg where it can earn a handsome interest rate. Then in the Fall, you may even opt to funnel your profits into the short-term financing of a fast-food business in Sao Paolo. All the while, you'll accumulate profits, expand your network of international financial contacts and — as an added bonus — enjoy a fair amount of international travel, from the capitals of Euorpe to the sun-drenched beaches of South America.

Does it sound interesting? Then read on....

CHAPTER TWO

The Offshore Solution

"The legal environment provides total freedom to carry on intermediary business in foreign currencies with no central bank regulations, no controls on the movement of capital, no bookkeeping requirements, no access to records for foreign authorities, no reserve or liquidity requirements, and, best of all, no taxes."

—George D. Moffett III
on the lure of an offshore center

How can you side-step the economic consequences of an unpredictable domestic market? How can you guard against the extreme personal and professional hardships that would result from a total financial collapse in your country? How can you avoid the tax collector's unblinking and prying eye? And, at the same time, how can you earn big investment profits that are safe from excessive taxation?

The answer: you can go offshore.

"Offshore" is, today, an integral and accepted part of intelligent financial planning for individuals around the world. In fact, there's literally a mass market of offshore money havens serving high net worth men and women from every continent and country. Having participated in its development, I am convinced that it is the single best option for virtually any investor.

The new world of international money havens is a non-stop, fast-moving arena of profit where success depends on your ability to master trans-border movement of funds. Today's players (regardless of the size of their account) pay little if any attention to national boundaries or to the geographic origin of an investment opportunity. It's irrelevant whether they live in the United States, Japan, or Europe; they're all concerned with the same things. Will any given investment generate an acceptable profit? Can it produce that profit quickly? Can they earn the money without paying too large a portion of it back in taxes? And can they conduct the transaction without undue government scrutiny?

Modern-day investors are aware that money can be made — is there to be made — day or night, and they are not afraid of split-second decisions. They know how to take command of high-speed technology and make it work to their financial advantage. Most important, they have found the secret of profit-making in the 1990s:

keeping their assets in perpetual motion, always making sure money is working where it can them the most good.

■THE OFFSHORE INDUSTRY

Consider this: *American Banker* estimates that international private banks have deposits that now total more than $700 billion. Yet this figure accounts only for money held in the world's four top tax havens. Now add in other safe evironments — places like the Bahamas, Hong Kong, Liechtenstein, Panama, Bahrain, and the Channel Islands — and the total swells to over $1 trillion!

"Offshore" is an integral and accepted part of the intelligent financial planning for individuals around the world. I am convinced that it is the single best option for virtually any investor.

We're talking about an enormous growth industry. The *Financial Times* reports the extent of that growth will depend on the industry's "ability to provide a range of flexible investment vehicles that are not available through onshore vehicles to investors and the growing pool of overseas and expatriate savers." That's a tall order involving a great many people. But, let's face it, with so large a market (so ripe for service), offshore opportunities will undoubtedly expand, diversify and proliferate.

This burgeoning offshore industry did not develop by accident. It has resulted from the needs of major corporations from around the world — entities with the money and means to survey the global environment, identify lucrative investment opportunities and "set-up shop." These corporate interests were the ones big enough to risk a loss. If the offshore approach had failed, they could have nursed their wounds and gone on to other international activities.

The problem never surfaced because the offshore business approach proved to be a virtual gold mine.

At the same time, consider the eagerness with which small, foreign countries and tiny island-states embraced the idea of servicing multi-million dollar clients. These small governments could never hope to generate industries profitable enough to raise them out of poverty and into international recognition. For these states, it is extremely advantageous to attract and nurture financial associations with prosperous investors from around the world.

When you look at the extraordinary success of those early foreign investments and the social and financial needs of small offshore governments, it's clear why the offshore option became so popular so fast. Capital standing on one side — constantly searching for safety, profit and privacy. On the other side numerous small countries hungering for economic development and hard currency. Combine the two and, voila, a genuine international money haven market is born.

Who can benefit from these financial santuaries? Most people assume they're utilized only by the ultra-rich, the billionaire jet set. The truth is, offshore havens are attracting more and more upper-income investors, people whose personal net worth ranges from between $500,000 to $5,000,000. Eight million people from every corner of the globe now qualify for international private banking services. Together, these customers represent a $7 trillion market.

Offshore enthusiasts often come from the most unexpected places. For example, I recently came across a personality profile of an internationally recognized musician. Here's an artist whose albums are sold throughout the world, a celebrity who could do his work anywhere. Yet, as he explained, "in the present-day music world, geography is no longer decided by place but by local taxation." He sensibly argued that "recording is moving away from New York, L.A., and London because of taxes." As another musician put it, "the equipment is the same the world over. It's the taxes that matter."

The offshore market has always included the mega-rich — people with more than $50 million in investible funds. By and large, these are people who want (and need) to move their money out of high tax jurisdictions or unstable political environments. These investors usually seek safe tax havens.

The mysterious Egyptian financier Mohamed Al-Fayed falls into this category. He used his company on the offshore center based on the Channel Island of Jersey to buy the Paris Ritz hotel. Another of his companies, in the fabled money haven of Liechtenstein, holds ownership of Al-Fayed's Scottish castle. For the mega-rich, offshore havens are simply part and parcel of international deal-making.

Another group that's becoming more and more involved in the offshore alternative is the "old money" people. Coming from families with inherited wealth that often goes back many generations, they want to use offshore centers to carry out regular, routine financial transactions. These clients are most often attracted by the privacy and discretion of offshore centers. It's been my experience that they also appreciate the speed and special handling that comes with offshore services.

On occasion I've met families that are so rich and have had money for so long that they've taken on the aura of royalty. It's not uncommon for people in this group to actually turn their holdings into havens for the benefit of others. Prince Rainier Grimaldi's family of Monaco is a case in point. Other examples involve Luxembourg and Liechtenstein — quasi-democratic countries that their owners/operators (Crown Prince Henri and Prince Franz Josef II respectively) have helped turn into money-making havens.

With greater frequency,, I meet people from still another offshore consumer "market." These are the up-and-comers, the young U.S. entrepeneurs who want to explore efficient alternatives to the traditional, slow-paced investment approach that dominates in this country. Dow Jones averages are of little interest to these people. They're more interested in building their businesses and moving at warp speed pace toward the mega-rich category. As a group, they are investing on two levels: the business and the personal. Consequently, they use offshore centers for commercial as well as private reasons.

I recently learned of a successful art gallery owner in Los Angeles. For convenience, I'll call him Richard. As someone involved in the high-stakes world of fine art, he understands the importance of long-range value and profit. Most of his clients purchase art for both its aesthetic worth and its investment potential. Therefore, he needs to stay one step ahead of their purchasing tastes.

Richard decided that he wanted more return on his personal investment income. So, he took funds from various conventional and low-yield sources and transferred them into an offshore company he had purchased specifically for this purpose. Because his offshore corporation was conveniently based in a Caribbean island haven, Richard was able to quickly and efficiently invest in a number of limited real estate partnerships and a few import/export ventures. He also placed some of his resources into international mutual funds. Within eight months, he had increased the return on his money to the point where he was considering opening a satellite gallery in the pricey Soho district of Manhattan.

Richard is part of this new, innovative investment market — people in their 30s and 40s who are gathering the investible financial resources required for offshore investment. I call this new breed of emerging investors the "inventurers." Like the adventurers of past ereas, they are bold and self-confident, proving that you can do business around the world and come out ahead, time after time.

■ AN OFFSHORE MONEY HAVEN — WHAT'S IN IT FOR THEM?

More than once, a new client has come to see me, listened to my ideas for an offshore investment strategy and then, looked straight across my desk saying, "It all sounds too good. What's in it for them? Why should that island offer me so much service when my own government gives so little?"

These are valid questions. We're accustomed to a financial environment that bows to government regulation. That can make it difficult to explain a government that tailors many of its laws and regulations to create an appealing financial environment. Nevertheless, that's exactly what offshore money havens are all about. They're social, political and economic entities that have been tailored to attract your investment dollar.

For instance, Malta is a country composed of three small islands in the Mediterranean Sea, just south of Sicily. Like many other havens, it's small (122 square miles) with a modest population of a few hundred thousand residents. Its citizens also include U.S. and European expatriates. That's because Malta offers a generous tax system. For almost 25 years, this former British colony has been independent. Consequently,, it also attracts a good number of high-rate tax exiles from the United Kingdom.

Malta's economy (like any other) requires capital. Following independence, its government needed to generate money to fund economic development. Unfortunately, the fledgling state went through a period of political upheaval during which its financial stability went from bad to worse. It learned its lesson, however. By the mid-1980s, it had established a sound government that sought to secure an influx of capital by offering an impressive tax break to wealthy individuals who purchased island property.

In early 1988, the Maltese government announced new regulations designed to compete with other money havens. The first one cuts the jurisdictional income tax rate in half, from 30 to 15 percent for foreign investors residing on any of the three small islands. Another regulation modified the local inheritance tax rules to ensure that estate duty is payable on only a small percentage of a deceased resident's assets. Again, the government's aim is obvious: to attract wealthy people from around the world who want to save taxes and leave the largest possible estate to their heirs.

Not every offshore money haven contours its local law and enforcement practices to this particular market. Still, these accomodations are reflective of the economic benefits that are available through offshore financial centers. Typically, each haven — whether it's located in the Pacific, the Caribbean, the Mediterranean, or inland, like Luxembourg — specializes in a particular financial area and services a specific onshore market.

Haiti, for instance, has recently gained international recognition for its unique divorce laws. It allows individuals to legally divorce their spouses in a matter of minutes and marry someone else the same day. With

California and New York among the states that recognize these divorces, Haiti is enjoying a booming business!

The bottom line is this: offshore havens want the spending power that foreign investors and residents can bring to their struggling economies. Without that wealth, they would be forced to depend almost exclusively on tourism for capital. And tourism could not begin to compete with the profits they earn by attracting foreign capital and hard currency. The result is that many places — Malta being one example — deliberately and carefully develop into financial centers offering tax efficiency and state-of-the-art financial services.

■ JAPAN'S MONEY HAVENS

As I've already explained, "offshore" investment does not work just for U.S. professionals and businessmen. It works for intelligent people everywhere. Listen to one of the greatest success stories in financial history. It's a saga built around the consistent and profitable use of foreign money havens.

Today Japan is referred to as an "economic miracle." And for good reason. It's clearly on the cutting edge of global economic might — with enough momentum to make it the world's financial giant. Most of the world's top ten banks are Japanese. In fact, the world's very largest bank, with assets over $300 billion, is the Tokyo-based Dai-Ichi Kangyo. By 1992 Japan's net external assets (which will approach $700 billion) will be five times greater than America's peak international creditor position of $180 billion in 1981!

The point is, Japan is rich and getting richer. Without exaggeration, it has earned its new-found status as the earth's wealthiest nation.

It's also fair to say that, in general, the Japanese people

are woefully underdeveloped as consumers. As a recent issue of the newsletter *Swiss Economic Viewpoint* noted, "the rest of the world has greater respect for the Japanese economy than they do themselves. Indeed, for such a rich nation, the Japanese quality of life still falls abysmally short of Western standards. They crowd together in tiny and absurdly expensive apartments. Public amenities such as galleries and parks are scarce."

How is it, then, that this previously poor island nation — with its relatively low standard of living and its utter lack of natural resources, defeated and humiliated in a world war — has become a financial giant?

Part of the answer involves Japan's clever (often brillant) use of offshore financial centers.

By sheer necessity, the Japanese have developed the right perspective in terms of offshore internationalization. Simply put, they have had to go offshore to earn profits. Their whole economy is based on the offshore solution. For them, the rest of Asia, the United States, Latin America and Europe are "offshore." There is an obvious logic to the fact that Japan would be an offshore triumph, because its onshore market could never produce the economic wealth that is contemporary Japan.

The American investment vision is not at all like the Japanese, as one internationally experienced U.S. executive explains. "America's large geographic expanse and huge domestic market have worked against our developing an international perspective."

I agree. We Americans can travel thousands of miles — from east to west, north to south, through deserts, mountain ranges, different climates and scenery — and still not have moved beyond the continental United States. That speaks highly of the expanse and beauty of our nation. Unfortunately, it also suggests that we are rarely reminded of a world beyond our borders.

The Japanese have realized for quite some time that there is a world outside their borders. According to the highly respected *Japan Economic Journal*, Japanese companies have been regularly using offshore tax havens since the early 1970s. Within the last decade they have established numerous offshore companies, using international money havens for profit as well as tax protection.

One of Japan's top financial strategists, Mitsuyo Hanada, Director of the Center for International Studies at the Sanno Institute, maintains that Japanese businesses have moved irreversibly into the globalization stage of economic development. He also argues that offshore money havens will become increasingly popular throughout the 1990s because through these service centers, Japanese investment interests can move more efficiently and more autonomously. "Even head offices may be moved to tax havens," Hanada predicts, "as Japanese enterprises spread out across the globe."

A cornerstone to Japan's offshore success lies in its diversified international strategy. As if playing championship chess, the government (as well as its corporations and individual citizens) has made a series of economically methodical moves — each based on the ones before it. Any new offshore venture moves its backers a bit closer to their ultimate goals of profit and operational flexibility — two business necessities that are unattainable at home.

With government approval (and sometimes with its support), Japanese business has invested billions in various tax and money havens. Panama, the Cayman Islands, the Netherland Antilles, Luxembourg and Hong Kong head the list. By and large, each of the ventures has been unique, entirely legitimate and impressively profitable.

Euromoney reported that way back in the late '80s major Japanese banks began transferring more than $60 billion in loans to Latin American countries from their own books "to those in a new shell company, JBA Investment, Inc., registered in the Cayman Islands tax haven." The strategy was devised with a full blessing from the Japanese Ministry of Finance (MoF), and its purpose was straightforward: to offer the banks tax relief. The report explained, "Under Japanese law, banks can set off only 1% of doubtful loans carried on their books against taxes owed...But by selling their sovreign loans at a discount to the Cayman Islands shell, the 28 banks participating in the scheme can take paper losses on these loans, thus entitling themselves to tax credits equal to their writedowns."

They couldn't get those tax credits by operating under the usual rules and laws of Japan. By going offshore they could. It's this kind of progessive thinking that explains why 17 of the world's top 25 banks are Japanese. Don't expect similar measures for American businesses and investors!

Another example of Japanese offshore skill centers around their involvement in Panama. As stated in *Tax Havens of the World*, "Panama does not assess any income tax on income produced from sources outside of Panama." Needless to say, this has made it a very attractive haven for business and investors from around the world. Japan is no exception. In fact, the Land of the Rising Sun is one of Panama's major trading partners, and has a $3.2 billion trade surplus with the Central American nation.

In recent years, Japan has appeared to value its Panama connection over an amiable relationship with the United States. At the height of the political turmoil swirling around General Noriega, Panama's former drug-dealing dictator, our government put subtle but considerable pressure on Japan to spurn this tax haven. Japan, however, chose to ignore our pleas because its economic interests in Panama are simply too valuable to abandon.

The Associated Press has reported that "Panama is not only a major consumer of Japanese goods, it also controls the Panama Canal, a vital link for Japanese cars headed for the eastern United States and agricultural products returning to Japan...Panama is Japan's largest export market in Latin America, as well as the top recipient of Japanese direct investment in the region."

In one single year, Panama received $2.4 billion (more than 50 percent) of Japan's private direct investment in Latin America. Many of Japan's biggest and most powerful companies and investors use it as a convenient offshore financial center. Most important, Panama's banking laws guarantee almost complete financial privacy. *The New York Times* has said that "Panama's banking laws are so secret that even United States branch banks in Panama have failed to provide records requested by the Internal Revenue Service in cases directly related to drug trafficking." For the Japanese — who place great value on confidentiality — such laws are quite alluring.

Almost as compelling for them is the freedom from government regulation that exists in Panama. In his book, *The Limits of Victory*, George D. Moffett III, writes that the Panamanian legal environment provides "total freedom to carry on intermediary business in foreign currencies with no central bank regulations, no controls on the movement of capital, no bookkeeping requirements, no access to records for foreign authorities, no reserve or liquidity requirements, and, best of all, no taxes."

These offshore centers are also being utilized in still

another popular Japanese investment tactic: the captive insurance company. Manufacturing giants such as Honda Motor Co., Matsushita Electric Industrial Co., Suntory Ltd. and the Sony Corp. have all set up "captive" insurance companies to provide liability insurance that is unavailable from a regular, onshore insurance firm. As a "bonus" benefit, of course, these foreign-based captives also provide a convenient means of tax management and cash flows.

Here's another example: The *Japanese Economic Journal* reports that in 1985, Orient Leasing Co. (a Japanese corporation) successfully "avoided taxation totaling some 10 billion yen by using its Dutch subsidiary and an affiliate built in the Netherland Antilles." Now that was a tremendous tax savings! Within months, scores of other major Japanese companies had flocked to the Netherlands to create similar financial subsidiaries.

Offshore finance is the next frontier where you can blaze a profit trail without undue regulation; capitalize on innovative ideas without excessive taxation; and control your own assets without burdensome disclosures.

Masao Nishio, an executive with Nippon Steel Corporation, a company that created a financial subsidiary in Amsterdam in wake of the Orient Leasing news, says "foreign exchange regulations are very lenient in the Netherlands, the country is extremely convenient for Japanese corporations to raise funds in such forms as Euro-commerical papers and other financial instruments."

The possibilities are literally endless, and Japan is willing to explore them all.

One more success story merits the time involved in

telling it. Perhaps more than any other, it helps clarify the ever-widening role of offshore money havens in Japan's international investment portfolio.

In the late '80s, Prince Henri (heir apparent to the Grand Duchy of Luxembourg) led a high-powered economic delegation to Japan. All of Luxembourg's top political and economic leaders accompanied him to Toyko. Their goal: to lure Japanese investment into their small but strategically-based Western European tax haven. As a lure, the Prince promised to help lessen the tax burden of Japanese companies.

How do you think the story ends? Within a year, some 15 Japanese life insurers established investment companies in Luxembourg! During the same period, nine Japanese bank branches also opened their doors in the little grand duchy.

The point here is not to praise the Japanese. The point is to prove that you — the affluent individual investor — can do what Japan's banks, corporations and high-ticket individuals have done for nearly two decades: use offshore money havens to your own financial advantage. If the Japanese have shown the world anything, they've shown it how to profit from globalization. Don't ignore that lesson.

■THE LIST GOES ON AND ON

Japan is not the only foreign country using money havens. The British have made an art of offshore business and investment. For decades, the Isle of Man (in the Irish Sea), the Channel Islands (in the English Channel), the British Virgin Islands (in the Caribbean), Hong Kong (in the South China Sea) and other strategic jurisdictions have served as financial offshore centers for British financial needs.

The haven most often associated with the United Kingdom is the Channel Islands. Wealthy individuals and select banks and corporations from England have been capitalizing on the benefits offered by these three tiny islands (Jersey, Guernsey and Sark) since 1960. By the 1970s, the island trio off the coast of England had become a fully operational and convenient money haven for most of the British upper-crust.

It didn't take long for international funds, corporate subsidiaries, bonds brokers, commodities traders and currency exchanges to set up operations to facilitate tax-free investments for this wealthy market. By the end of the 1970s (and with the tacit approval of the British government), banks such as the Bank of India, Banque Nationale de Paris, Bank of Bermuda, Manufacturers Hanover, N M Rothschild Bank of Switzerland, Bank of America, Chase, Citibank, Hong Kong Bank and major British banks (as well as a smattering of Spanish, Dutch and other European banks) had set up offices on Jersey.

Large U.S. securities firms (like S.G. Warburg, Lazard Brothers and Morgan Guaranty Trust) followed suit. By the 1980s, the Channel Islands — Jersey and Guernsey, in particular — had become ultra-modern offshore financial centers. Their market? Rich investors from around the world with a sustained emphasis on British wealth.

More recently, a growing flow of British tax exiles (as well as Canadian and American expatriates) have started streaming into another money haven: the British Virgin Islands. *The Economist* reported in 1988 that "so many offshore companies have been incorporated in the islands that there is now one of them for every two of the 12,000 inhabitants."

The story continued by saying that, in 1984, the British Virgins decided that they wanted a slice of the Caribbean offshore capital business. So, "the self-governing islands' legislative council adopted a law that made it both cheap and simple to register businesses there. With solid British law behind them, the islands offer the convenience of dealing in United States dollars, their official currency." Their effort was an immediate success. By 1988, the number of incorporations in the British Virgins had rocketed. "Between January 1st and April 30th, 2,211 new business were added to the list..."

Over the past few years, the British have also managed to set up a number of lucrative international funds. As of now, they hold something like 1,050 overseas funds worth over $80 billion. The Channel Island haven of Jersey is home to more than 300 of these funds. Other major beneficiaries, according *Forbes* magazine, are Guernsey, Luxembourg and Bermuda. It's worth noting that the institutions which manage these offshore funds are major international players — like U.S.-based Citicorp, which manages 43 offshores funds worth approximately $250 million. So the strategy must be a lucrative one for everyone involved.

Germany, a nation that has developed into an exporting dollar giant, also uses havens. One of its most recent offshore ventures was born out of the need to avoid newly-imposed taxes on all investment earnings. Here's a sense of how bad the tax burden is: one experienced consultant placed an advertisement in a Bonn newspaper offering expert advice on how to deal with the new withholding requirements. He found that a great many German companies and banks have finally been pushed too far, and are moving subsidiaries into the haven of Luxembourg, which has no withholding tax.

Another large German bank, Dresdner Bank AG, "has unveiled plans for a new Luxembourg fund concentrating on investments free from the tax." The point, said a spokesman for an investment group set up by German savings banks, is to increase the international weighting of their funds. He said, "By stronger internationalization of these funds, we can largely avoid the withholding tax."

The Germans are also discovering (along with the British, other Europeans and savvy Americans) that there's a ready-made haven in their own backyard. Monaco, with its relaxed attitude toward taxation, is a promising new offshore center.

Evidently, the secret is out because the London-based *Financial Times* recently ran a story with the eye-catching headline: "Monaco: A Fiscal Paradise for Foreigners." It appears that Monte Carlo has become the site for regular cocktail parties with guestlists that include high net worth investors from all parts of the world. These posh "get togethers" are hosted by competing bankers, fund managers and brokers — all of whom want to provide financial services to rich individuals and companies seeking tax protection.

How much can they offer? A lot. At the moment, income tax is not imposed on anyone other than French citizens. Further, companies which meet certain guidelines do not have to pay any corporation tax. There are no capital gains taxes and absolutely no estate or death duty between husband and wife or between parents and children.

One British tax exile explains with delight, "all you need is a carte de sejour (residence card), and you don't have to pay any income tax at all.

"What's more," he added, "this is a sophisticated and convenient place with all the modern communication equipment you could ever want for running a worldwide business empire from a sunny balcony...."

The *Financial Times* succinctly says: "Monaco's fiscal system has enabled it to transform itself quietly and discreetly into a leading offshore business center as well as a tax haven for wealthy individuals. It is no coincidence that tennis stars like Bjorn Borg or Boris Becker have decided to take up residence in Monte Carlo and that numerous high net worth individuals from countries such as Italy, Greece, Britain and Lebanon have made the principality their base."

Offshore money havens are usually set up for a specific purpose. A most interesting haven is the Emerald Isle, Ireland. In fact, Ireland is the European Economic Community's biggest tax haven. Right now, over 900 foreign investors use it as an offshore money haven. Among them: Coca-Cola and Pepsi-Cola. According to *The Economist*, Ireland's biggest edible export is cola concentrate. And Coca-Cola's largest plant outside the United States is based in Ireland, in a town called Drogheda.

From the corporate offices of Tokyo to the bank vaults of London, from the villas of Monte Carlo to the conference rooms of Bonn, one message keeps recurring: people throughout the world seek offshore money havens as a legitimate and necessary element in today's fast-paced, globally-linked financial market. Governments, corporations, banks, trading companies, trusts and partnerships as well as individuals use them to make money, reduce taxes and ensure financial privacy without concern for national boundaries.

THE NEXT FRONTIER

Offshore finance is the next frontier where you can blaze a profit trail without undue regulation; capitalize on innovative ideas without excessive taxation; and control your own assets without burdensome disclosure. Be aware, however, that to be successful, you must be guided by the best advisors armed with the right information. And always be wary of false steps.

As I travel to various international financial centers around the world, read the relevant research and talk with key offshore investors, I am more convinced than ever that now is the time to move into the offshore market. A *New York Times* article explains that the offshore trend marks a big change for Americans and other international investors. Traditionally, we have kept the overwhelming preponderance of our assets close to home. But more and more, the value of foreign currencies, the likelihood of superior investment performance and the promise of true financial privacy will stimulate the flow of American investment into offshore centers.

The ultimate lesson to be drawn from this chapter is a lesson in international diversification. That's the significance of the offshore solution. Before an economic shutdown destroys your financial standing, I urge you to consider the money haven approach. It allows you to spread your money out over several markets, hedge your investment bets and ensure privacy as well as tax protection.

CHAPTER THREE

The Open Door: Doing Business Offshore

"By all measures, we are launched on a new era in which the entire world is to become the investor's oyster."

—The Global Money Game

As you prepare to internationalize your own assets and holdings, bear in mind that many investors and entrepeneurs have paved the way for you. That means there are role models out there and success stories to help guide your offshore strategy. Remember that there have also been abysmal failures in the global marketplace. So, approach every potential offshore venture with a combination of enthusiasm and caution.

Whenever I meet with a potential client, I offer a panoramic view of the rugged but beautiful financial terrain that can be found offshore. My advice is always the same. First, believe that there are limitless financial opportunities outside our borders, because there are. Second, know that to benefit from them, you must adopt an entirely new business style; a style that mixes entrepeneurial savvy with a well-conceived business plan.

I try also to highlight my strongest belief in global diversification: the time to aggressively pursue offshore investment has arrived. Given the current global economic picture (and reliable forecasts of tomorrow's), the offshore option is an absolute prerequisite for financial success. As recently as ten years ago, that was not the case. However, as we move through the 1990s, a healthy step outside your country's borders will be essential to your financial security and, of course, profitability.

Let me share some interesting facts which form the basis of a persuasive argument for offshore investment. In less than 20 years, the world's stock-market inventory has grown 700 percent from roughly $1 trillion in the late 1960s to more than $7 trillion in 1990. How much of that market do you suppose is contained within the United States? In a few short years the equation has shifted. In 1970, U.S. equities comprised fully two-thirds of the world's stock-market. Today, less than one-third are American. Nearly 70 percent of the world's stocks (and more than 55 percent of its fixed income) are invested in overseas markets. Therefore, it makes little sense to limit your investing sphere to just the continental United States.

Still a bit confused? Let me offer a simpler definition. In understandable language, an offshore venture refers to any business that is controlled by a U.S. citizen but located and operated outside the jurisdiction of the United States. (Of course, you can substitute your country for the U.S. because offshore means any place outside your national borders.) As you can see, that allows for a lot of different business plans. And when you look at the contemporary offshore environment, you quickly see very distinct projects, each one of them highly reflective of the individual who owns and runs it.

In the present economic climate, the offshore option can give you considerably more than Swiss bank accounts. In fact, it really does offer something for everyone. Your options are unlimited, from owning your own offshore bank to operating your own international money fund, or serving as an international broker for industrial spare parts. It's entirely up to you. Your only obstacle is the boundary of your imagination.

■THE WINDOW OF OPPORTUNITY

Until quite recently, the U.S. government did not encourage businesspeople to go offshore. It didn't necessarily discourage them, but (for a variety of reasons) Uncle Sam practiced a kind of benign neglect when it came to international diversification. Now that's all changed.

Part of the change came about because more individual American investors began to see the light. As James Thorneburg, a businessman from Statesville, North Carolina, put it, "I looked at the marketplace and convinced myself that you're either going to be global or you're going to be nobody."

Recently, leafing through *Business Week*, I came across a very expensive special advertising section. There it was — a multi-page, full-color section that had been purchased by the U.S. government to sell the offshore concept. The point was to encourage American business people to go offshore. The idea was endorsed in a letter from the Secretary of Commerce who wrote that it is time to enter the offshore market.

I smiled at the spread. In fact, it made my day. Here was a member of the President's Cabinet giving exactly the same advice that I've been giving since the mid-1970s. Go offshore. Now.

The Secretary went on to say:

> The dollar has declined substantially against the currencies of our major trading partners, and government efforts to open world markets to U.S. goods are paying off....Recognizing that today's economic climate is ideal for improving our position in the world markets, the President has launched...a major new campaign to take advantage of a window of opportunity that has opened...

Of course, the real story had to be read between the lines. Americans have not successfully managed to keep the dollar strong. The domestic economy has been going haywire for sometime. So it's important to get out there and do something now, before it's too late.

The Secretary's comments reinforced my own thinking about offshore investment. The "window of opportunity" that he referred to is opening wider every day. More and more individuals, companies and investment groups are benefiting from the offshore option.

It seems that everyone is trying to get in on the act. I've been an international financial advisor for nearly 15 years and I've never seen so many people waving the offshore banner. I believe the international marketplace has never been so ripe for profit-making. In part, the surge of activity results from recent data on the size and purchasing power of the international market. Experts tell us that the rest of the world produces four times the U.S. GNP. Fully 95% of the planet's population lives outside the U.S., and it's growing 70% faster than we are.

Sam Ferguson, president of Ferguson Industries, is an example of the new breed. His company helps finance and set up fertilizer plants in various foreign countries. With close-cropped hair, dark horn-rimmed glasses and classic white Stetson, Ferguson looks more like a small-town businessman than an economic trailblazer. But aside from his Texas manner, he's an offshore activist. "If I weren't in international sales today, one of three things would have happened: I'd have closed my doors when the domestic market dwindled away; I'd have developed an entirely different line of products; or I'd have a very small company with a very small staff and take what we could sell."

I am constantly amazed by how many intelligent, hard-driving businesspeople simply will not acknowledge that financial opportunity exists outside their national borders.

Ferguson's business style is straightforward. "We simply recognize no geographical boundaries," he explains. "Any country is a sales prospect....In our first year of exporting, foreign business was about two to three percent of sales. Today, about two-thirds of our business is export, and, overall, we make a better profit on our international business than we do on domestic sales."

Kathleen Bond, an experienced hand in offshore business and the manager of the international division of EIL Instruments, Inc., believes people like Sam Ferguson are still in the minority. She says that far too many Americans continue to have a "border mentality." They don't understand, she argues, that "you can do business as easily in Saudi Arabia as you can in Chicago."

I don't know if that's totally true. Doing business abroad does require special skills. Nevertheless, they are skills that can be easily acquired and honed. Too many people wear border blinders about doing international business. I am constantly amazed by how many intelligent, hard-driving businesspeople simply will not acknowledge that financial opportunity exists outside our continental borders. I suspect their myopic vision may really be a defense. Maybe they prefer to deny the offshore market rather than admit they're afraid of it.

Everyday I encounter more evidence that the offshore option is the way to go. For example, recognizing that more and more people are conducting worldwide business from their U.S. telephone, AT&T recently inaugurated an "International 800 Service." As its promotional material explains, "It's a fact that today's economy is not local, regional, or even national. It is global."

AT&T's International 800 Service acknowledges the pivotal role of offshore centers in today's international economy. Of the nearly 30 countries that can utilize the service, almost half are bona fide offshore jurisdictions, with all the relaxed legal and tax laws that are associated with such foreign financial centers. These include the Bahamas, the British Virgin Islands, the Cayman Islands, Hong Kong, the Netherlands, Panama and Trinidad & Tabago.

AT&T has no genuine need to help you reach out and touch someone. So, they wouldn't be pumping money into trying to sell this service if they hadn't researched their potential market. They've glimpsed the future, and they know that it will be supported by a booming offshore economy.

■OFFSHORE'S FINANCIAL GIANTS

Aside from international corporate activity, I've seen a tremendous increase in the number of individual financiers who roam the world in pursuit of profitable business deals.

One whose profile is most visible is the Australian communications magnate, Rupert Murdoch. His empire is spread over four continents: Europe, Australia, North America and Asia. Although he is not a run-of-the-mill

The Murdoch Empire
$7 Billion

offshore investor, I believe we can learn a lot by observing some of the masters of the game.

Let me also point out that Murdoch has recently been sideswiped by the economic downturn I discussed in Chapter One. His net worth has gone down. Even so, it is still helpful to take a close at his global portfolio. He began with two struggling newspapers that had belonged to his father. Today he owns — among other things — more than 100 newspapers and magazines, a satellite cable outlet, book publishers, his own airline, and a U.S. television network. He recently purchased Triangle Publications, publisher of *TV Guide*, for $3 billion. He is, in a word, big.

What interests me most about Murdoch's style is the way he can manipulate and enhance his financial standing by simply exercising the international option, and using national tax and legal differences to his advantage. With money strategically located around the world, he can take advantage of opportunities that are possible only with interglobal linkages.

For example, when he purchased Metromedia, he financed the deal by having his company (the Australia-based News Corporation) issue shares on another of his holdings (the California-based 20th Century-Fox). At a price of $2 billion, the project was an expensive gamble. But by financing on a global basis, Murdoch made it work. As *Business World* put it:

Murdoch's luck held. When interest rates dipped, his company was able to raise $800 million by floating several bond issues in Europe and stretching its bank credit lines....

Several differences between American and Australian accounting principles have made it easier for Murdoch to borrow. In the United States, for example, the Fox preferred shares were treated as debt and the dividend pay-out was deducted as though it were an interest expense; but Down Under, these shares were lumped with shareholder equity. On paper, this reduced News Corp.'s debt load and enabled it to exercise more leverage. Asset revaluation is another Australian accounting technique that facilitates borrowing. Periodically, News Corp.'s mastheads and television licenses are reappraised. If they have grown in value, the increases are added to shareholder equity, thus strengthening the balance sheet....

That's the beauty of international investing. By moving offshore, you can expand your pool of available capital and, in the process, strengthen your own investment power. Of course, few of us are Rupert Murdochs. Nevertheless, his sense of scale and ambition are an inspiration to any aspiring offshore investor.

Another fascinating investor, rapidly moving into offshore ventures, is William E. Simon, the former U.S. Secretary of the Treasury. Considered by many people to be a true financial genius, Simon recently moved away from the American financial market because, he says, it's become too erratic. His sense of timing is uncanny.

Simon has an interesting sensibility as far as investing is concerned. "I'm a market man," he recently declared, "and a good market man stays ahead of the power curve. People used to wonder how I could operate out of New Jersey. Simple. Just give me a handful of dimes and a working phone, and I'll make money."

Staying ahead of the power curve means having the ability to predict the future. That prediction does not have to come from a sixth sense or from an astrologer's tip. It can come through diligent, hard work. It can result from staying abreast of the economic indicators and understanding how they point toward forthcoming ups and downs in the world economy.

At any rate, Simon is obviously a man brimming with confidence. And with good reason. He was one of the pioneers and top beneficiaries of the leveraged buyout and made hundreds of millions of dollars in the 1980s. Now worth more than $400 million, he's turning his eyes to the next frontier: offshore investment.

Not long ago, a profile of Simon appeared in *The New York Times Magazine*. In it, he spoke of his new "Pacific Initiative" which involves creating "a new entity — comprised of a merchant bank, a couple of commercial banks and a handful of savings and loan institutions (or thrifts) picked up on the cheap, all of them on the West Coast or Hawaii." Together, Simon explained, these financial entities are "meant to serve as a mighty bridge of capital spanning the Pacific Basin, drawing on the huge pools of money accumulated in Asia, pursuing targets of opportunity worldwide while channeling a bonanza of foreign investment into the United States."

In the short run, he says, his banks will enable him to weather the economic catastrophe that he regards to be "the inevitable consequence of the Reagan Administration's bizarre management."

Individual investors like Murdoch and Simon aren't the only ones getting in on the international financial boom. *Euromoney* reports that "offshore investments by U.S. tax-exempt pension funds are estimated to have grown from $3.8 billion in 1979 to over $70 billion by the end of the 1980s — a compound growth rate of 47% per year. More important, many institutional investors are just beginning to make investments in the world's smaller capital markets."

By and large, these institutional investors are known for their conservative style. So, why are they going offshore? Primarily because their risks are lower overseas — especially in the smaller capital markets that aren't tied to the returns generated within the giant markets.

Dollar returns, even after currency exchange, are rather high. You can also obtain company shares at a lower price on the local market, whether or not the company competes internationally.

Increasing numbers of investors are taking heed of the offshore market's potential. Murdoch, Simon and the pension fund managers are only a few of the seasoned investors who scan the globe for financial opportunity. They are joined by tens of thousands of men and women throughout the world; part of a rapidly expanding new breed of investors and entreprenuers. They have erased the concept of national borders from their operating manuals. For them, the global economy is simply one vast, interlocking financial playing field.

■ANYONE CAN PLAY

I want to make it clear that anyone can become part of this offshore bonanza. Certainly, it's important to be aware of the global investment giants and to realize that their fortunes depend on the offshore option. But for most of my clients and readers, it's easier to identify with the many middle market investors and businessmen who have grown rich from international ventures — people whose assets range between half a million dollars and $20 million.

One particular success story involves a man named Charles McKay, a 54-year old entrepeneur who lives in Florida.

Based in south Dade County, McKay has worked hard to be successful. A 23-year veteran of offshore investment and business operation, he's weary of the economic wars that he's experienced and the accompanying tough times. But when he talks about international money-making, a gleam comes to his eyes and his face beams. "There's nothing quite like it," he says proudly. For him, the initial allure was travel and big money. Always enjoying foreign places, he was determined to find a way of turning that enjoyment into money.

McKay started out in 1963 with a small-sized company that manufactured building materials for Florida-based contractors. There was nothing particularly remarkable about the company, nor about McKay. But he had two things going for him. He spoke a little Spanish, and he had a good idea. He wanted to take his product line and market it throughout Latin America. In the beginning, he hit the pavement himself — actually walking the streets of various South American nations, meeting potential clients and drumming-up business.

His efforts succeeded. Today, he trades commodities — everything from used factories and lumber to exquisite marble and frozen American orange juice. Like other modern global players, he doesn't need to speak Spanish anymore. And he doesn't have to leave the United States unless he wants to. Instead, through sophisticated communications technology and various methods of instantaneous fund-transfer, he monitors each of his offshore investments — which span the Western Hemisphere and the Middle East — from his own home office.

That's the essence of the offshore option: being able to manage your business and personal affairs from the onshore location of your choice while continuing to enjoy the legal and tax benefits of offshore locales.

McKay's current offshore operation is a company called ternational Equipment Services, which he describes as a turnkey operation. It's a multi-faceted venture based in Miami with activities that shift from country to country depending on need. He might operate for awhile in Ecuador, then move to Venezuela or Guatemala. He may make a deal to purchase a plant in one country, ship it to another for dismantling and refurbishing, and then to somewhere else for reassembling.

Like many offshore strategists, McKay prefers to move fast. As a result, many people find it difficult to keep pace with him. "He's a crazy man," one observer says. "He's running off in all directions at once and you think this guy is nuts, until you see him bringing home all the bacon." That bent toward fast investment turnaround and the willingness to act immediately on a good idea are qualities he shares with most offshore enthusiasts.

Perhaps best described as an "international trader," McKay lives by one simple motto: "innovate or evaporate." By having a stake in the offshore market, he has managed to do more than survive erratic shifts within the U.S. economy. He's capitalized on them. In effect, he is poised for the future — wherever it looks the brightest.

The offshore option provides Charles McKay and every other offshore player with another attractive benefit: flexibility in all aspects of their business and personal financial affairs. It doesn't matter whether you're a huge, medium-sized or small investor. It doesn't matter whether you're seeking a safe harbor for your over-taxed assets, or a relaxed legal environment where you can increase your profit margin by as much as ten-fold. An offshore involvement guarantees you a flexible business tool.

For example, what if you wanted to sell your U.S.-based business? How much could an offshore involvement contribute to the process?

In 1987 international buyers acquired an estimated 3,750 American businesses for prices ranging from $1 million to $50 million. All reliable indicators suggest that the future will bring more of these trans-national purchases. According to R.M Rodnick, chairman of an international merger and acquisition company based in California, "The volume of mergers and acquisitions of smaller to mid-sized, privately held American companies by international investors represents a growing trend."

At one level, an offshore involvement would put you in close and continuous contact with an international network of businessmen — all of whom are look for appealing investments; some one of whom may find your business to be exactly what he's after. More specifically, by having an offshore holding company or bank, you can structure the sale of your own company to an international buyer while maintaining confidentiality, avoiding uncessary tax burdens and earning a generous profit.

Perhaps the easiest way to understand the idea of doing business offshore is to note some of the classic examples of offshore uses and benefits. These include offshore research & development activities, offshore foreign trade, offshore ship registration, offshore aircraft registration, offshore manufacturing, etc. Whatever your individual goals and needs, you will more likely meet and satisfy them in an offshore setting. That fact has been recognized by everyone from AT&T to the U.S. Department of Commerce to Charles McKay. Now it's your turn.

■STAYING AHEAD OF THE POWER CURVE

Although I have known a few investors who all their assets within the United States and still become marginally involved in offshore activities, it usually makes more sense to establish an offshore presence. You will probably want to select a specific base for your operations. Make sure that you choose well because the establishment of an offshore business base is expensive and time-consuming. Time and money are what you want to conserve. So, make your choice carefully. (Chapter Five is guide to the various offshore centers.)

Once you've decided to diversify your assets and initiate an offshore investment strategy, it's important that you consider the project a major commitment. Don't neglect your offshore investment when domestic concerns develop. Having ventured into the international arena, you must give the same personal attention to those interests as to your onshore activities. If you don't, you risk the loss of money and credibility. You also become vulnerable to being left in the lurch if and when onshore financial options falter.

With this in mind, you should move on to a major business decision — one that will affect your profit and loss statements for years to come. Do you want to be involved in an offshore project that is owned and operated by someone else? Or would you be better served by owning your own private international financial institution or corporation?

Let me be honest about my own bias. I think that, given the deteriorating situation in this country and expanding opportunities abroad, most U.S. investors would be wise to purchase their own private offshore bank or corporation. In this way, they will be free to take advantage of the various international benefits that are often denied to individuals.

Even if you opt for your own bank or company, you have other choices to consider. For instance, do you want to establish (or purchase from a previous owner) a private international bank? Or a private international investment company (PIIC)? There are appealing advantages to both. A small, private brass-plate bank located in an active financial center can combine freedom from traditional banking regulations, relief from heavy taxes and almost total financial privacy with most of the convenient services we associate with major onshore institutions (i.e., MasterCard issuance and interest-bearing checking accounts).

On the other hand, owning a PIIC will enable you to become involved in a multiplicity of international activities. Your corporate charter will authorize the company to engage in a wide variety of financial activities (including the right to buy foreign stocks, CDs, real estate and currency). The charter will also permit the company to engage in import and export trade as well as financing (extension of loans to third parties). Some investors use their corporations as holding companies to provide tax protection for such intellectual properties as patents and trademarks.

The point is — whether you want to ship cattle to Japan like one California rancher who loads a 747 jumbo jet with Black Angus heifers every two weeks, or buy stocks on the London exchange because, as one investor explained, you like to do business at 3 o-clock in the morning — using a privately-held international institution can be satisfying and cost-effective.

Once you enter the international arena, it's crucial that you learn to identify the best offshore opportunities. To stay ahead of the power curve that William Simon talks about, it's important to spot them before they "peak."

Through the years, I've seen various foreign sites come into vogue and then pass out of favor. Usually, they become popular because their government actively pursues outside investment. Offshore center policy and practice is specifically tailored to attract money from around the world. Then, after a time, another foreign government designs an even more appealing investment environment. And the whole dynamic repeats itself.

For many years, I have been a strong believer in Pacific Basin growth. Yet, there are also other regions that allow assertive offshore investors to enjoy a high rate of return on any number of investments or activities.

It's easy, for example, to use your offshore base to invest in Japan, Great Britain, France, Mexico, the Netherlands, Hong Kong, Spain, or Singapore. Or, you can decide to base your offshore operations in a British Commonwealth location, where you are positioned to take part in some very interesting developments. One of these recent opportunities is the Canadian market.

Internationalizing doesn't always transport you to one of the world's exotic financial markets. Sometimes it can take you to neighboring nations, like Canada. Recent economic growth and new legislation have made it much easier (and more appealing) for U.S. investors to become a part of the Canadian financial boom. Since mid-1984, when the Progressive Conservative party came into power, the government has given foreign capital every incentive to enter the country. One of the first steps that the government took was to abolish the agency that screened and sometimes stopped foreign investment. As a result, more astute investors are looking north for opportunity.

Keep in mind that the Canadian stock market performs better than the U.S. market. The Canadian securities market is the sixth largest in the world. What's more, Arthur Johnson, author of *Breaking the Banks*, has found that the largest North American market for venture capital is the Vancouver Stock Exchange. In today's fast-paced market, that's vital information.

Johnson also notes that "More than 30 percent of the shares traded in Canada are those of resource companies. Metals, oil and forest products are the mainstay of the economy. Traditionally, the profits of these companies rise at the end of a booming economic cycle and on expectations of rising inflation; hence the market's takeoff after the bull has been on a global tear."

Two other high-potential areas are Australia and New Zealand. Large sums of money are starting to flow throughout this region, primarily because both nations can offer higher interest rates than those tendered in the United States.

New Zealand recently passed new tax legislation that will help give it a competitive edge over Australia. In October of 1988, the corporate tax rate was cut from 48 to 28 percent for resident companies and will be reduced to just 33 percent for foreign corporations. A series of cuts in import tariffs will reduce rates from a whopping 50 percent to just 16.5 percent! And double taxation on company profits paid as dividends will also be eliminated.

The offshore option provides every player with flexibility in all aspects of their business and personal financial affairs. It doesn't matter whether you're a huge, medium-sized or small investor.

As you may have already guessed, these Commonwealth-associated locales are not the only game in town. For instance, any international investor would be wise to remember that, in 1992, Western Europe will remove all trade barriers between neighbor countries to create one gigantic market. All together, the unification of the European Community (EC) will create a market of more than 320 million consumers. This will, in turn, create further opportunities for investment. Securities, bonds, stock options and other vehicles will increase in volume and in value as companies prepare for the restructuring through creative mergers and acquisitions.

As these businesses expand to meet the new challenge, competition for funds will accelerate. That suggests the probable need for international investors who can lend money, fund bond issues and finance expansion. There will also be opportunities for U.S.-controlled projects that offer specialized financial services such as international banking and insurance. As the new European market expands, so too will its profit potential.

Looking south to Latin America, there is growing investor interest in the conversion of international bank loans into equity investments. This occurs when a bank trades the loans it holds in a particular country for an equity position in a company based in that nation. As reported in *Euromoney*, "The obvious reason for making such investments is that the realized value of an equity investment may eventually exceed the expected value of the loan converted. Such is the beauty of an equity investment: the upside is unlimited."

Bear Stearns is a leading U.S. investment and trading firm that serves international corporations, governments, institutional and individual investors. A few years ago, it saw the loan conversion market in Latin America as a potentially big money-maker. So it set up a Latin American Finance Group intended solely to arrange complex debt swaps among multiple counterparties in Latin America. The result has been impressive, and Bear Stearns' clients are elated. The point is, this firm used its expertise to anticipate an opportunity and to capitalize on it earlier than the competition. That's the real secret to success in the international market: Keep your eyes and ears open, and move with certainty as quickly as you can.

THE THREE STEPS TO OFFSHORE SUCCESS

It's dangerous to over-simplify anything. The process of internationalization is not without its challenges and risks. Nevertheless, I think there are three basic steps to making a prudent and profitable move offshore.

THE FIRST STEP is to shed your border mentality. If you continue to see the world in terms of artificial lines and boundaries, you will fail to take advantage of the new international economic climate. I like the way Sam Ferguson phrased it: "We simply recognize no geographical boundaries."

THE SECOND STEP is to watch what the big money is doing, and learn from its successes as well as its failures. Investors and businesses with deep pockets can afford to stake out new territories and take greater risks. Hoever, by tracking their moves, you can shape your own strategy. The masters of the game usually offer fascinating insight into what works and what doesn't.

THE THIRD STEP step is to explore the landscape in all directions. Currently, there's a rush to capitalize on Pacific Rim activity. However, remember Canada up north — just waiting to be mined with the proper strategy and, by 1992, unique profit opportunities will abound in the European Community.

■THE TIME HAS COME

If you're still wavering about whether or not to conduct business offshore, consider the following points. During meetings with potential clients, I find these points to be the most persuasive argument for establishing an offshore base.

First, remember that tens of thousands of small and mid-sized business people and investors are involved in the global economy. The recent devaluation of the dollar, higher yields in overseas markets, relaxed legal regulations and a greater international flow of money — all have created more investment and business opportunities for Americans.

Secondly, going offshore should not depend on the

domestic economy. As one successful offshore investor put it, "international diversification should be part of any investor's portfolio. Waiting on domestic opportunity could mean lost opportunity." In my view, the state of our current domestic economy suggests that waiting for good times at home could mean waiting a very long time.

Third, information on offshore investment is available from several sources. More new information on offshore business is being generated. Whether it comes from the government, international organizations, the media, specialized advisors, international newsletters or computer databases, the amount of information and resources available is rapidly increasing.

Fourth, language is no longer a barrier. Twenty years ago, when Charles McKay took the offshore initiative, his ability to speak Spanish made a decisive difference. Today, there are a sufficient number of English-speaking offshore centers to satisfy any business need. Many offshore investors work through English-speaking agents or brokers that they hire abroad. Keep in mind that foreign business people often speak some English, or have access to people who do.

Fifth, international licenses, tariffs and certificates are manageable. Offshore advisors, international brokers, agents and distributors (both here and abroad) know how to deal with locally-based bureaucracies. At the outset of any offshore involvement, it is wise to work with an experienced firm or individual in order to insure that all the proper paperwork is in hand and in appropriate form.

Finally, moving your money is not a major problem. One tried-and-true method is to work by letter of credit. These are issued by a bank at the request of a party to a transaction. The letter identifies the seller of a bond or product and the amount of money to be paid. The issuing bank promises to pay upon receipt of those documents which certify that the conditions of the transaction have been met. Remember: a letter of credit is irrevocable; the bank must pay you even if, for some reason, the buyer defaults.

Going offshore, whether it's to conduct your own business or to invest in international markets, may seem overwhelming at first. So, talk with a consultant. Weigh the benefits and the risks. But don't hesitate too long. Make the move before it's too late.

CHAPTER FOUR

The Profit Incentive

"Uncertainty is a fact of life...but you can prepare for the unknown." "

—Harry Browne
Investment Advisor

CHAPTER FOUR

The Profit Incentive

The number one concern among virtually all my clients is profit. People always want to know how much money they can make offshore, and how fast they can make it. They want to see the bottom line, and they want it to clearly point toward substantial economic benefits.

One man who comes to mind as a prime example of the profit motive is Federico Solis. In 1980 he walked into my office wearing an exquisite Italian suit carrying an elephant hide briefcase expressly made for him in Africa. He cut an impressive figure. Beneath the stylish international exterior was a man intent on making a financial killing.

Freddy had a great idea. He wanted to serve as an intermediary for big money on a global basis. To accomplish his aim, he bought a private international bank based in the Caribbean. Before owning his own bank, he couldn't get the right people (he called them the "big boys") to return his calls. Now doors were opening for him as never before.

The gist of the story is that Freddy made it work. He used his bank to obtain letters outlining a company's credit needs. These were written by the Chief Financial Officers of major corporations in the United States. Freddy guaranteed them better rates that they were getting.

With these valuable letters in hand, he flew off to Europe where he presented these letters to the directors of leading banks throughout the Continent. In particular, he found banks in France, Germany, Switzerland and England to be quite receptive. His one rule was to meet only with the top man at every institution. If Freddy couldn't meet him, there would be no deal.

The results were astounding. Nearly every banker committed to loans and credit lines at the rates Freddy had promised the borrowers. For him, the payoff came in large commissions on each single financial package that he put together. After one year of concerted effort, Freddy's plan paid off. He made $4.5 million and the profits have continued to go up siince then.

Today, at forty, Freddy Solis is a little graying at the temples but his assets have doubled. He estimates his net worth at $60 million. We recently spoke on the phone. He's now using his bank as a broker for loans between governments and banks. He told me that within the week he would be meeting with the finance ministers of two nations to help them negotiate loans for development projects in their countries. Then, with a chuckle, he told me that the commissions are bound to be astronomical.

The interesting thing about Freddy is that he came into my office with a simple idea: to make money on an international scale. He chose the offshore route as the means to test his idea. It worked because he worked at the idea, every day for nearly a year. He once told me, "Success is a combination of the desire to succeed and the use of the right tool at the right time." For Freddy, that tool is an offshore entity. Day in, day out, this financial tool gives him a competitive edge. Freddy was transformed from someone with a great dream to someone who could put his dream into action and realize a great profit.

People like Freddy are after one thing. Without difficulty, I can help give them what they're after. The first step is to understand with every fiber of your being that the U.S. market and its economy is drying up. The real opportunities are now outside our borders. In fact, over the past 20 years, the argument for offshore investment has become almost irrefutable.

First of all, it hardly makes sense to limit your investment game to domestic options. I also tell them that the entire offshore industry was built on a single principle: let your money work wherever it can work best. A quick look around the international financial scene should tell you all you need to know about how this nation compares to the rest of the world. Since Black Monday in 1987, the U.S. market has remained virtually comatose. By mid-1988, the Dow Jones industrial average had barely advanced 1 percentage point. In 1990, it fluctuated somewhat but ended the year, on average, on the downside.

During that same time period, however, Japan's stock market hit new highs. London's markets — badly hit by fallout from the mini-Crash — were surging again. And foreign mutual funds were outpacing their American counterparts by impressive margins. Global funds had generated average gains of over 6 percent, and international funds were boasting almost 10 percent increases.

The entire offshore industry was built on a single principle: let your money work wherever it can work best.

I predict that over the next few years, words like "dull," "lethargic" and "boring" will be used more and more often to describe the U.S. investment scene. By contrast, offshore financial activities will continue to boom. That means the way to wealth in the 1990s will inevitably lead you outside this country.

While I'm at it, I'll make a second prediction. Become a part of the global marketplace and, like Freddy Solis, within one year, your pocketbook will show the difference!

■THREE WAYS TO MAKE IT OFFSHORE

If you plan to be among the winners in tomorrow's international economy, you must do three things. First, you must explore the options available to you offshore because there are lots of ways to make money abroad.

Some people like to approach the global market one step at a time. That's fine. It can be reassuring to see profits inch up, little by little.

Other investors want to plunge ahead, pumping a larger share of their assets into higher-risk, higher-yield projects. That's fine too. They are typically well-rewarded for their daring. Most of the people I work with want something in-between these two extremes. Only by learning about the various opportunities that exist can you design the offshore investment plan that's right for you.

As a second prerequisite to global success, you must diversify your portfolio. A first major step in this direction is, in fact, to move assets offshore. When you're used to a domestic investment plan, it is an essential transition to send those first funds outside the United States.

But after you've made the mental shift and expatriated a portion of your money, you must take it the next step. Big offshore profits always come from global diversification. Don't keep all your eggs in one basket, they say. I've found that to be a good motto in the international marketplace. If you spread your money across a multitude of markets and keep it busy in a number of nations, you position yourself to earn money on the big bonanzas — wherever they occur.

Finally, offshore profit demands that you take action. It's not enough to read all the right books, subscribe to all the right magazines, and talk with the best consultants. You must gather together as much information as you feel you need and get started. I firmly believe that the most modest offshore approach is better than none at all. So don't convince yourself that you aren't prepared to begin. If you've found your way to this book, you're ready.

When these three essential elements come together,

you have the makings for a genuine offshore success story. And somewhere along the line, an amazing thing will happen. In a subtle but unmistakable way, you will become a different person. Ultimately, that's what I like best about my work: watching people take on a unique sense of confidence that can come only from seeing their ideas and effort turn into bottom line profits.

Bill Hollings, a client of mine, is a perfect example of this transformation. From our first meeting, after a two-day seminar that I conducted in Dallas, Bill struck me as a classic American entrepeneur. Everything about him — his beige gaberdine suit, his neat dark-brown mustache, his modest manner and cool Texas drawl — conveyed an image of honesty and exactness. He instantly came across as the kind of guy you'd trust with your money.

Over a drink that evening, Bill explained the outline of a fairly simple international business plan. He intended to purchase an offshore bank and use it for two things. First, he wanted to increase his personal assets. Second, he sought to increase his company's visibility. At that time, Bill was operating a first-class limousine service in the Dallas-Fort Worth area. By establishing an offshore presence, he figured he could hob-nob with the rich and famous. In the process, he hoped to expand his client base.

Within a few weeks, Bill had received the official license and charter for his bank in the Pacific Island of Nauru. Within months, he had built it into a thriving, full-service financial center. To begin with, he developed three zero-risk investment programs for people who wanted to benefit from an offshore involvement but who were too hesitant to purchase their own company or bank. These investment programs were structured to let every client find his own level of comfortable risk.

Like most good businessmen, Bill had a sixth sense about promotion. It wasn't long before he had produced some really persuasive yet understated outreach materials. These brochures and postcard mailings added a level of professionalism and credibility to the well-conceived nature of his three offerings. For many investors, the promotional pieces were an initial contact with Bill's bank. What they saw was a serious, sensible service institution that addressed their needs.

After only a year of successful operation, Bill decided to concentrate more of his energy on the offshore marketplace. It had already been very good to him, and he was convinced that it could offer him more than a better limousine service. His bank could be a phenomenally successful business in and of itself. So he started delegating a lot of his Texas business operation to associates, and devoting the bulk of his time to offshore ventures.

He also began to get creative. His tendency to do things in the most traditional manner gave way to a more innovative business style. For instance, he started using his Nauru-based institution to structure and broker large transnational loans. It didn't take long before he was bringing together borrowers and lenders from all over the world in a wide array of interesting partnerships, mergers, acquisitions and start-up ventures.

It wasn't too long before Bill grasped that he was armed with an amazing financial instrument. He had a weapon that could get him through any door. Soon after this realization hit him, Bill read in the Dallas newspapers that the famous Hunt family was running into some major financial problems. Specifically, they were facing the threat of bankruptcy. He instantly saw an opportunity. Never one to waste time, he picked up the phone and called them directly. Not only did he get through, but he designed a loan package that made him a bundle of money.

I recently talked with Bill over the phone. He told me that since buying the bank, he's earned over $25 million. Not bad for three year's work and an initial investment of $30,000. Still, what I like best about his story is the way it shows that offshore business can make millionaires out of fairly ordinary people. Most important, it reveals the way that global money-making affects people.

Bill did not enter the international marketplace as a dynamic man. He was an intense, methodical entrepeneur who had very modest goals for an offshore banking business. Nevertheless, the power and vitality of the offshore environment itself had an effect on him. It freed him from the excessive restrictions that characterize business operations within the United States, and it gave him the tools to make more money than he himself had ever envisioned.

A few months ago Bill was invited to a high society ball in Dallas. He was surprised but elated to receive a gold-engraved invitation to one of the premier social highlights of the year. The word had spread that William T. Hollings was a man to be reckoned with and respected. Through the brillant use of his offshore bank, Bill had positioned himself in such a way that within a short period of time he had moved up into another social stratum. As a banker, he now commands a Texas-size dollop of influence and prestige.

STEP ONE: AN OFFSHORE BANK ACCOUNT

Especially for beginners, it may be reassuring to learn that offshore finance does not need to involve high-stake ventures. In fact, it can be as simple as opening a bank account in a foreign country. You don't have to take the bulk of your assets and move them half way around the world. By doing nothing more than establishing a personal checking or savings account with a bank outside the United States, you can earn a significant profit. Even more important, you can get a taste of the amazing financial opportunities that exist outside the domestic marketplace.

If you're thinking about the possibility of an offshore account, be aware that every foreign financial institution (regardless of its size or jurisdiction) must provide certain services in order to maintain its legal status as a bank. That means your business is extremely important and desirable to any offshore bank. They need your money and your confidence in order to stay in operation. So they'll go far out of their way to keep you satisfied.

It's a very different story here in the United States. All major domestic banks stay in business because of their investment portfolios. In other words, your individual checking or savings account is not a matter of great consequence to them. They're glad to have your business, of course, because it means more money in their coffers with which to invest in real profit-earning ventures. Nevertheless, if you walk out the door today, taking all your money with you, nobody is likely to lose sleep tonight over your departure. This discrepancy between on- and offshore banks results in real benefits to anyone who maintains an account in another country.

To begin with, offshore banks are safer. The myth that U.S. banks offer safety because the government provides insurance for all deposits up to $100,000 means that banks here have the option of being bailed out by the government if they don't follow good management practices. At one time, this insurance was a real protection. But, today, with the whole banking industry experiencing failure after failure and the federal government short of funds, we are facing the prospect of little or no protection. A U.S. bank that fails today may return, at most, twenty-five cents on every dollar to its depositors.

A depositor also has to factor in the additional cost of operating a bank in the United States. Ten to twenty

International Bank of Commerce

Bank Services

Deposit Form SR-1

percent of a U.S. bank's earnings are now allocated to regulatory compliance. At this time, American banks are spending upwards of $100 billion a year to comply with a labyrinth of federal, state and local laws it needs to spend money on these kinds of things? By patronizing these banks, you support the outlay for regulatory compliance and get back less in return.

Conversely, offshore banks do not have the regulatory burden. In fact, as independent entities, they must operate efficiently and economically or they will fail and fold. They don't have the option of falling back on government. In addition, unlike the domestic banks, offshore institutions must maintain a higher ratio of liquidity—the ratio of liquid assets to debts. Their reserve requirements are much higher than onshore banks. In other words, offshore banks are now financially stronger, safer and better managed as a whole than most domestic banks.

Basically, when it comes to the protection of your property, assets and capital, you're the one who has to set the standards. In terms of banks, the higher standards most of us require in today's economic environment is being provided by offshore banks.

Furthermore, offshore banks offer a very attractive interest rate — several percentage points above what you can find at the best U.S. institution. Normally, the longer you keep your money on deposit, the more interest you earn. I know of one private offshore bank that provides its customers with 14-percent-per-annum interest on funds held for at least seven years. Granted, you may not want to tie up your money that long, but the story serves to illustrate just how appealing the offshore banking environment can be.

Float time is another benefit that comes with offshore bank accounts. Have you ever wondered how all those travelers checks turn into big profits for American Express? It's simple, really. Everyday, people around the world exchange their cash for insured American Express Travelers Checks. Literally millions of dollars are cycled through this process week after week, and believe me, that money doesn't sit idly for months while happy vacationers cash one $50 check at a time. Instead, it is intelligently invested into high-interest T-bills and money-market accounts. In other words, during the time between purchase of insured checks and actual onshore bank clearing, American Express is earning interest on your money.

As an individual offshore customer, you can make money from float time in a similar way. For example, if you establish an interest-bearing checking account in a foreign jurisdiction, you can use it to pay your domestic bills. Then, when checks are deposited by your creditors, they begin a long trip back to your offshore bank for clearing. Ordinarily, you can expect that process to take between 30 and 40 days. During that time, you will earn interest on the money you maintain in the account.

It's fairly easy, actually, to open a foreign account. You can do it yourself — by sending a money order or cashier's check made out to the bank along with instructions on what kind of account you want to establish. There are a lot of international investment magazines and journals available now, and all of them contain ads for offshore centers that would like nothing better than to get your unexpected check in the mail one day.

The problem, of course, is your nervousness while you wait for a letter of confirmation from the bank. So I suggest that you let technology do the work faster and with more reliability. Work with a consultant who can implement the initial transaction for you via FAX machines. This also gives you someone nearby to whom you can turn to with questions and concerns during the early days and weeks of managing your foreign account.

You may also be interested in opening "twin accounts" with your offshore bank. This is a specialized service that combines a "current" (checking-type) account with a high-interest deposit account. Most of your money is held in the high-interest deposit, but a small balance is kept on hand for everyday withdrawal. In addition, if you are ever overdrawn, the bank automatically transfers money from your deposit account to cover the difference.

For the slightly more adventurous, there are also fiduciary accounts to consider. They let you use your offshore bank as a proxy investor and earn interest profit at the same time. For instance, let's say you maintain a savings account in a private Liechtenstein bank. You can direct your banker to invest all (or part) of your holdings in U.S. dollars and West German marks. The dollars will be purchased in New York and held in a U.S. bank under the Liechtenstein facility's name. The deutschemarks will be held in a German bank in Frankfurt.

For the record, it appears as though your offshore bank is acting on its own behalf. Nevertheless, all profits earned on the currency exchange and any interest earned on the deposit are paid to you. The Liechtenstein bank makes a commission for the fiduciary service and you make tax-free money because all your profit was earned outside the United States.

STEP TWO: HOW TO DEVELOP AN INTERNATIONAL INVESTMENT GAME PLAN

When you're ready for the next step in profit-earning potential, I would suggest you think about investing in a number of offshore funds. All these funds are straightforward mutual funds based in tax haven jurisdictions or in low-tax nations. Since they operate outside the investor "protection" and tax regulations of this and other major countries, they are able to invest in a broader range of instruments than onshore domestic investment companies. This flexibility makes them extremely attractive to investors worldwide.

To get the most from global diversification, I agree with other financial consultants who recommend that you put at least 15 percent of your portfolio into non-U.S. securities. You can choose either cash or fixed interest securities (like bonds). You can transform your U.S. dollars into any of the world's major currencies or into equities.

Frankly, though, too much choice can be difficult to handle, especially if you're a beginner and operating in unfamiliar territory. For example, can you trust yourself to know the right moment to switch from Japanese to European funds? And picking the big winners from among some 50,000 stocks and bonds traded on more than 100 exchanges in three dozen countries can be overwhelming — even for the most experienced offshore investor.

So, again, my advice is to rely on professionals. If your offshore financial consultant knows this field, let him handle it for you. If he doesn't, he should know someone who does because the size of the market is astounding! There are now at least 70 U.S.-based international equity funds, and more than 500 offshore funds. In addition, there are numerous global funds investing foreign bonds, currencies and other types of securities.

In general, I recommend these international mutual funds because they offer you a kind of one-shot investment strategy. They make it possible for you to put your money on the table and then sit back while experts place it in precisely those locations where it's most likely to make a fast and handsome profit.

Do be aware that there are differences among international funds. Some are what we call "closed-end." That means they invest only in the stocks of a single country. So, in a way, they restrict your money-making power. Nevertheless, some of them have done very well. In fact, one closed-end fund (the Taiwan Fund) recently outperforming all international funds by returning a phenomenal 228.2 percent!

As you might expect, the funds with a heavy focus on the Asian markets — especially Japan's — have been the best performers over most of the past decade. While U.S. stocks rose about 6 percent in 1988, Japanese equities, for example, were up almost 26 percent! And the South Korean stock market didn't even feel a ripple effect from Black Monday. Stocks never fell after the U.S. market plunge and have been at or near record highs for over a year.

Still, some investment pros fret that the Tokyo Stock Exchange is defying the laws of economic gravity. So their advice is to switch out of Japanese equities now. I think the Japanese market best years are behind it. Worldwide mutual-fund dynamo John Templeton, for example, has sold most of the Japanese holdings in his $9 billion fund portfolio. These days, he says, it's better to target resource-rich countries such as Canada and Australia. Other experts suggest that you put your money in Germany and the Netherlands, where stocks are dramatically undervalued. Still others favor Spain, where inflation and interest have fallen and capital investments have picked up.

In my view, the Pacific Rim nations — where double-digit hikes in corporate profits and GNP gains of 6 percent have become commonplace — are also good bets for the 1990s. To help keep tabs on this area, I recommend that you subscribe to the *Far Eastern Economic Review*, a monthly publication covering business and investment activities in the nations of the Pacific Rim. The articles and advertisements featured in each issue can be of enormous help to any investor with interests overseas. Also, the magazine regularly gathers corporate annual reports from many of the world's leading companies, and offers them to readers at no cost. By sending away for reports on Asian-based firms, you can get a very good sense for just how well their stock is likely to do over the coming months.

The point is, nearly all the international funds have surpassed U.S.-based global funds, largely because they face less regulation and fewer investment restrictions. So jump in because the water is warm. And the profits are hot!

STEP THREE: MAKING A TACTICAL DECISION TO OWN AN OFFSHORE COPORATION

If you follow steps one and two that I've outlined above, I guarantee that you'll rapidly feel ready for something more substantial. Once aware of what the offshore marketplace can offer, investors become extremely eager to broaden their horizons. In other words, you'll want to begin running your own offshore operation instead of participating in someone else's.

Like all aspects of offshore business, private ownership abroad comes in various shapes and sizes. One of your options is to set-up or purchase an offshore corporation. What would you do with it? That's entirely up to you. Frankly, you don't have to do anything with it if you don't want to. You can just let it operate as your broker in the international marketplace.

Once you assume ownership of an offshore corporation, you'll be legally entitled to use your firm for a wide variety of activities. For example, it can invest in stocks, commodities, CDs, real estate or foreign currencies. It can also import and export all around the world and serve as a holding company to protect patents and trademarks.

Moreover, many companies based in offshore jurisdictions are used for manufacturing. Starting a company in order to manufacture products can also serve to bring you many benefits such as providing a vehicle for raising capital. However, you usually have a legal obligation to manufacture the product in question: computer parts, clothing, toys, etc. Unless this is your intent, I suggest you stay away from offshore corporations purchased on the basis of proposed manufacturing of goods.

Some individuals have also started offshore safety deposit companies. These are designed to serve individuals who want to keep their valuables safely stored offshore. These companies operate in a similar fashion to safety deposit companies in this country. Owners are able to charge fees for their service.

If this whole process seems a bit overwhelming, don't worry. You can enjoy all the benefits (and disadvantages, unfortunately) of an offshore corporation without having to personally run the company. Reputable and well-connected offshore consultants can make professional management services available. Typically, they'll refer you to a firm based outside the United States. Montreal and Hong Kong are home to a number of these financial managment groups offering a full line of investment and administrative services as well as insurance for the tax-free status of the corporation.

One you assume ownership of an offshore corporation, you'll be legally entitled to use your firm for a wide variety of activities. It can invest in everything from stocks to foreign companies.

Working with one of these firms offers another important benefit. It makes your firm "legitimate" in the eyes of Uncle Sam. You see, without an offshore management firm, it might appear that you are running your offshore company from within the United States. That could prompt the IRS to claim your business is nothing more than a "paper corporation" designed to avoid taxes. However, with overseas management, there's no doubt that your firm is truly a foreign entity — a mandatory prerequisite to convincing the federal government that it has economic substance along with technical form.

There's another offshore business that you may want to investigate. Reinsurance firms — or "captive" insurance companies as they're more often called — have been in business for years all over the world. To benefit from them, you must have a company here in the United States that purchases liability insurance.

By establishing an offshore insurance firm, you can instantly insure yourself against a number of high-risk contingencies: malpractice, striking employees, fire, flood and the like. Instead of paying premiums to a U.S. insurance company, you simply pay them to yourself, in the name of your offshore company. Your domestic corporation will save a lot of money because it won't be contributing to the profit and administrative overhead of an underwriter. And, perhaps best of all, since insurance premiums are tax deductible, you will begin writing tax-deductible premium checks to yourself! The more insurance you buy, the more money you make.

Talk with your consultant about the captive concept. Obviously, it won't be useful to most individual investors. Even small consortiums are probably out of this picture.

You should be aware that if you establish one of these entities, you will need to function as a bona fide reinsurance firm. That's thanks to tax authorities here in the United States who got so upset by the captive concept that they pushed through legislation to force all U.S. corporations to accept third-party reinsurance risks into their foreign insurance pool. In this way, they prove themselves to be true reinsurers and not just ingenious tax evaders.

STEP FOUR: ACQUIRING YOUR OWN BANK

The next step in offshore diversification is to acquire your own offshore bank. This move will allow you to benefit from many of the profit vehicles talked about so far, and will open the door to even more sophisticated profit possibilities. It offers, in my view, a very flexible offshore money-making tool.

For starters, virtually every offshore bank services its owner's personal financial needs. That means that as a bank owner, you will enjoy all the customer benefits associated with offshore banking. And you won't pay a thing to get them because you'll be servicing yourself. In addition, you will gain an appealing new level of financial privacy because much of what you transact will be processed in the bank's name rather than in yours. In a sense, you will become an invisible economic entity protected from the radar-like vision of Uncle Sam and his investigators.

There are, however, more sophisticated profit perks that come with bank ownership. For example, all banks — foreign and domestic — borrow money from their depositors. When you open a checking account at any commercial bank, you are really loaning that institution your money in exchange for a checkbook. Currently, U.S. banks are paying about 5 percent interest on checking accounts. That means that the bank earns at least as much profit on the initial deposit if it is to break even.

Needless to say, the bank's goal is to do a lot better than break even. So, it takes your money, loans it out to third parties at the prime lending rate (today, that's between 9.5 and 14.5 percent depending on the borrower and the situation), and keeps the difference as its profit.

Your private international bank can work in exactly the same way. Deposits can be accepted; loans can be made. The beauty of the concept, from your perspective, is that your bank makes money from both transactions. You earn a little bit from your depositors' money and you get a little more from everyone who borrows from you. In my view, this is the basic concept behind a two-way street to wealth and prosperity in the 1990s.

Once you get enough depositors — who learn about you primarily from aggressive advertising in international financial publications and from third-party associates — your bank can begin to extend credit. It can issue letters of credit and financial guarantees. In other words, it can allow borrowers to deposit a fixed sum of money for a specified period of time (usually ten years). The interest on that deposit is paid into a "sinking fund" which enables the bank to issue money amounting to the deposit plus interest to the borrower.

You profit in three ways. First, your bank charges a nominal fee to issue the letter of commitment. Second, it charges several percentage points to actually issue the loan guarantee. Third, it gains the use of its client's secured deposit during the period of time the guarantee is pending. If the borrower doesn't have enough capital to make the initial deposit, your bank can lend him the money at a higher rate of interest than it pays to establish the sinking fund. Or, if the loan is obtained from a third party, your bank can charge an additional handling fee. So you stand to make money in still a fourth way.

Your offshore bank charter also allows you to provide back-to-back loans. In this particular transaction, funds deposited by one corporate subsidiary are used as collateral for a loan to another subsidiary of the same parent company. It's a fairly common banking process that lets diversified corporations transfer their profits from one business arm to another — usually from a high-tax base of operation to a low-tax jurisdiction. When the parent company is the owner of the offshore bank, the profit incentive is even more compelling because all handling costs and percentage point charges are kept within a kind of revolving money door.

Finally, your offshore bank can offer secured lending. Nearly all offshore banks take advantage of their right to lend money. The most frequently issued loans are for venture capital, high risk projects involving high interest rates. Within the United States, strict laws restrict lending activity at extremely high interest rates. Private offshore banks are not limited by these legal parameters. Instead, they can lend at whatever the free market will allow — sometimes 10 percentage points higher than loans made by conventional lenders.

▌THE MAGNIFICENT SEVEN

Aside from the profits that you earn taking deposits and making loans, your offshore bank provides seven distinct money-making benefits. I call them the "magnificent seven" because, like the movie, they are an unbeatable combination. Each one of them calls for its own skills and financial connections. So, as an offshore bank owner, you will want to work with a professional consultant who can help you network with the right foreign representatives in your chosen jursidiction. Then your only responsibilities will be to serve as the bank's North American Advisor and to dream-up new and creative ways to spend the money you make.

Let's see how many of the magnificent seven appeal to you.

PROFIT BENEFIT NUMBER ONE: INVESTMENT

When all is said and done, offshore banks make money because they invest their deposit reserves in high-yield ventures. Intelligent investment inevitably earns the bank more money than it is required to pay its depositors — no matter what rate of interest it offers. This earning power is possible because foreign banks are not bound by the investment restrictions that limit onshore banks. Instead, they can invest in any number of opportunities, from real estate to high-ticket consumer goods and securites. In my opinion, this single benefit is reason enough to purchase your own offshore bank.

PROFIT BENEFIT NUMBER TWO: CURRENCY EXCHANGE

Many offshore banks offer a currency exchange service to customers living in countries like South Africa, where currency conversion is prohibited by law. The bank earns a profit because it charges a handsome commission (sometimes as high as 20 percent of the deposit) on the transaction.

PROFIT BENEFIT NUMBER THREE: COMMODITIES BROKERAGE

If you like fast-paced business, you might enjoy the wheeling and dealing that comes with this service. I have one client in Tampa, Florida who makes it a cornerstone of his offshore profit strategy. He uses his expertise as a fresh produce distributor to broker commidities to a wide array of North and South American businesses. Through his offshore bank , he issues letters of credit to coffee merchants and produce distributors throughout Columbia, Guatemala and Venezuela. When one of them has a significant surplus, he simply issues his own credit to the dealer. The terms specify that delivery will be made to one of the bank's clients, to be named at a later date. He then shops his network of Latin American and U.S. businesses until he finds an interested buyer, and has his bank negotiate a profitable sale. He tells me he earns between $50,000 and $400,000 on more than a dozen such transactions every year.

PROFIT BENEFIT NUMBER FOUR: SECRET NUMBERED ACCOUNTS

I've probably already made it clear that these anonymous accounts are not my favorite aspect of off-shore finance. Frankly, I think that from a customer's perspective, they're an over-rated dinosaur from the off-shore Stone Age. Nevertheless, a lot of people around the world put considerable value in them. Usually, they are residents of politically turbulent nations who feel a real need to keep a sizeable portion of their assets in a secret account that cannot be linked to them or their familiy members.

Not all foreign jursidictions allow for the Swiss-style numbered bank account. So if you want to provide this customer service, be sure to pick a locale that does. It will definitely help you attract an entire community of international clients and the profits that go along with their business.

PROFIT BENEFIT NUMBER FIVE: TRUSTS

Most offshore banks find it profitable to offer trust-company services. Acting as a trustee under deeds of settlement or will, receiving assets on behalf of clients, and managing them in accordance with their instructions can be a lucrative business. I know that some offshore banks charge up to $10,000 to administer a trust.

PROFIT BENEFIT NUMBER SIX: CASH MANAGEMENT

The goal of any bank is to ensure that capital is legally invested and utilized in high yielding opportunities like commodities and real estate. Unfortunately for U.S. institutions, onshore bank laws prohibit financial facilties from making such investments with their long-term deposit reserves. Offshore banks are far less constrained. They can legally invest all their capital — long- and short-term — in any opportunity they choose.

PROFIT BENEFIT NUMBER SEVEN: ARBITRAGE

"Arbitrage" means the simultaneous buying and selling of the same (or equivalent) securities in different markets. A smart offshore banker can monitor various currency values in a number of markets and take lucrative advantage of the arbitrage process. To put it simply, he can buy low and sell high — all in the same moment. And he can keep the difference as a profit.

For example, an offshore bank might buy deutschemarks for its account in Frankfurt and immediately sell them for Italian lire. Then, if it can find a broker (perhaps in Zurich) who needs lire, the bank can trade again. And this time, it will get more value than it started with.

▌THE BOTTOM LINE

By this point, many of you are wondering how you can become part of the offshore market. For some of you, this is as easy as sitting down and writing a check for the purchase of your own bank. For many others, it takes a level of creativity to go out and actually obtain your very own offshore bank.

One of the most encouraging examples of individual determination I've ever encountered took place at one of my seminars. One of the attendees was a young entrepeneur named Eric Foxman. Although he was very excited about the propsect of offshore banking, he was personally unable to purchase a bank. However, to his credit, he came up with a way that allowed him to become a bank owner.

He convinced a number of investors at the seminar to place a certain amount of money down on the bank. When Eric had enough funds, he purchased the bank in his name with the investors as his partners. The point is that you don't necessarily need the money to own a bank. There are always ways to obtain what you need if you are creative and determined.

A few months ago I received a letter from Eric. He wrote that "everything has gone better than he dreamed." His partners are happy, he's earned enough managing the bank to purchase a substantial percentage of the bank and customers are flocking to its services.

Now as far as you're concerned, how much money can all this put in your pocket? It depends on which offshore financial options you combine in your international investment plan. If you choose to work with just a single foreign bank account, you can probably count on several percentage points more interest than you're earning here in the United States. If your deposit reserves are high, that could mean thousands of dollars a year.

If you add to that foreign account a number of intelligently selected global mutual funds, you've up'ed your profit potential by tens of thousands of dollars. This two-pronged effort is probably a good plan, in fact, for the extremely cautious.

I hope for your sake that you decide to be aggressive because by purchasing your own private international bank, you can surpass those modest profit projections by leaps and bounds. Remember, Bill Hollings made $25 million in just three years! And, Freddy Solis doubled his worth. For each of them, all it took was a modest investment up front, some creative thinking, and one offshore bank.

CHAPTER FIVE

In Pursuit Of True
Financial Privacy

*"The greatest degree of privacy in this society is achieved by
the very rich, the very poor, and the very crooked."*

—Bill Petrocelli, Author
Low Profile

There is a second major concern that brings prospective clients into my office: financial privacy. Over the years, I've heard a staggering number of horror stories from people whose lives have been indelibly marked by corporate and governmental intrusion. Based on what they've told me and on what I've read about U.S. law and economic policy, I am convinced that there is a complex, seemingly invisible information system in this country that has been set up to unearth, store and disseminate even the most personal facts about your life.

If you're like many Americans, you probably assume that the Constitution ensures your unalienable right to privacy. Unfortunately, you're wrong. The Fourth Amendment — the national guarantee most often cited when people talk about confidentiality — specifies only that "the right of the people to be secure in their persons, houses, papers, and effects against unreasonable searches and seizures shall not be violated and no warrants shall issue, but upon probable cause...."

The men of 1787 who drafted this legal tenet clearly meant to protect privacy as it pertained to property. They wanted a right to unthreatened ownership of land and personal possession. But as an article in *Time* magazine recently pointed out, our founding fathers lived in a world where people shared common norms of morality. They didn't need to sort through the questions that plague a global information-service economy. They didn't need to worry about how one man might decide to use (or share) private financial information about another. They didn't foresee an era in which sophisticated communication systems could instantaneously interact, calling up, comparing and exchanging information about you or me within a matter of minutes.

In other words, they didn't foresee the 1990s. Today, the greatest threat to your individual privacy has nothing to do with property theft. It has to do with access to information about you and your activities. Where you live and work, the names of your children, your medical and psychiatric history, your arrest record, the phone numbers you dial, the amount of money you earn, the way you earn it, and how you report it to Uncle Sam after it's yours — these are the information tidbits that will undoubtedly remain stored in lots of different places as long as you keep your money within U.S. borders.

An offshore financial involvement offers you the one and only escape from this government-endorsed conspiracy. Just as you can legitimately make more money oversees than you could ever hope to earn in this country, you can also look forward to enjoying your foreign profits in an atmosphere of complete confidentiality. In money havens scattered from Hong Kong west to Aruba and south to the Netherlands Antilles, you can benefit from iron-clad secrecy laws that strictly forbid any bureaucratic review of your personal financial records. That means you can legally guard your assets from the overzealous inspection that has become part and parcel of U.S. banking and investment portfolio management.

■HOW DEEP CAN THEY DIG FOR DIRT?

If you're like most upper- and middle-income Americans, the federal government alone maintains nearly 20 separate files on you. According to one recent analysis, Uncle Sam currently has computer tabs on three billion files, a virtual treasure trove through which an army of eager bureaucrats can search and snoop. The state in which you reside probably holds another dozen or so active computer files on you. And the Census Bureau routinely updates its records. Any minute of any day, its computer system can spit out your basic data: sex, race, ethnic origin, marital status, employment situation and place in the household pecking order. Most important, it can legally pass any or all of that information along to other interested branches of government.

Then, of course, there's the Internal Revenue Service. The IRS knows how much money you make, and where it comes from. The Social Security Administration probably knows more than you do about your employment earnings history. If you served in the armed forces, you're permanently listed in the archives of the Veterans Administration as well as your service branch.

Are you a borrower? If so, then at least one credit bureau (and probably several) keeps a file on you. Lenders nationwide can request from any one of these independent business operations a slew of information about your income, debts, employment history, marital status, tax liens, judgements, arrests and convictions. The largest of these data collection firms is TRW Inc. maintaining files on some 120 million Americans at any given time.

Still another category of consumer investigation companies collect information about the health habits and lifestyles of likely employment and insurance applicants. How do these agencies get their information? Mainly from the friends, neighbors, employers, landlords and other casual professional associates of those they are investigating. The big daddy of this business is Equifax Services, Inc. based in Atlanta. Equifax sells reports to prospective employers and insurers on well over 20 million people each and every year.

This booming information industry has gone the way of all big business: toward specialization. For example, the Chicago-based Docket-Search Network, Inc. sells a service called "Physician's Alert." It consists solely of information on patients who have filed civil suits. Its clients, naturally enough, tend to be doctors in high-risk specialties like obstetrics and orthopedics.

Then there's Moscom Inc., the world's leading supplier of call-accounting computer systems. Through Moscom's software system, employers can connect their workers' telephones to a personal computer system and track all on-the-job phone calls. The idea is to give executives a bird's eye view of their monthly telephone bill. But in the process, they are spying on who their employees call and how long they talk. Is it such a stretch to envision a future decision to eavesdrop on what they're talking about?

Today, the greatest threat to your individual privacy has nothing to do with property theft. It has to do with access to information about you and your activities.

Sometimes, the information that's conveyed through these systems is painfully accurate. For example, I was once hired by a professional caterer who had spent years living with the negative financial consequences of a past mistake. Jackie was still fairly young when I met her — maybe mid-thirties. She came to see me because her five-year-old business (a good catering service primarly used by the L.A. entertainment industry) had finally taken off and she was becoming quite successful. Along with her partner, she had nurtured a select clientele and they were grossing about a million dollars a year. They wanted to take a percentage of their profits and invest them off-shore. Their goal was a healthy return coupled with a fast turnaround.

During our second meeting, Jackie happened to mention that she had actually started the business out of her small West Hollywood apartment. Now she leased a separate facility, but still lived in the apartment. It seemed odd to me that someone making her kind of money (and obviously aware of strategic financial planning) wouldn't own a home. So I asked her about it. It turned out that while she was still in cooking school, she had bought a brand new Porsche sports car. "It was great while it lasted," she told me. "But on an assistant chef's salary, I couldn't keep up the payments for long." Before she could get out from under a mound of unpaid bills, the car was repossessed.

In hindsight, of course, it's obvious that Jackie shouldn't have bought a car she couldn't afford. But by the same token, it doesn't seem fair that six and a-half years later, her credit rating was still suffering a death blow from that earlier mistake. She had tried to buy a house, she told me, but the past repossession stood out like a glaring red light to every potential lender. None of them were willing to take the risk.

I think it's even more shocking to learn about the victims of inaccurate information transfer. Like one California woman who was unable to buy health insurance because an emergency-room physician treating her after a diabetic attack wrongly diagnosed her as being an alcoholic.

Not long ago, I also read a story about a guy in New York who had received a notice of his dishonorable discharge from the Army — an odd occurence since he'd never been in the service. Finally, he found the source of the problem: a former college roommate had been using his name. "I realized that my Social Security number was stored in I don't know how many data bases across the country," he said. His ex-roommate had everything from bad credit to jail records — all under his name. Unable to persuade credit agencies to change his records, he was in the process of applying for a new Social Security number and driver's license. How's that's for adding insult to injury?

■TECHNOLOGY: BOON OR BANE?

The extent to which misinformation exists is, unfortunately, a matter of sheer speculation. According to some estimates, as much as 50% of all FBI records are inaccurate or incomplete. State criminal records are said to be anywhere between 12 and 49% accurate. And only 13% of all federal agencies bother to audit their own systems for accuracy.

That is particularly alarming when you stop to consider the following: it's Uncle Sam himself who weaves the most complex web of information on U.S. citizens. There are about 85 federal data bases on 114 million people. And it's not just the volume of information that's frightening. Advances in computer technology are making it easy to do what was impossible just a decade ago: cross-match information at the touch of a keyboard.

A network of 15 federal regulatory and enforcement agencies routinely mix and match data — ostensibly in an effort to detect fraud and waste in welfare and social service programs. Divorced fathers who fail to pay child support can be identified. The Education Department can compare data that comes from various record systems to locate wage-earners who have defaulted on their student loans. By comparing its lists with state drivers license records, the Selective Service can ferret out the names of young men who have failed to register for the draft. And the IRS can flag taxpayers who underreport by matching tax returns with information from employers, stockbrokers, mutual funds, and insurers of stocks and bonds.

In fact, the government's most aggressive investigating agency is the IRS. Its debtor master file, created in 1986, is routinely used to withhold tax refunds owed to borrowers who default on federal loans. So far it lists about 750,000 people who owe money to the Education

Department, the Housing & Urban Development Department, the Veterans Administration, and the Small Business Administration.

Business Week reported that Uncle Sam even experimented briefly with buying lists from direct-mail companies, just to find out if the spending habits of targeted individuals were in sync with their reported income.

The program was dropped almost immediately, but the basic concept behind it — computer profiling — is now common practice within government. The idea is to spot combinations of data that characterize the types of individuals likely to engage in specific behaviors or activities. The Drug Enforcement Agency, for example, has worked up profiles of the types of people who are most apt to violate drug laws. The IRS knows the characteristics and behavior patterns of people most likely to underreport income. All this collecting, computerizing, searching, matching, merging, sifting and reporting is meant to spot criminals, cut costs and increase efficiency. Fine. But what about risk of error and federal abuse?

Uncle Sam would like to convince us that the benefits outweigh those risks. And, in fact, national computer monitoring has produced some impressive results. IRS officials argue, for example, that the new technology helped them recover $2.5 billion in 1985 taxes alone — money that would have gone uncollected without the computer cross-matching. From the perspective of a typical U.S. taxpayer, however, the system means that the federal tax man has added one more trick to his already long list of investigation tactics. By flipping through an array of different computer information files, he can now pinpoint even more Americans who owe another few thousand dollars. Or more.

■THE LETTER OF THE LAW

What does the law have to say about this blatant invasion of privacy? What are your rights when it comes to keeping your financial life confidential?

I hate to be the one to tell you, but you don't have many. And the ones you do have are steadily eroding. The bottom line is that while the U.S. Supreme Court has recognized your constitutional right to privacy in some cases, it has repeatedly failed to extend that right to "informational privacy." In other words, you have very limited ability to curtail the collection, exchange or use of information about you or your personal financial situation.

There are, in fact, laws that authorize the invasion of your privacy. One of them is The Bank Secrecy Act of 1970 (Public Law 91-508). Its name is a deceptive misnomer because instead of protecting confidentiality, it gives our government outrageous authority to review and investigate personal and business bank accounts. The law requires all U.S. banks to maintain records of deposit slips and the front and back of all checks drawn over $100. Since it would cost so much to keep these records on hand, banks are allowed to routinely microfilm all your checks — regardless of value. So they do. All of them!

The law also demands that banks maintain records of any credit extension (other than a real estate mortgage) that exceeds $5,000. Banks must report all cash transactions, deposits or withdrawals, in excess of $10,000. They are required to ask you for your Social Security number or taxpayer identification number before any new checking or savings account can be opened. If you do not supply this number within 45 days of the request, your name, address, and account numbers are put on a list for inspection by the Treasury Department.

The law takes routine government inspection a few steps further by requiring that you supply federal officials with your own share of sensitive information. For instance, you must report any transfer of money across U.S. borders if it exceeds $5,000. You must also acknowledge the existence of any foreign bank accounts when completing your annual tax return.

Advocates of the Bank Secrecy Act like to say that it aims at fighting organized and white-collar crime. Maybe. But I seriously question who suffers most from the letter of this law. Criminals and thugs, who are often masterminds at circumventing legal mandates? Or innocent Americans who have never heard of the laws that conspire against their rights to privacy? I have to agree with the late Supreme Court Justice William Douglas who said, "I am not yet ready to agree that America is so possessed with evil that we must level all constitutional barriers to give our civil authorities the tools to catch criminals."

Several individuals and groups have challenged the constitutionality of the Bank Secrecy Act, but in each case, the Supreme Court has ruled in favor of the federal government. In one of the most significant of these rulings, the highest court in this nation said categorically that we are not entitled to any "expectation of privacy" in bank accounts or records. In fact, one of the Justices wrote that in each and every one of our banking transactions, we "take the risk...that the information will be conveyed by the [banker] to the government."

On the bright side, some action has been taken to reduce what privacy expert Mark Skousen calls the "wholesale government inspection of bank records." In his book, *Mark Skousen's Complete Guide to Financial Privacy*, he reviews a few of them. The most important, I think, is the Financial Privacy Act, passed by Congress in 1978. It requires that government investigators notify an individual and give him the opportunity to challenge the search of any bank, savings and loan association, or credit card record before that record is turned over to the government. If Uncle Sam wants to review records without notifying the customer, he must seek a court order barring the bank from notifying its customer of the investigation.

In actuality, a lengthy time delay is the only benefit of the law. Some of the people who have challenged the government's request to see bank records have waited up to nine months before their case was heard in court. And once heard, virtually every judge has ruled in favor of Uncle Sam.

You should also know about the Anti-Crime Act of 1986. In my view, it has given ominous new powers to U.S. Customs, allowing agents the right to search through baggage and mail without a warrant or permission. This new authority applies to departing as well as returning travelers. So, at their discretion, airport Customs officials can now rummage through the things you take out of this country as well as the things you bring back into it.

The Money Laundering and Drug Control Act of 1986 is another frontal attack on personal privacy. This one makes it illegal for bank employees, stockbrokers, real estate agents, automobile dealers, jewelers and other businesses to accept deposits from a "known drug dealer." Granted, it sounds fair so far. But the law also states that deposits are outlawed even before legal conviction. In effect, businessmen and bankers are being told to discriminate against anyone who *appears* to be guilty! That, it seems to me, is diametrically opposed to the principles upon which this nation was founded. Yet it's now the law of the land, passed by Congress and upheld by the courts.

The conspiracy continues even as I write this book. In

mid-1988, the Crime Subcommittee of the House Judiciary Committee approved a bill to amend what it termed "money laundering laws" passed by Congress in 1986. In effect, the bill would take us back to the worst consequences of the Bank Secrecy Act because it would let the Treasury Department and other federal agencies forward to the Justice Department records on any "suspicious financial transactions" without notifying the bank customer.

The panel may also revise and offer at the full committee level a legal amendment which would let banks provide more information to the Treasury Department than is currently permitted without prior customer notification. The new law, if it's passed by Congress, would let your bank and the federal government work behind closed doors to find any wrongdoing in your financial activity — whether it was intentional or not!

By going offshore, you can give yourself an immediate escape valve. You can stop chasing the elusive goal of onshore privacy.

Don't be mistaken about why all this concerns me. I don't condone illegality. I don't think people should evade the taxes they owe to this country; and I certainly don't think that white-collar executives should be allowed to use public or private corporation funds to make outrageous and underhanded profits for themselves. On the other hand, I wonder why our government has decided that the only way of identifying bad guys is to snoop around freely through the personal business matters of law-abiding citizens.

Even more to the point, I wonder why any American with the economic option of moving offshore and into an atmosphere of utter financial privacy would chose to stick around and take the abuse. You deserve something better, and there are plenty of foreign financial centers willing to make you an offer that's hard to refuse.

■ AN OUNCE OF PREVENTION...

To ensure your own financial privacy, you must do two things. First, you must minimize the amount of information that gets created about you. Second, you need to verify and limit access to the information that already exists.

That may sound like elementary advice, but remember, the experts say that we ourselves provide government and private industry with most of the data they maintain on us. In fact, one study concludes that more than 72 percent of the time, investigators obtain their information from the very people they are monitoring.

So, out of respect for the fact that you will probably want to keep some portion of your assets within the United States, I urge you to take a minute and consider ways that you can protect yourself from unnecessary invasion of privacy. Just to get you thinking along the right track, here are some practical suggestions...

First, be aware that that not all domestic banks are alike. They all fall under U.S. banking regulations, but some are more privacy-oriented than others. For example, a number of financial institutions have recently started photographing and fingerprinting customers before completing even the most routine transactions. Don't do business with that kind of place! Instead, look for a bank that's willing to ensure the highest possible level of financial confidentiality.

A good way to identify the right institution is to ask for a written contract that sets down the ground rules for your professional relationship. Make sure your contract includes at least these two provisions: the bank must notify you whenever anyone asks to see your records; and you reserve the right to periodically see and correct any records the bank may keep on you.

A second rule of thumb is to conduct low-profile banking. Think about it. By reviewing nothing more than your monthly checking account statement, an investigating agent could learn a lot about you — where you shop, the restaurants you frequent, the names of friends and relatives, your religious and political affiliations, even the private clubs at which you have a membership. In essence, the account provides a panoramic view of your everyday lifestyle.

You should aim to reduce the clarity of that view. For instance, use your checking account for only ordinary, everyday expenses — mortgage or rent payments, utility bills, car loans. Then, for more sensitive purchases, open and maintain a second account — preferably offshore. Better yet, handle these through a registered trade name. Simply set-up a company and conduct your discreet transactions through its checking account. It's easy to implement this strategy. Your business must be registered, of course, either at the county or state level (or both). It's perfectly legal as long as you register it and use it without intent to defraud, and it will give you a flexible, low-key way to legitimately preserve your privacy.

To keep a low profile, you should probably avoid the wide array of privacy-insurance gimmicks that are around these days. Ultimately, things like invisible ink (meant to protect your checks from the bank's photocopy machine) and red checks (again, intended to limit reproduction) are only going to work against you because they bring attention to you and your account. That's not your goal. You want to preserve privacy, so, you must try to blend in, become invisible within a system that constantly searches for the slightest deviation from routine procedure.

When it comes to investments, be forewarned that some — like interest on bank accounts and dividends from a brokerage account — are automatically reported to the government. Others are known only to brokers, bankers, and fund managers. Still others are not reported to anyone. Within this last (and most appealing) category, there are a number of sub-divisions. For example, information about your commodity futures, options, and non-dividend-paying stocks must be made available for disclosure, but only if someone asks for it. Data relevant to a foreign bank account is reportable to the government, but you are the one who reports it. And investments such as municipal bonds, gold and silver, foreign currency, diamonds, art and other collectibles are not reportable to anyone, not necessarily known to anyone, and not available for disclosure until the investment is sold.

Offshore involvements allow you to have as much privacy as you need. By moving assets offshore you regain control.

Again when it comes to investment, consider the benefits of working through a registered trade name. Brokerage firms accept corporate accounts, and these accounts are used by individuals as well as by large corporations. A professional coporation can trade under its own name, and if titled properly, will ensure the anonymity of the real owner. You should know that your privacy is maintained only at the trading level. Outsiders can still gain access if the brokerage firm chooses to reveal the true owner.

To maintain financial and personal privacy in your correspondence, consider renting a post office box. This, together with a registered trade name, can do a lot to ensure at least a significant amount of confidentiality.

Finally, keep tabs on your credit records. There are about two thousand separate credit bureaus in this country, and they all carry data that could potentially be used against you. Under the Fair Credit Reporting Act, you can demand to know what is in your file. If you disagree with any of the information you find in it, you can insist that another investigation be done. If that second go-around doesn't resolve the matter, you can enter your own statement of explanation as a permanent part of the credit file.

■ IN SEARCH OF THE REAL THING

I opened this chapter with a quote from Bill Petrocelli's excellent book, *Low Profile*. In essence, his entire argument is wrapped up in that short excerpt.

Within the United States, it's possible to work like a dog, diligently and ferociously safeguarding the limited privacy that our legal system still allows. Frankly, the incredibly rich don't need to bother. They're already protected by sophisticated investment plans — usually they include offshore involvements. The very poor don't make much effort either. They're too busy making ends meet, and Uncle Sam isn't vigorous in pursuit of information about them. They don't have enough money to make it worth his while. Finally, of course, there are the very crooked. They don't spend time protecting a legal right to privacy because illegal activity keeps them pretty well-occupied and camouflaged.

That still leaves a lot of people. People like you — upper-income professionals and businessmen whose level of success makes them aware of how the government systematically deprives them of personal financial privacy but who hesitate to take any drastic action.

It's for all those people that I've written this book. By moving a portion of your money offshore, you can give yourself an immediate escape valve. You can stop chasing that elusive goal of onshore privacy, and in the process, you can walk away from the frustration and aggravation that are part of that quest. You can find out what life is like on the other side of excessive government regulation and bureaucratic redtape. You can, for the first time in your life, discover what true financial freedom feels like.

Again and again throughout this book I've said that if you want to design an international investment plan that's tailored to your specific needs, you must establish a one-on-one, professional relationship with an experienced offshore financial consultant. When it comes to structuring a foreign involvement that's sensitive to your genuine concerns about privacy, the same advice holds true.

Nevertheless, there are four basic privacy benefits that apply to almost every offshore venture and can be, implemented in virtually any foreign financial center. Maybe you'd like to review them.

PRIVACY BENEFIT NUMBER ONE: You Can Buy Insurance Against A Banking Or Economic Crisis In The United States

Domestic banks are in bad shape — worse shape, in fact, than most foreign banks. More banks failed in 1987, 1988, 1989 and 1990 than at any other time since the depths of the Great Depression. Of course, your money is insured up to $100,000 by the FDIC, but what would happen in the event of a universal banking crisis? Federal agencies could never handle the massive run on banks that would ensue. Having some money tucked away, in a safe and secure foreign account may be just the protection you need.

Remember, too, that in times of trouble, governments tend to persecute the financially independent by means of price controls, rationing, foreign-exchange controls, prohibition of foreign accounts, confiscation of property, and high taxes. War, and sometimes just the threat of war, can bring with it the sting of government restrictions.

History has also taught that discrimination can rise up and attack even the powerful within a society. At various times, in various places, Jews, Blacks, Asians, Protestants, Catholics and many others have been singled out for disdain. Unfortunately, governments are not immune to their own prejudice. Under federal authority, people around the world have had their property taken away. Sometimes they have also been imprisoned and even killed.

That's why smart investors living in politically and socially explosive countries often keep the bulk of their money offshore. Overriding (and rational) fears of government expropriation push them into a no-choice position. As Americans, we can be far less fearful. Nevertheless, there is growing concern about creeping federal authority over individual economic liberty. As a result, quiet transfers of money and assets have become common.

If the essence of financial privacy means limiting the information that is available about you, then it seems wise to act before the fact. Don't wait until a period of unrest brings you and your assets under federal scrutiny. By then, it will be too late. You won't be able to protect what you've got because Uncle Sam will probably decide to "protect" it for you.

PRIVACY BENEFIT NUMBER TWO: You Can Protect Your Bank Records

If you have the proper government credentials and just

$50, you can gather the following information and material on just about anyone: checks (both front and back copies), bank statements, signature cards, loan applications, deposit and withdrawal slips, and all bank communications. Even more to the point, you can get it without your suspect ever knowing about the probe.

Domestic banks typically release records in the event of civil litigation, court proceedings, and in some IRS audits. A private foreign bank, on the other hand, can protect you from any such invasion. By owning your own offshore bank, for instance, you ensure that all your financial decisions (and the papers that authorize them) are beyond the reach of domestic rules and regulations. Provided your dealings are structured as bank transactions rather than as individual or corporate ones, Uncle Sam has limited authority over the size or frequency of your transactions.

PRIVACY BENEFIT NUMBER THREE: You Can Limit Excessive And Unfair Marketplace Competition

One of the most important privacy benefits you get from an offshore involvement is protection against overly aggressive competitors. Countless fights have taken place in U.S. courtrooms, many of them involving large sums of money and vengeful antagonists. The inclination to sue at the least provocation is on the verge of becoming an epidemic. And the likeliest targets are the people with the most money.

Let's say you become involved in a business situation that ultimately leads to a lawsuit. If you bank within the United States, a court may award your competitor legal access to any or all of your financial records. In the prooess, your privacy may be seriously jeopardized. If, however, your records are kept offshore, they are impervious to court orders.

Another important benefit involves the right to maintain a healthy distance between creative ideas and your competitors. For example, let's say you have a formula or patent that you want to protect. If you decide to copyright the idea here, you must disclose it to the Copyright Office, Immediately, your million-dollar concept becomes part of the public domain. Before you have time to establish a firm market, the idea can be reformulated with minor revisions and translated into your strongest competition.

Instead of going to the appropriate onshore office to file your formula, why not convert it into financial information? Call it "the exhibit to an agreement between a scientist and the formula's owner." If the formula's owner just happens to be an offshore entity, the exhibit is likely to be protected under the bank secrecy laws of the foreign jurisdiction.

PRIVACY BENEFIT NUMBER FOUR: Your Can Separate Your Present From Your Past

Have you ever been the target of ugly gossip or intentional misinformation? It's sometimes based on nothing — just lies and innuendo. Other times, the story has a kernel (or more) of truth. And that's even more difficult to handle.

Most of us have a few skeletons in our closet. When it comes to financial privacy, however, those bones take on particularly ghoulish contour. Past mistakes — from a car repossession to a personal bankruptcy, draft evasion, or a minor criminal record — can haunt you for a very long time. Credit bureaus maintain all their information for at least seven years; and often for even longer.

The truth is, we do not live in a perfect world. People do not dismiss the past from the present. They are not willing to judge associates only on the grounds of firsthand experience. If, for whatever reason, you are interested in separating your past from you present, financial privacy is a must. You will never have it within the domestic financial environment. Offshore centers, however, can guarantee that today is what matters. Yesterday is essentially irrelevant.

There is a more subtle concern that some people have about separating their personal identities. Even if they have no past mistake to hide, they want (and need) to make a clear distinction between various current financial involvements. For example, doctors have a very particular professional image in this society. To protect their medical practice they must appear above and beyond many of the investment projects that the rest of us can implement.

What would you think of a doctor who decided to invest in a bar? Probably not much. Yet he has every right to experiment with profitable ventures. By handling his affairs offshore, he can keep a desirable distance between his Manhattan medical practice and his Miami Beach bar and grill.

■AS MUCH OR AS LITTLE AS YOU LIKE

Privacy is a relative concern. It can mean virtually nothing to one person while it means everything to the next. Only hermits know complete confidentiality, and they pay a high price for it. They're isolated from everything. Nobody knows anything about them but, then, they don't know about anybody or anything.

Most of us don't want privacy when it costs that much. At the same time, very few of us want to just hand-over the details of our financial lives to the government. Instead, we want some middle-ground, some halfway point between hyper-sensitive secrecy and flagrant economic exposure.

Offshore involvements — everything from a checking

account in some Carribean tax haven to a private international bank or corporation — allow you to have as much privacy as you need. If you want to declare everything to Uncle Sam, there's no law forbidding you from doing so. If, on the other hand, you want a strict guarantee of confidentiality in all your personal financial dealings, you can have it.

The point is, by moving assets offshore, you regain control. Within the United States, you must play according to federal rules — rules that get a little less citizen-oriented every year. Offshore, there are entire jurisdictions organized to play by your rules. You design the game, and you get to be the winner.

CHAPTER SIX

Offshore Tax Protection

"Domestic law and tax provisions are the least personal, coldest, and most complicated aspects of placing funds abroad. These are the most critical...criteria in the whole issue of tax haven use."

—Robert Kinsman

Someone once said that there are only two absolutes in this world: death and taxes. That's certainly true for U.S. citizens. In fact, concern over excessive taxation is the third major motivation for offshore banking. Well over half my clients initially move into the global marketplace — at least in part — to legally reduce their tax load.

Rob and Bonnie Marsh are a perfect example. About two years ago, they walked into my office and related an all too typical tax nightmare. For nearly four years, they had owned and operated their own business, leasing office equipment (such as FAX machines, copiers, computers and cellular telephones) to small companies and private individuals. When we met, they had two locations in Los Angeles and were planning to open a third.

Everything had been going well, they said, until a recent meeting with their accountant. Due to changes in the tax law, they owed an enormous corporate tax. I didn't ask them for an exact figure but Rob kept mentioning the "unfairness of a $75,000 tax bill."

That was only the first level of their problem. Rob and Bonnie also faced a huge individual income tax. They asked me about the consequences of not paying the debt promptly. I told them what I tell all clients in that situation: the worst creditor in the world is the IRS. Beg for the money. Borrow it. Even sing for your supper if you must. But pay the IRS what you owe them because they can make your life miserable until you do.

I sat there, watching and listening as they explained their situation, and I was reminded that success brings a lot of complex responsibilities. Rob and Bonnie were both very smart, and obviously industrious enough to transform a good business idea into a thriving company. Yet they had forgotten an essential part of good business operation. They had forgotten to tax plan. They had done a great job at making money, but they had completely overlooked the task of safeguarding their profit.

They had become successful, but they hadn't managed their success very well. And for that error, they were going to share a lot of the money they had earned with an unfeeling relative: Uncle Sam.

After a couple of meetings and some in-depth conversation about the international market, Rob and Bonnie decided to purchase an offshore entity. On the one hand, they reasoned, a privately-owned facility would be a boon to their business. For example, they could use the bank or corporation to finance the leasing of their equipment offshore. Since most of it was made in Japan or Korea, anyway, they could save themselves the mark-up that comes with buying imports.

On the other hand, their own offshore financial tool could offer a convenient, legitimate way to structure both personal and business tax savings. Specifically, they arranged to make it the sole owner of their onshore business. In the process, they divorced themselves personally from the company's profits but still ensured themselves total control over its financial management. The end result: at last our meeting, Rob and Bonnie said they had cut their overall current tax burden by more than 60 percent!

■SURVEYING THE TERRAIN: TAX REFORM

Speaking from a tax perspective, things have come a long way since 1776. And you might say they've moved in the wrong direction! It's ironic, really, to think that this country was born out of history's most successful tax revolt. Until 1913, there was absolutely no income tax levied against any U.S. citizen.

Yet, as this book goes to press, the United States is home to the most complicated and burdensome tax laws in the world. A New York City Tax Committee Report from the late 1960s found that this nation's tax code was beyond the understanding of most tax specialists. And that was more than 20 years ago! The situation has only worsened since then. Indeed, the tax problem is now considered so severe that every federal administration, each new session of Congress, and virtually all political candidates make the promise to work toward relief for individuals as well as businesses, and to simplify the tax code. When Ronald Reagan ran for President in 1980, one of his major platforms was tax reform and simplification. Yet, most experts agree that his 1986 Tax Reform Act did not manage to deliver what he promised to ensure: lower taxes for most Americans. Granted, the law does represent the most massive overhaul of our tax system in decades. But for a piece of legislation that was described as both simple and fair, it's turning out to be intimidatingly complex and arguably just for tax lawyers.

According to a recent study by the Congressional Budget Office, the tax reform will not have a positive impact on most taxpayers. The study reveals that, on the whole, Americans will continue to pay the same portion of their income (about 25%) to the federal government as they paid in 1977. That means no real tax relief in more than a decade!

The *National Review* has put the situation into even clearer focus. "Recent research has worked through the net impact of the total tax package," the journal reports. And the evidence is overwhelming: "all income brackets above $50,000 pay more in taxes under the new tax laws. Considerably more." Let me translate that into concrete figures. Taxpayers who earned $200,000 and above in 1988 saw their tax liability rise as high as 12.9 percent over what they would have paid under the old law.

Unfortunately, the outlook for the next few years is not uplifting. All indicators suggest that tax rates will continue to rise, with a significant jump expected in 1991 and 1992. Many of you have already learned that the promised tax rate of 28 percent for 1988 was actually a phantom pledge because the Congress sneaked in a surtax of 5 percent on income over $43,150 for individuals and $71,900 for couples filing jointly.

In addition to higher income tax rates, a number of other tax hikes have been proposed and are already on the table for discussion. Although I won't predict the specific outcome of that discussion, I suspect that increases will most likely come in the form of higher excise taxes, increased energy taxes, the probable value-added tax also known as a VAT.

Tax avoidance and tax evasion are two very different things. When you avoid tax, you decide to use all legal means available to reduce your tax burden.

Regardless of the specific tax hikes, one thing seems certain: there will be further tax increases levied against U.S. citizens. After a decade of borrowing money and running up annual deficits of more than $200 billion, the federal government literally has no choice but to tax its citizens as harshly as the law and legal system will allow. For those who keep assets within the domestic economy, that means more income passed on to Uncle Sam and less available for lifestyle, children, business and savings.

But perhaps the most frightening thing about the 1986 Tax Reform Act is its impact on the U.S. capital gains tax. In fact, for a country that is supposed to believe in capitalism, America — thanks to the '86 reform — has become nothing less than hostage to a pathetic capital-gains tax structure.

To fully understand the significance of the transformation, let me remind you that there are two distinctly different ways to earn money in this country. The first way is return on labor: salary, wages, and fees for professional service. This is your income, the money you live on and a portion of which you pay the IRS as your personal income tax. The rate at which you are taxed on personal income depends on how much you earn. I suspect that most of my readers are likely in the 28% tax bracket, meaning that once all legitimate deductions are subtracted from your income, you pay Uncle Sam a little less than one-third your total earnings.

There is a second way to earn money. It's called return on capital, or "passive" income. It's the money you make each year on your investments. Those investments can be interest on savings deposits, loans or bonds; rental income; patents; stock dividends; or royalties. Put simply, the 1986 Tax Reform Act has played havoc with the tax rate imposed on this second kind of income. It has resulted in the largest increase in the capital-gains tax rate ever imposed by the federal government.

Before the tax reform measure became law, the top rate of capital-gains tax in America was 20%. That's outrageous enough, if you ask me. Many countries, in order to encourage capital investment, do not even tax capital gains. But in 1988 — just two years after passage of the new law — the maxiumum rate shot up to a staggering maximum effective rate of 38.5% for short-term investment profits. As of January, 1988, capital gains were taxed just like ordinary income and, so, were permanently linked to each taxpayer's personal income tax bracket. For affluent Americans, that means millions and millions of new dollars tucked into Uncle Sam's pocket each and every year.

In my opinion, the federal government has gone way over the edge on this matter. Right now, Americans pay one of the highest tax rates in the world on income generated by capital. That's one of the major reasons for our longstanding stock market stall, and a key reason why American business has been so slow to invest in new factories and equipment. I don't think our economy can function for long under the weight of this new capital gains tax structure. Something will have to give. And soon.

A study done by Arthur Andersen, an accountancy firm, reveals that of the 11 industrial nations, only Australia and Great Britian have higher long-term capital gains taxes than the United States. Germany and Japan, for example, don't impose any capital gains tax. In the desperate attempt to reduce its insurmountable debts, the United States is trying to implement a tax law that would be laughed out of virtually every other capitalist nation on earth.

President Bush is on the record for wanting to cut the tax rate on capital gains to 15% on assets held for at least one year. Although this still seems high to me — when offshore options offer so much more appealing a tax structure — it's definitely a move in the right direction. At a time when most of the capitalist world is moving toward cutting capital-gains taxes in an effort to promote equity investment, we need to get in touch with economic reality.

■ EXPLORING THE OPTIONS

So what are intelligent Americans supposed to do with their money? Fling open their wallets, pockets and checkbooks to pour it into the lap of the IRS?

Some experts argue that you might as well because it's becoming harder and harder to protect your onshore assets from the government's invading eye. So hard, in fact, that even smart guys have started to make stupid mistakes. For example, the *Wall Street Journal* reported a few years ago that one well-respected investment banker kept $700,000 in cash in a closet, and he used it to pay his babysitter.

Aren't there better ways to deal with that kind of cash?

Not nearly as many as you might think. To show you what I mean, let's run through some of the choices that would confront you if you woke up tomorrow morning with just that amount of cold cash sitting on your dresser.

The obvious place to put $700,000 cash, you might be thinking, is in a bank account. But remember, we've already established that there's a law requiring banks to tattle on anyone who deposits or withdraws more than $10,000 in currency. So why not hire runners to open accounts at 75 different banks and deposit just under $10,000 in each? Because there's also a law which makes that practice illegal. And each deposit increases your chances of being caught because banks are also required to report under-$10,000 transactions from anyone who "looks suspicious."

Once upon a time, bearer municipal bonds offered a way to invest a big "stash." No more. The 1982 tax law bans new issues of bearer tax-exempts. A shrinking pool of pre-1982 bearer munis can be bought secondhand, and banks are not required to report depositors who cash in the coupons. But the game is up when the bond matures. Redeeming the bond at either a bank or a stockbroker causes a 1099-B report to go directly to the IRS.

Buying stocks won't work, either. Just like banks, brokers are required to report deposits over $10,000. Charles Schwab, a leading stock brokerage firm, won't even take cash at its teller cages. Merrill Lynch won't take more than $100.

What about using that $700,000 the old-fashioned

way? You could spend it. The truth is, you could try. Theater tickets and restaurant meals are safe. But that's a lot of Broadway musicals and caviar. So what about bigger purchases, you say. Well, don't try to buy a Mercedes with it because car dealers (and all businesses) must file a form 8300 with the IRS on all cash purchases over $10,000. Large winnings and purchases of gambling chips at casinos are also reportable.

On a final note, let me pass along one more news item. The IRS hired 2,500 auditors every year for the last three years. That means Uncle Sam is increasing his "police force" by a hefty 26 percent!

As you may have already suspected, I do have another solution to propose. You could take your $700,000 and move it offshore. By purchasing your own international corporation or bank, and making it the owner and manager of your assets, you would side-step the whole IRS mess and save a lot of the money you'd make in a more profitable environment than the U.S. market.

■THE OFFSHORE TAX ADVANTAGE

Is offshore tax protection really feasible, given the government's increasing mania for stricter enforcement? Of course it's feasible! And you know why? Because in today's economy, it's necessary. Americans, on the average, are better-educated and more self-directed than ever before. In growing numbers, they see the possibility of a genuine transnational economy. Like never before, they're learning to shop around for the best investments and the best places in which to make them. Typically, that takes them outside U.S. borders.

With billions of dollars at stake, foreign jurisdictions are extremely eager to create low-tax enclaves for disgruntled Americans and other high-tax nation residents. It's the simple law of supply and demand. A lucrative foreign market has nurtured tax havens that have existed for many years, and it's led to the creation of a number of new tax sanctuaries.

There's another important reason why offshore tax protection exists. It's the reflection of a basic human instinct: positive self-interest. Intelligent men and women who work hard to achieve something usually want more success and more protection for the sucess they've already achieved. Perhaps it's true that a fool and his money are soon parted. But smart people want to hold on to theirs.

Isn't that what you'd want to do with that $700,000 sitting on your dresser? You'd want to protect it as best you could from taxation and creditors, and if possible, you'd want to make it earn you even more money. To show you how offshore economics can help achieve both goals, let's examine one scenario for managing just half of that imaginary fortune. I'm cutting the figure down because I want you to see that it takes only a reasonable investment to produce amazing offshore results!

It is not illegal to place your money outside the government's sphere of authority.

First, you should take about $40,000 and purchase an offshore bank charter and license in, let's say, in the Caribbean money haven of Aruba. I suggest that you commission an experienced native resident to work as your part-time bank agent. I also urge you to set-up a well-equipped home office — complete with xerox machine, a FAX, two telephones and a top-notch computer system.

Once your office and the offshore facility are operational, you can really get to work. You would be wise to have your agent work in tandem with one of the better international investment management firms to identify lucrative foreign investment and partnership opportunities. Canada is home to a number of these firms, so ask around. And check out the possibilities with your offshore banking specialist. After careful review of your options, and within six months, you might aim to spend in the neighborhood of $200,000 on intelligent selections.

All of your investments would technically belong to the offshore entity, of course. So any profit made on them falls under Aruba rather than U.S. tax law.

I suggest you start to quickly borrow money from your offshore company or bank. The bank, of course, will charge you the highest possible interest rate. You pay the interest, which is wholly deductible, and deposit the money back in the bank. Immediately, the bank can extend another loan to you. Now you'll begin paying the bank interest on the second loan as well as the first, and it, too, is wholly deductible. The interest payments received by the bank are tax-free, so as they accumulate offshore, you can reinvest them over and over again with no tax penalty. (The United States imposes a 30% withholding on the interest paid to a foreign corporation or financial entity. This withholding can be eliminated with proper tax planning.)

You need not be content with a bank that has only you for a customer, though. Through professional advertising in a number of international investment journals, you can also begin attracting depositors to your offshore bank. Using the same six month timeframe, I would say $100,000 is a very conservative estimate of what might come your way. That money, in turn, could be used to make loans to individuals and small businesses.

So, at the end of one year — for an initial investment of around $300,000 — you could have established an international presence, entered into a number of lucrative foreign business ventures, avoided tens of thousands in taxes, and actually earned some cold cash in the form of deposits and interest income.

What about the money that's left over? If you're smart, some of it will have gone to a top-notch international financial consultant. Plan, too, on all the extravagant meals you can want at your favorite restaurants. And by all means, figure in money for at least one quick trip to your Caribbean tax haven. I can tell you from experience, vacation spots don't come much better!

HOW TO STRUCTURE OFFSHORE TAX BREAKS

From a tax expert's point of view, a single and important distinction rests at the heart of offshore banking's appeal. Tax avoidance and tax evasion are two very different things. When you avoid tax, you decide to use all legal means available to reduce your tax burden. When you evade tax, you opt to use illegal means to achieve the same end.

Any reputable accountant will encourage you to avoid taxation. In fact, if your accountant isn't working with you to plan intelligent tax avoidance strategies, I'd suggest you look for a new accountant. His job, after all, is to help you design legal and appropriate ways in which to reduce your taxable income and increase your untaxable investments.

If, on the other hand, your accountant were to sit back while you intentionally failed to report a part of your income so as to reduce taxes, he would be tacitly going along with a criminal action. It is against the law to hide any percentage of your money — no matter how small — from Uncle Sam. It is not, however, illegal or immoral to place your money outside the government's sphere of tax authority. And that's where the beauty of offshore investing comes into clear focus.

A privately-owned corporation or bank in a foreign jurisdiction lets you have the ultimate in business confidentiality. It separates you from your money in a way that protects you from the reach of IRS. At the same time, it allows you absolute control over the movements and activity of your money.

An offshore corporation or bank is as much a legal entity as yoy are. Therefore, to the IRS and other governmental agencies, its assets, liabilities, and income are its own. In practical terms, that means you can sell your investments —subject to certain rules — to a foreign company bank (which, of course, you own) and immediately make the bank responsible for any tax due on the profits from those investments. In addition, any future appreciation will be transferred to the bank.

You also limit your liability. Again, the key is proper tax planning. You will also not be subject to current tax laws and if you repatriate your assets later, you will be able to use them. In other words, the bank or company is a business. It accumulates assets. It can be used to finance local operations and to fund export activities.

By establishing the bank or corporation offshore, in a jurisdiction that imposes little or no tax, you prevent confiscation of profits by the host nation. And, best of all, you deny Uncle Sam — ravenous as he is for additional tax dollars — any claim whatsoever to those profits. After all, even the IRS cannot levy U.S. tax on a foreign business operating outside its jurisdiction!

In order to make this offshore tax avoidance formula work for you, remember the three basic characteristics of any true "tax shelter":

• They are separate from their creator by guaranteeing that the income they receive from their investments cannot be considered part of his or her income;

- They are domiciled in countries where the tax situation is much better than in their creator's home country;

- They can be indirectly controlled by their creator, and their assets managed by him as he sees fit, without tax liability in his home country.

I should point out that the economic perfection of this tax avoidance strategy will not last forever. The U.S. federal government is not blind to the realities of offshore investing, and it's not thrilled that foreign financial centers are offering U.S. citizens a legal way to circumvent taxes. Nevertheless, for the time being, Uncle Sam can't do much about it.

Over the past several years, the United States has extended tax treaties to a number of well-known tax haven nations. In each case, the aim has been to establish an open dialogue between our government and theirs on the subject of U.S. investor involvement in the offshore financial community. There's a major obstacle to the treaties' usefulness, however. Tax haven jurisdictions have far more to gain by protecting owners (who pay handsome licensing fees and governmental service charges on certain transactions) than by finking on them to the IRS.

Historically, tax loopholes are short-lived. Chances are, the offshore "loophole" will eventually fade to a mere shadow of what it is today. Still, for U.S. investors who act quickly, there's time for incredible tax savings. And, quite frankly, even if the U.S. government does manage to gradually suffocate offshore investing's tax appeal, it would take decades — perhaps an entire century — for the offshore tax situation to get half as bad as it has already become here in the United States!

Put simply, the longer you wait to plan your tax avoidance program, the more money you lose. Every day that you delay costs you a percentage of your earnings. I always tell my clients to view taxes in concrete terms. Just like the money in your pocket, taxes represent your time, your energy, and your talent. What percentage of those personal commodities are you willing to give the IRS? Once you've made that determination, you must assertively act to protect the rest.

If you feel that you are working to build something that will last; something that will be there when you decide to retire; something that you can count on in an emergency; something you can pass on to your heirs — then tax planning, with an offshore instrument as the centerpiece, must be a priority.

THE "BARRIERS" AND THE "EXEMPTIONS"

There's an interesting history behind the tax advantages of offshore investing particularly the banking aspect. Back in the late 1950s and early 60s, federal officials became alarmed by the alluring tax benefits to be had by U.S. investors involved abroad. Their fear was simple enough: if too many investors moved assets offshore, the IRS could lose millions in annual revenue. So, as a precautionary move, President Kennedy urged Congress, in 1962, to prevent Americans from using tax havens. Within months, legislation was introduced which taxed every American citizen who owned a controlling interest in any foreign corporation.

It wasn't long before the U.S. banking industry got wind of the proposal and quickly moved to modify it.

Virtually every major bank in this nation lobbied against the tax law. If their foreign subsidiaries were taxed at a shareholder level, they explained, then they would be unable to compete effectively against their foreign competitors.

Congress was convinced, and basically built in a series of tax breaks for American-owned banks operating outside the United States. These special privileges continue to apply to any merchant bank that purchases and sells stocks as an underwriter; acts as an investment advisor, merger consultant, or business manager; or engages in a broad range of manufacturing and business activities outside U.S. borders.

Let's take a look at some of the taxes that you can effectively avoid by owning an offshore facility. I think the list is impressive.

- *The Controlled Foreign Corporation (CFC) Tax* is a major barrier to tax avoidance. It applies to all foreign corporations closely held by either a U.S. corporation or individual. Normally, when no more than ten U.S. citizens own such a foreign company, they are all subject to the current federal tax on their proportionate share of that company's worldwide interests, dividends, and royalties. In other words, the CFC tax allows Uncle Sam to take a hefty share of "passive income" from each of these shareholders — all of whom are treated as if the corporation (as a seperate legal entity) did not exist.

- *The Foreign Personal Holding Company (FPHC) Tax* was adopted many years ago to attack incorporated pocketbooks which operate in tax havens and which receive passive income. The tax is imposed only in the case of passive income generated by a foreign corporation that is owned by no more than five U.S. citizens. In such cases, each shareholder is taxed as if the corporation did not exist.

7 Barriers & Exemptions

1. Effectively-Connected-with-U.S. Tax:
   Offshore Bank is Exempt
2. PFIC TAX:
   Offshore Bank is Exempt
3. FIC Tax:
   Offshore Bank is Exempt
4. PHC Tax:
   Offshore Bank is Exempt
5. AE Tax:
   Offshore Bank is Exempt
6. FPHC Tax:
   Offshore Bank is Exempt
7. CFC Tax:
   Offshore Bank is Exempt

Typically, this barrier to tax avoidance is insurmountable, but under the provisions governing it, foreign banks receive special exemption from the IRS if they can show that the bank was created for some express purpose other than pure tax avoidance.

- The Accumulated Earnings (AE) Tax applies to both foreign- and U.S.-based corporations that are owned by U.S. citizens. Put simply, it taxes all accumulated earnings that are considered "unnecessary" for the business of the corporation. The AE tax burden can be as high as 38% on undistributed U.S.-source accumulated earnings in excess of $150,000 per year. It also imposes a penalty tax on those earnings that cannot be justifiably retained.

An offshore bank can qualify for exemption from this tax because all banks — in the everyday course of business operation — accumulate earnings. That's the way they make the portfolio investments that keep them afloat.

- *The Personal Holding Company (phc) Tax*, imposed at the rate of 70%, applies to foreign- as well as U.S.-based corporations that are owned by less than ten Americans. It is incurred directly by the company and not by its shareholders. In the case of a tax-haven corporation, it applies to closely-held haven businesses, and is imposed on all relevant U.S. source passive income.

Offshore banks may avoid this tax because their income is not technically considered to be "passive."

- Foreign Investment Company (FIC) Tax is imposed annually on U.S.-owned foreign corporations that exist primarily to invest in stocks or commodity futures.

An offshore bank is exempt from this tax so long as it functions as more than an international brokerage house.

- *Passive Foreign Investment Company (PFIC)* was enacted in 1986 because the U.S. Congress was concerned that some taxpayers were able to avoid many of the IRS traps by careful tax planning. The PFIC rules add a surtax on all distributions to U.S. shareholders from a foreign company unless the company was actively engaged in business and most of its assets are used in that business. A foreign bank registered in the United States can avoid the PFIC rule. Also, the PFIC rules can be avoided or their impact minimized through careful tax planning.

- *Effectively-connected-with-U.S.. Tax* is a nebulous-sounding federal practice. It basically imposes a tax on the U.S. source income of any foreign-based but

U.S.-owned corporation if that income is "effectively connected with a U.S. business."

An offshore bank is exempt from this tax because its activities, to a large extent, are treated as if they were conducted offshore through a resident agent.

■JUST A WORD OF WARNING...

Remember that even within the international market, laws apply. A vast majority of the people I meet in my work see offshore banking and business as a legitimate escape from our over-zealous U.S. tax system. Occasionally, however, I hear about someone who views it as something else: a way to conduct profitable but illicit business activity.

Howard Fisher, a well-known tax attorney, likes to tell a particular story about one of these offshore rogues. I'm going to borrow the tale because it has important lessons to offer. First, it shows how tempting it can be to break the law when you enter the foreign market. It's like being set free inside your favorite candy shop: with so much to choose from, it can be hard to watch your weight. I also like the story because it shows how offshore financial trouble can come from the least likely source. And, finally, the story shows how you can operate legitimately on all the major levels, but ultimately be destroyed by the small details.

Gucci is, for most discriminating shoppers, a familiar name. Luggage, briefcases, purses, and innumerable accessories all of them expensive — are the products made by the firm. Most shoppers don't know, however, that the company's founder, Dr. Aldo Gucci, made part of his fortune with help from an illegal offshore scheme.

When Gucci entered the offshore market, he was a successful middle-aged physician who wanted to use his hard-earned capital as a ticket into the lucrative world of foreign investment. So he hired a high-priced Manhattan tax attorney, and told him to establish a company called "Gucci USA." It would design and market some of the most expensive leather accessories in the world, he said, and market them throughout the United States and the rest of the world.

Next, based on some pretty "creative" advice from his attorney, Dr. Gucci decided to establish a foreign-based subsidiary. The foreign company was to develop concepts for new products, research the marketablility of those products, and attempt to sell the designs to interested manufacturers abroad. After considering the options, he selected Hong Kong as the offshore jurisdiction for the subsidiary because of its tax allure, and within a few months, he had signed a licensing agreement with his own Hong Kong company, stipulating that it would receive 10 percent of Gucci USA's gross annual income to use as operational funds.

It was a bold scheme. Imagine being able to take 10 percent of an enormous gross annual income, move it out of this country without ever paying tax on it, use it to make millions offshore, and keep the money within a foreign financial center that imposes no tax on capital gain. It was illegal, of course, because the Gucci subsidiary never really functioned at all. It was a paper front that allowed Dr Gucci to funnel unreported personal and corporate income into an offshore tax haven.

Nevertheless, the idea worked for 15 years.

And eventually, when Dr. Gucci was caught, it had absolutely nothing to do with a thorough IRS investigation. He was caught because his own children turned him in. They felt that they were not getting their fair share of his burgeoning financial empire. So they decided to make money another way. They matter-of-factly went to the IRS and gave them the name of their

Dad's front company. They also offered its bank account number and the name of its bank, Chase Hong Kong. In exchange, they asked to collect the reward that's typically given for such information: up to 10 percent of the amount of unpaid tax due on accumlated profit.

As long as they were at it, the Gucci kids also decided to tell Uncle Sam who held the shares of the Hong Kong Company: two Panamanian-chartered companies. And if that wasn't good enough for the government, they even told officials where the actual shares were held.

Guess what the IRS did with all this information? Went directly after Dr. Gucci? No, because the government couldn't convince its star "witnesses" to testify in open court. What's more, the IRS didn't have anything that could be used to indict Dr. Gucci. So, as small comfort, Uncle Sam went after his bank. The IRS went to Chase Manhattan in New York, the parent bank company, and asked them to make Chase Hong Kong provide records on Dr. Gucci's transactions. Chase New York refused to comply and, so, the IRS decided to sue them.

Of course, the bank lost their case. So they took it all the way to the appellate court. And, again, they lost. In fact, I suspect that they knew all along that they would lose. But they also knew that if they rolled over too quickly on a big client like Gucci, their name would be mud with every major international investor.

Just to end the story, let me tell you how Dr. Gucci was ultimately nabbed. When all the dust settled, they got him on a technicality. He was shown to have had a "defective license agreement." In other words, they showed that there had not been enough activity within Gucci's Hong Kong subsidiary to prove it a legitimate business entity. In fact, during the 15 years that the agreement was in place, only three drawings or plans for new products had been produced by the firm. They had all been sent to the United States for approval, but none of the three ever resulted in an actual product. And the killer was that all three drawings had been prepared by an employee in New Jersey!

As soon as Chase New York turned over its records on Gucci USA, Dr. Gucci pleaded guilty and he wound-up spending 18 months in a New York wayhouse.

I've shared this story because it illustrates the fact that offshore crime really doesn't pay. At least not very often. And not forever. Certainly there are international players who find illegitimate ways to make big money up front, but over the long haul, they pay a high price for the profit. They must constantly worry about exposure, and more often than not, they end up paying Uncle Sam anyway — from a prison cell especially designed for white collar crooks.

The longer you wait to plan your tax avoidance program, the more money you lose.

It's one thing to out-smart the IRS at its own game. It's another to break the law. How can you tell the difference? When you cannot comfortably trace your actions with clear explanations for why you did what you did, you've probably crossed the line from shrewd offshore venture strategy into criminal business operation. That's an extremely important distinction.

■ THE SPIRIT OF AMERICA

There are tens of thousands of people throughout this country who mind their own business, apply themselves, and make a real contribution to our economy. Yet, with the passage of each new tax law, they must hold on tighter in the effort to keep an equitable fraction of the fruits of their labor.

Every year, the President, the Congress, and the Supreme Court give IRS officials more money, more laws, and more leeway to collect revenues from us all. They get better computers, more agents, more auditors. It's a virtual army against each individual and each family.

Ironically, however, it's the very complexity of the U.S. tax system that offers wise Americans the one remaining way out from under excessive taxation. With the help of an experienced financial consultant, you can turn the ambiguities and inconsistencies of our tax code to your own advantage. You can break away from the uninformed majority and revolutionize your economic life. I believe that in making such a move, you reflect the finest spirit of this nation: individual ingenuity and the pursuit of personal betterment.

Right now, offshore banks and some foreign companies let you legally move assets outside the U.S. beyond the reach of Uncle Sam. The special tax breaks they provide may not last forever, but for the moment, there are fortunes to be made abroad.

CHAPTER SEVEN

Protecting Your Assets

"The simple answer to the question, 'Do I need to protect my assets?' is yes, unless you don't care about the wealth you have accumulated."

—Howard S. Fisher,
International Tax Attorney

Most successful Americans want a very basic kind of financial freedom. They want to be able to spend the largest possible percentage of the wealth they have accumulated in whatever way they see fit, and they want to be able to will what remains upon their death to their heirs.

There's nothing terribly complex or bewildering about such a liberty. In fact, it complements the economic ethics that built our nation: a guarantee of free enterprise and the promise that every generation might prosper beyond what it came from to ensure a better life for those it leaves behind.

Unfortunately, it's only a small minority of affluent Americans who ever manage to enjoy this kind of freedom. The reality for everyone else is far more sobering. Even upper-income professionals often find themselves working twice as hard as their parents just to accumulate half as many assets. Recent surveys find that only 20 percent of all U.S. citizens can afford to buy a home. Two-car families now require in the neighborhood of a thousand dollars a month just for mid-luxury transportation. Private education costs between four and eight thousand dollars a year per child — and that's for elementary school. As one friend of mine with two sons in college recently said, "Tuition means I have to deduct $45,000 a year from my income before I can even think about eating or keeping a roof over my head."

Put simply, true asset protection does not exist in this country. Just for starters, there's Uncle Sam to attack the kitty. Immediately after he takes his share, you've probably lost a full one-third of what you had to begin with. Then there's state tax to pay, social security tax, gasoline tax, consumer tax and, of course, estate tax on anything you inherit. Figure in the additional cost of liability insurance and loss — both of which are everyday components of business operation for a lot of wealthy Americans — and you begin to see why even highly-paid professionals don't live as well as their parents did in the 1950s and 60s.

You also build the strongest argument there is for developing an offshore financial strategy. Outside the United States, and beyond the reach of excessive U.S. government interference, there are little-known ways to safeguard what you have, and use it to make a lot more.

■WHEN IS SUCCESS A LIABILITY?

When I was a kid, my family lived next door to a man named Hal Leon. Mr. Leon was not a particularly exceptional guy, but he was one of the nicest people I've ever met. He seemed to love his family and like his neighbors. He was always the first to offer help when you needed it but the last to interfere otherwise. He was a lawyer, which in our neighborhood made him sort of a big shot, but he never held his credentials over anyone. As I remember it, his only apparent source of pride was an enormous backyard garden that he tended himself.

I was in the fifth grade when I first overheard my parents talking about Mr. Leon's car accident. Later it came out that the incident had left a young girl blind in one eye. I remember that everyone talked about it a lot, but nobody ever seemed to approach him directly. So it was only through the grapevine of neighborhood gossip that I learned, over the course of many months, that he had been sued by the girl's parents, lost his case and was hit with an overwhelming liability debt.

For a while, nothing seemed to change. But during my sixth grade year, I remember that Mrs. Leon went to work — an odd development in our suburban area, where wives were inevitably full-time homemakers. Eventually, I heard that they had gone bankrupt. Bankruptcy was a word only uttered in hushed tones when I was a child; and at the time, I wasn't really sure what it meant. I did know that it was the explanation for the Leons moving away and selling their big station wagon to someone else on the block.

When I was a child, lawsuits happened only to the very rich and the very delinquent. Millionaires were vulnerable because their pockets were so deep that they almost cried out to be pilfered. Ner-do-wells were vulnerable, too: drunks, quacks, and scam artists who either allowed bad habits to blur their better judgment or deliberately set out to deceive and steal.

Today, things are very different. Lawsuits happen to just about everybody. Experts predict, in fact, that one out of every four adults in this country will be sued during the coming year alone. Some of those suits will be for wrongful damages, like the one against Mr. Leon. But like all spheres of economic activity, lawsuits have "matured" over the past several years.

For example, there will probably be 50,000 personal injury lawsuits involving damages of $1 million and over filed this year — twice as many as were filed in 1975. Five years ago, the average general practice physician spent $8,000 a year on insurance to cover up to one million dollars in award damages. Today, that same doctor is paying around $50,000 for coverage of up to three million. And that's just for GPs! Medical specialists pay far more.

It's the newest craze. Litigation has replaced baseball as America's favorite pastime. People sue their doctors, their hospitals, their general contractors, their plumbers, electricians, gardeners and television repairmen. They sue their landlords and they sue their tenants. They sue their automobile dealers, and their insurance companies. One group of failed investors recently sued their bank for lending them too much money — the cause, they argued, for their financial demise. Another couple sued the Catholic Church when their son committed suicide because, they maintained, he had received inadequate counseling from his parish priest.

It's absurd, and yet it's not very funny. Lawsuits hang like a threatening cloud over most of us. Any successful businessman should fear them because at any moment, he might be slapped with a multi-million dollar suit. It might not even be his own mistake that gets him in trouble. Negligence on the part of one of his employees (or even his customers) can do the job just as well.

Litigation has replaced baseball as America's favorite pastime.

Consider the following scenario. A mid-size hardware store owner is sued for $1.4 million because a customer foolishly decided to test a power saw inside his store and hit another shopper — seriously cutting both his arms, leaving him unable to work for nearly two years and permanently disabled. The store owner, as it so happens, wasn't even in the store at the time of the accident. But as owner, he is sued for negligence. Does it sound far-fetched? It shouldn't. Cases like this happen all the time, and they wipe out hard-earned fortunes in the instant it takes a judge or jury to rule in favor of the plaintiff.

By the way, lawsuits don't always result from a little guy suffering at the hands of a big guy. Sometimes, in fact, it's just the opposite. Strategic Lawsuits Agaist Public Participation (SLAPP's) are good examples of what I mean. Citizens who campaign against local polluters or new developments are increasingly likely to be hit with one of these suits. They can be small — like the one filed against a West Virginia blueberry farmer. When he told local authorities that operators of a nearby coal mine had polluted a river and killed fish in it, the mining company sued him for $200,000.

SLAPP's can also be quite big — like the one filed against the League of Women Voters in Beverly Hills. In a recent election, the League supported a ballot initiative to stop a fully-planned condominum project. League officials also wrote two letters to a local newspaper criticizing the measure. The developers took decisive action: they sued the League for $63 million.

Perhaps the worst aspect of the lawsuit mania that plagues us is that it can be completely indiscriminate about who it destroys. A woman named Violet Hansen once came to see me, desperately wanting to take advantage of the offshore option. In conversation it came out that her house and life savings were likely to be confiscated to pay off angry creditors. I should admit up front that I have a hard time accepting the legitimate right of a creditor to take such personal assets — regardless of the offense. But what was particularly frustrating about this case was the fact that Vi herself had not done anything wrong.

Years earlier, she had co-signed on a loan that her son-in-law took out to start his own graphic design and printing business. The company had been doing well, at least apparently, and Vi had just forgotten about the loan. Well, in actuality, things were not going so well. The business failed, and along with her son-in-law's bankruptcy came her own. Vi's only crimes were a soft heart and poor judgement. But for those offenses, she paid through the teeth.

I remember how frantic she was. Her husband had worked his whole life to provide for their retirement. He had died just a few years before, and she was almost inconsolable at the thought of losing all that he had left behind. Her idea was to quickly establish a legitimate offshore presence and then transfer nearly all her holdings into a welcoming foreign center.

The trouble was, her good idea had come a little late.

Offshore asset conservation can be legally offered only if there are no judgments or liabilities against your assets. Vi's assets were already under attack. Fortunately, with some careful planning, I was able to deal with her predicament, but she was definitely caught in a bad situation.

Perhaps one of the worst cases I've come across had do with a client of mine named Oliver Webster. He had inherited some virgin land in rural Tennessee from an uncle. Soon after he inherited the property, he was sued for $75 million by the local townspeople. The land had a gas storage tank buried on it. The tank was polluting the whole area. The case went to court and Mr. Webster lost everything.

In a similar vein, it is possible to have all your assets frozen by police — not only for your own crimes but for other people's as well. By the stipulations of the Anti-Drug Act of 1988, authorities have the right to temporarily take or restrict your access to your own property (i.e., your house, car and all your bank accounts) if they think you received all or part of them from a relative or other associate who sold drugs. When will the assets be returned? When the suspect is found innocent or when you can prove that you had no reasonable way of knowing about the illegal activity and that the property were purchased with "clean" money. Even under the best of circumstances, that could take several months to prove. In the meantime, your financial ship is sunk.

A LITTLE PROTECTION IS BETTER THAN NONE

My advice is straightforward: move as many of your assets offshore as you can — still ensuring your own level of investor confidence and security. Why? Because the more you keep offshore, the better-protected you are from attacks by nuisance lawsuits, the government and the courts. Nevertheless, I realize that not everyone is initially willing to commit the bulk of their hard-earned assets to an offshore protection plan. Frankly, I suspect that's only because they're new to the game. The more involved you become in foreign investment and business opportunities, the more willing you will be to see your money leave the veritable seive that characterizes our domestic marketplace. The conventional means of protection — IRAs, savings accounts, etc. —, no longer offer any protection. In time, friends and relatives will be hard-pressed to interest you in any domestic project.

In the beginning, though, you will probably want to maintain a sizeable onshore presence. So for those just starting the offshore adventure, I would like to offer some advice on how to best protect the assets you keep here in the United States. The advice is limited, I know. That's only because, without extensive and creative planning, the possibilities for genuine asset protection are so limited here. There are, however, four rules you should follow in all your onshore financial activities. If you adhere to them, your accumulated wealth will be as safe as it can possibly be within the United States.

RULE ONE: BEWARE OF JOINT RELATIONSHIPS.

Marriage is a 50-50 proposition, right? And a ten percent interest in a new business ventures means a ten percent accountability for future losses and claims, right?

Wrong on both counts.

Most Americans suffer under the misconception that what is fair in one aspect of a relationship, whatever the nature of the association, is fair in all aspects of the relationship. Sadly, that doesn't hold true when it comes to the distribution of financial responsibility and accountability.

For example, a wife may have nothing at all to do with her husband's professional activities — in fact, they may be separated — but if his business gets into trouble, creditors will see her share of their jointly-owned assets as fair game in their quest for recompense.

Likewise, if you are a ten percent partner in a business venture that fails, you can be held 100 percent accountable for its losses. That means your home, your IRA, your stocks, bonds, savings accounts and valuable investments are all up for grabs in the scramble to pay off bad debts.

One of the cornerstones to all asset conservation is this: you have to separate yourself from your money in order to avoid paying it to people you don't like.

So be cautious. "Joint tenancy," the fancy term for co-ownership, between spouses and relatives can sound great in the beginning but it can turn very sour very fast. Pre-nuptial agreements, as unromantic as their are, can provide a good deal of asset protection down the line. Once dismissed in most court proceedings, many judges are now quite willing to review them and rule in accordance with the provisions they outline.

Be careful, too, about joint business ventures. Often, they are held to be nothing more than simple general partnerships with open-ended liability for anyone involved. If that "anyone" is you, it could mean big losses down the line.

RULE TWO: USE CORPORATIONS WISELY.

One of the cornerstones to all asset protection is this: you have to separate yourself from your money in order to avoid paying it to people you don't like. By establishing a U.S.-based corporation through which you handle your business activities, you distance yourself somewhat from the liability that might result from those activities. (There are other alternatives, too: limited liability corporations and limited partnerships that are available under special laws in Wyoming and Florida.)

I remember years ago, when I first became involved in offshore financial consulting, I met a man at an international business seminar who kept telling me to incorporate. "Don't let the bastards get you," he said. "Make one mistake and you'll lose a little blood." Then he said something I'll never forget. "And they're all like sharks. They smell that little bit of blood and they go crazy."

He gave me good advice. I'm happy to report that I have not encountered trouble with my business associates. But that doesn't mean I couldn't. So for me, and for millions of other consultants and businessmen, it's wise to operate through a corporation. If the time ever comes that a client or business associate does sue, all personal assets are independent of the business. Ultimately, they're still vulnerable by virtue of the fact that the same person owns them both. But they're not as immediately vulnerable.

By the way, it's possible to need more than one corporation. This would certainly be true if, let's say, your business has two facets, and one of them is far more likely to bring on lawsuits. For someone who manufactures construction equipment and operates an architectural firm, two corporations would be in order. One for the relatively low-risk architectural venture and another for the high-risk construction business. With this arrangement, one business could remain (at least temporarily) unaffected while the other withstands the shock of a legal battle and possible liability.

RULE THREE: SPREAD YOUR WEALTH.

There's one sure-fired way to avoid paying costly tax and liability bills: technically rid yourself of your most valuable assets. Give a lot of your money to your children, other relatives, or worthy social causes; put it in trust; transfer it to a limited partnership (of which you officially own just a small part). But get your name off of it. In this way, if financial disaster hits, much of the wealth you have accumulated will be beyond the reach of your business or personal adversaries.

The problem with this arrangement is pretty obvious. How can you enjoy the pleasures of wealth you give away? Well, for starters, most people work hard — at least in part because they want to pass along economic security to their kids, extended family, and important non-profit causes. In addition, it is quite possible that assets given to children (especially through an ir-revocable trust) can be relied upon in times of future economic need.

For example, if you place 100 percent of your real es-tate assets in a trust for your kids, you could easily have more than a million dollars in equity stashed away for your heirs' financial future. If, however, you run into financial trouble yourself — even if you lose everything you own — the trust and all that's in it will belong legally and lawfully to your children. Creditors will have no claim to it.

Assuming you have a good relationship with the trust's beneficiaries, you can count on them to instruct their trustee to loan you some money to get started again. If, on the other hand, you don't get along, you've got little recourse because nothing in the trust belongs to you. You have little or no control. As always, the key is planning.

RULE FOUR: INTELLIGENTLY DISTRIBUTE ASSETS BETWEEN SPOUSES.

Just as a couple can, to some extent, safeguard their assets by entrusting them to their heirs, they can also protect against potential loss by intelligently dividing their assets within the marriage. Let me use an example to illustrate my point.

Lauren and Jake were in their early forties when they decided to initiate some careful estate planning. In talking with a number of consultants, they decided that Jake's sports equipment rental business left him relatively open to devastating lawsuits. So, they strategically set up two trusts. One was established in Lauren's name, and into it they placed the bulk of their assets. The other was set up in Jake's name, and it held his office equipment and their two cars.

It proved to be a brilliant move. Six years later, Jake was sued for more than four million dollars when two customers had a fatal car accident in a dune buggy he had rented to them. Their widows won their case and had legal right to everything owned by the business and by Jake. That meant the cars, of course. But virtually everything else was held in trust under Lauren's name. As a result, it was safe, and provided a second economic chance for the couple.

Thousands of married people lose everything each year because of a lawsuit brought against just one spouse. Don't let that happen to you. Plan wisely. And, while we're on the topic, remember not to put 100 percent of your assets in just one spouse's name. Courts would probably find that to be an attempt to defraud creditors. If so, you could still lose everything.

THE OFFSHORE ADVANTAGE: A FOREIGN ASSET PROTECTION TRUST

Admittedly, there are limitations to each of these domestic asset protection plans. And in effect, all the limitations result from two mutually-supportive conspiracies against American businessmen and investors.

First, in any attempt to safeguard your money within the continental United States, you are up against the power of the federal government. Put simply, Uncle Sam doesn't want your assets to be protected because he wants to get at them himself.

Second, there is an insidious relationship between the U.S. financial sector and the U.S. government that works against your efforts to keep assets free from excessive taxation and regulatory interference. At one time, American banks could operate independently of the federal bureaucracy. Today, they cannot. The reporting requirements and legal restraints placed upon banks and savings and loans makes it truly impossible for you to have a private relationship with your financial institution. In fact, whether your onshore banker likes it or not, he is the greatest obstacle to your asset protection plan.

In the effort to circumvent these intricately intertwined problems, many investors have established onshore trusts, into which they've placed the bulk of their assets. "Living trusts" are the newest rage, it seems. (These revocable trust agreements usually specify that all trust income be distributed to you, as the trust creator, during your lifetime. Then, upon your death, the trust's principal assets are left to your heirs.) I've personally seen a number of how-to paperbacks marketed specifically to affluent Americans who might want to investigate the trust as an appealing alternative to simple bank accounts and stock or real estate investment options.

True, living trusts do offer one real benefit: they let your heirs avoid the inconvenience, delay and cost of the probate experience. (Many people are unaware that probate can be extremely expensive — up to 11 percent of the gross value of the estate in some parts of the country.) Nevertheless, if you are considering one, my advice is to beware. For starters, a revocable "living" trust will not escape estate tax because, by their very nature, they let you keep control over the property — by being able to revoke or amend it any time and by retaining the power to withdraw any portion of the trust property at any time.

If that's not enough to dissuade you, there are other serious drawbacks to domestic trusts. For example, the U.S. courts consider any trust that has been created by an individual for his own benefit (even if actual control of all assets has been surrendered) fair game in a creditor's quest for recompense. In other words, if you place your assets in trust, but continue to benefit in any way from them, then someone who wins a legal judgment against you can go after those assets. And in most cases, get them.

Conversely, the U.S. courts have held that creditors can go after the assets in a domestic trust if the trust creator retains any measure of control over them — even though he may not actually enjoy the benefits of the trust assets. For example, if you set up a trust and maintain nothing more than the right to amend the original trust agreement, the courts would be likely to hold that your creditors could go after whatever assets you have placed in the trust.

For all these reasons, I suggest that if your estate is worth $300,000 or more, you strongly consider one of the best asset protection strategies I know about: the Foreign Asset Protection Trust. Properly executed and intelligently maintained this single offshore venture can provide you with an unparalleled level of tax protection and financial invisibility. It may not protect you from becoming the target of a lawsuit or other claim. But it may place your assets substantially beyond the reach of any U.S. court, and severely limit anyone's ability to enforce a money judgement against you. In the process, it will also discourage potential creditors from making bogus claims, and save you the emotional and financial cost of addressing such claims.

One of the keys to a successful foreign trust is the selection of a friendly host country. By that I mean you should establish your trust within an offshore jurisdiction that, first and foremost, maintains stringent laws against enforcing foreign judgments. The whole notion of the trust is based on common law, which applied in only some countries — those formerly or presently associated with Great Britain. Most other countries operate under a separate set of codes, and while they have vehicles similar to trusts, they have different names and varied structures.

Properly executed and intelligently maintained, a Foreign Asset Protection Trust can provide you with an unparalleled level of tax protection and financial invisibility.

For example, the British Virgin Islands (BVI) has a well-established body of trust laws which protect any BVI-based trust from the scrutiny of foreign courts and creditors. Yet, like the United States, the BVI recognizes a properly structured trust as a separate legal entity — independent of its creators — and will not allow creditors of any of the parties to the trust to obtain the trust's assets.

It's also critical that your preferred foreign site have nothing equivalent to the U.S. "statute of frauds." In other words, you want to be sure that if you were to physically transfer your assets to the offshore center and then place them in trust there, courts and creditors here in the United States would be unable to claim fraudulent intent. Why? Because the laws that govern the creation of trusts in your chosen foreign center do not recognize such fraud.

A basic foreign asset protection trust can be set up with anyone as the direct beneficiary — including you as the creator of the trust. However, for maximum protection, it's better to choose someone else for that role. (Otherwise you could be seen to have too much of a beneficial interest in the trust and its activities.) If, however, you do decide to make yourself the beneficiary, be absolutely sure that you are entitled only to the trust's income and have no claim to its principal. That way, a creditor can theoretically attack only your income stream from the trust, not the actual assets.

Just like domestic trusts, all foreign asset protection trusts have a "trustee," someone to administer the trust and hold its assets for the benefit of the beneficiaries. I have worked with clients who insist on being the trustee to their own foreign trust, but I have to tell you that in every one of those cases, I advised against it. Serving as your own trustee can be extremely dangerous. A court is much more inclined to invalidate a trust if its creator is also a trustee or a beneficiary.

So select an independent foreign trustee, either an individual familiar with your personal life and business needs, or a financial institution with which you have an ongoing relationship. If neither of those options seems appealing or appropriate, you can turn to one of many professional international management firms that specialize in the supervision of foreign trusts and other offshore entities.

When you initially establish the trust and name a foreign trustee, you should also name a committee of one or more "trust protectors" to serve as advisors to that trustee. And you should serve on that committee. Why? Because the protectors have the right to remove or replace the trustee, so, by remaining a part of the protector committee, you keep indirect but effective control over the trust's assets. And if a creditor should later decide to pursue you, you can simply resign as a protector, leaving the foreign trustee in sole control of the assets. (That way, there can be little merit in the argument that your resignation was somehow impermissible transfer of assets after the creditor's claims were made.)

Establishing a foreign asset protection trust is not a terribly complex or lengthy undertaking, but it does require expert legal advice from a trust attorney. There are a number of special features that should be included in the trust agreement: anti-duress provisions and a spendthrift clause are just two examples. Don't risk making a mistake. Bring in a qualified specialist to work with you on the project. It will necessitate a financial outlay upfront, but it's likely to save untold headaches and expenses down the line.

Finally, because it is generally required that you transfer title or ownership to the property to the offshore jurisdiction before you actually establish a trust there, the foreign asset protection trust is usually best for holding liquid assets: cash, stocks, bonds and certificates of deposit. In addition, assets transferred to a simple foreign asset protection trust should generally be those not needed for your daily living or business needs. In other words, they should be your "nest egg," which you have been setting aside for future security.

ADDITIONAL LAYERS OF PROTECTION

A foreign asset protection trust can be a vehicle for people seeking nothing more than the basic right to safeguard their money. As an irrevocable trust, it is an entirely independent entity, and recognized as such under the laws of all 50 states and the U.S. federal government. That means, if you take care to distance yourself sufficiently from the trust — so that a court will not find that the arrangement is a sham for holding assets under your direct control — no judge or jury can legally give your creditors assets that you earlier contributed to the trust.

A number of recent court cases demonstrate exactly how the use of these irrevocable trusts can work. In one of those cases, a women with two grown children established an irrevocable trust into which she transferred most of her assets. The trust provided for the distribution of the entire net income to the woman for life, with the remaining principal to go to her children upon her death. When the woman was later sued by a creditor, the court refused to set aside the trust, saying that "a creditor has no more rights and can secure no greater benefit from a trust than the beneficiary of the trust can obtain for himself." In other words, since the woman herself could not ignore the provisions of the trust or regain the principal for herself, then neither could her creditors have it set aside to obtain the assets it contained.

Still, for some people, an offshore trust alone does not offer enough asset control. Despite its protective advantages, some people want (and need) more direct authority over how assets are maintained and put profitably to work. In particular, if you run your own business, have a professional corporation or own real property within the United States, you will probably want to combine a foreign asset protection trust with a domestic limited partnership. Using both, you can ensure that your assets remain completely safe from creditors, and that you keep constant and total control over them.

Here's how it works. You establish a foreign asset protection trust within a welcoming offshore jurisdiction, and you contribute virtually all of your property to that trust. Then, you set up a domestic limited partnership, personally taking just a one percent interest in the partnership but designating yourself as general partner. The foreign trust takes a 99 percent interest and pays for that interest by contributing to the partnership your operating business, your family home, title to your investment real estate and any other non-liquid assets.

Once the trust and partnership are funded, your total assets will consist of just a one percent interest in the limited partnership and the few personal belongings that you have not contributed to the trust. As a result, very little of your total net worth is available to any potential creditor. Technically, 99 percent of that net worth belongs to the foreign trust and has been contributed to the limited partnership.

So if a creditor were ever able to obtain a judgment against you, your only asset would be a small interest in the partnership.

Another big part of the system's appeal lies in the control it gives you over assets that cannot be attached. Specifically, because of your role as general partner, you will still be able to do with the trust's assets whatever you please as long as it's in the furtherance of the partnership's purpose. And as an additional perk, there is no authority that could allow a creditor to remove you as general partner of the partnership. So you would continue to control all of your assets all of the time.

You may even be able to get money out of the limited partnership held in your offshore trust if you have the ability, in arm's-length transactions, to draw funds from it as salary for services performed and as fringe benefits. (If you go this route, however, be aware that these wages and benefits are vulnerable to creditors in any judgment against you.)

Even if a creditor does attack you, the most he can obtain would be a so-called "charging order" against your partnership interest. True, he could go after all the benefits that flow to you from the partnership, but because you own so small an interest, very little does flow to you. This charging order would also mandate that you treat the creditor only as an "assignee." That means, he would have no vote in the management of the partnership and would not be able to force you to make distributions from the partnership.

This final provision allows you to create the "poison pill" — something to discourage even the heartiest of creditors. You simply include a provision in the partnership agreement that allows the general partner to retain the earnings of the partnership and not make cash distributions. If a creditor gets a charging order against the partnership, you can stop making cash distributions. This move will no doubt irritate the creditor. But, frankly, that irritation pales alongside what lies ahead for him. Let me explain what I mean.

Under U.S. tax laws, a limited partnership is deemed to have distributed its income to the partners at the end of each fiscal year — even if no cash distributions were made. Thus, the creditor is faced with the prospect of having to pay taxes on the income generated by his assigned share of the partnership's income despite the fact that he has not received any money at all! Faced with such a prospect, most creditors will not even bother to attack your interests in the foreign trust or the domestic limited partnership.

Finally, because 99 percent of the partnership belongs to the foreign trust, the assets from the partnership all flow automatically offshore and back into a trust that is governed by extremely favorable foreign laws.

I should mention that there are even more elaborate offshore asset protection plans. Of course, they involve more initial research and additional start-up revenue. Nevertheless, for investors with a lot of vulnerability and a high public or professional profile, they can be very desirable. Unlike the foreign trust alone, a trust, partnership and offshore bank can work hand-in-hand, forming a powerful triad. These complex protection strategies are not fixed plans. Instead, they constantly evolve and change to inhibit potential challenges of lawsuits directed against you. In essence, by keeping your money on the move, and circulating it through creative combinations of various offshore financial ventures (trusts, consulting companies, holding companies, and banks), you can obliterate all traces of your financial activities.

Realize that for this total invisibility, you relinquish virtually all personal affiliation with and claim to your assets. You can control them. In fact, you can make them grow beyond most people's wildest dreams. But you can't call them your own because they're all absorbed by the offshore plan, never to emerge for future creditors to see.

■ HAVE YOUR CAKE AND EAT IT TOO.

There's a popular expression making the rounds these days: Less is more. Well, when it comes to conservation and responsible ecology, that may be true. But when it comes to money, only more is more.

So as you find yourself successfully accumulating more, don't forget that unless you do something to protect yourself, a hefty chunk of what you've worked to acquire will be sacrificed to the U.S. taxman. And what's left could be lost overnight in an ugly (and perhaps even unfair) lawsuit.

But take heart. Asset protection is available. To a very

limited extent, it's even available within the domestic market. Unfortunately, however, as citizens of the world's great experiment in free enterprise, we Americans have to look abroad for any true safeguards.

That's the bad news.

The good news is that there are places where you can protect your assets. And with some careful pre-planning, control them too. All you need is the commitment to give offshore money havens a try, and the willingness to work closely with a well-qualified professional consultant.

CHAPTER EIGHT

Eight Steps To Offshore Success

"Spontaneous innovations in the marketplace arise to avoid government regulation and taxation..."

—David Glasner
Free Banking and Monetary Reform

Offshore money havens are no longer a luxury reserved for the ultra-rich. Within today's global economic system, they are the prime investment option for anyone whose assets total a quarter of a million dollars or more. That includes tens of thousands of Americans — all of whom want tax protection, impressive profits and financial privacy.

Why do you think so many investors — large, small and in-between — are moving toward this global business approach? Why have they decided to compete (and win) at the offshore game?

In part, the offshore boom results from a wide array of technological advancements. Thanks to sophisticated telecommunications and computerized banking services worldwide, people can make, spend, win, lose and transfer money faster than ever before. A conscientious investor may, for instance, assess the value of currency in any nation on a given morning, decide when it has reached a danger point and complete a cash-out program on all liquid investments held in that country by the following afternoon! This fast-paced movement of funds has made offshore investment very appealing to numbers of domestic businessmen and entrepeneurs.

But there is an even more profound reason for the trend toward offshore investment, which involves the changing profile of today's financial players. Regardless of their individual differences, the economic winners of the 1990s will share a common view of the global marketplace. They see it as a wide-open environment from which to pick and choose the most lucrative investment options. They have taken what I perceive to be the most important step in attaining genuine financial independence: learning to see the world without national borders. That gives them an almost limitless profit arena.

If you take only one message from this book, I hope it will be the enormity of your potential investment sphere.

You no longer need to restrict your financial activity to the traditional Swiss bank account, or to a paltry selection of onshore tax shelters. Conventional investment vehicles (such as bonds, commodities and securities) have become relics of another time. The entire world offers lucrative ventures, and you can become a part of any or all of them. You just need to broaden your own investment horizon.

Experience has shown me that, for many reasons, we Americans tend to see the world as a neatly divided assortment of cultures, countries and currencies. We think of east as east, and west as west, and only at the United Nations do the twain meet. I can't tell you how many times I've worked with extremely successful professionals and entrepeneurs from around the country, all of whom want to add offshore investments to their financial portfolio. Nevertheless, their personal sense of economic nationalism limits their ability to reap the benefits of the offshore solution.

They pay a high price for this limited vision. They miss the benefits inherent in the international option. From those who have avoided offshore activity altogether, I most often hear about profit margins that are far less than satisfactory. From those who have severely restricted foreign investments, I learn of stymied venture activity and meager earnings. In each instance, I find myself thinking of the more assertive investors (from the United States and around the world) who have entered the offshore market, who are constantly taking part in creative new ventures and who are sharpening their global edge.

THE BIG MYTH ABOUT OFFSHORE BUSINESS

Despite it's proven benefits, the international option

still lacks a level of public credibility. For too many people, the words "offshore investment" conjure up images of money laundering, drug trafficking, arms smuggling, insider-trading schemes and tax evasion. The media is partly to blame for this false impression. Every television network, newspaper and weekly news magazine in the country has run stories on illicit foreign financial ventures. After all, these complex intrigues make for attention-grabbing headlines.

Admittedly, there is some truth behind the hype. Illegal activity has occurred, and continues to happen. Although this criminal element accounts for only a tiny fraction of the total offshore investment community, it has managed to tarnish the reputation of an entirely legitimate financial option. Why? Because the global market is so inviting, and so well-tailored to unregulated profit that it has easily fallen prey to those with less than honorable intentions.

For example, the Iran-Contra scandal of the late 1980s uncovered a world in which the profits from illegal drug and arms deals ended up in secret Swiss bank accounts. From endless hours of televised hearings, we learned that Col. Oliver North (a member of the President's National Security Council who worked out of the basement of the White House) was funding the contra rebels of Nicaragua with money from international drug sales and arms deals to the Iranian government.

It marked the end of President Reagan's amazing and unquestioned popularity. It also added fuel to the fire of "offshore" illegality. How ironic that the most famous of all international financial scandals should involve the U.S. government itself! Federal authorities have been nothing less than rabid in their search for individual investors who may have improperly circumvented the law. All the while, the biggest scheme was happening right under their noses.

The complicated narcotics mess with now-deposed General Noriega of Panama also contributed to negative myth-making about offshore activites. Here was a man — the leader of his nation who accepted millions of dollars in bribes to allow the safe transport of drugs through his country. He also tolerated the laundering of drug profits through Panamanian banks. *Southern Banker* magazine reported that "$200 to $300 million a month" was laundered through 140 Panamanian banks for the notorious Columbian drug cartel. Noriega personally pocketed "$10 million a month in protection fees."

When we learned that the late President Ferdinand Marcos of the Phillippines may have taken money from his country's budget and used it in the international market for personal profit, the myths became legend. It's now estimated that during his reign, Marcos may have stashed upwards of $10 billion in secret accounts throughout the world.

During the late 1980s, news broke that the Securities and Exchange Commission was investigating an insider-trading scheme and the use of Swiss banks. We learned that such respected firms as Morgan Stanley, Goldman Sachs & Co., First Boston Co., Merrill Lynch & Co., Shearson Lehman Hutton, Inc. and Charles Schwab and Co. were all subpoenaed in the case.

I've related these stories not to aggravate an already sensitive nerve among prospective offshore investors. I've covered them because I want to honestly confront the fact that international business does include an underworld of illegitimate activity. What financial environment is without its bandits? Wall Street certainly has its share of thieves. So do the venerable financial houses of Hong Kong.

The point is, when there is money to be made, some people will try to take more than their fair share by opting to break the law. As a rule, our government does not engage in illegal arms trades. Most heads of state are honest and concerned with the betterment of their people. Most business conducted by top U.S. securities firms is legitimate, open and above-board. It is unfair to allow isolated exceptions to these rules reflect negatively on the entire offshore option.

The global marketplace is a wide-open environment from which to pick and choose the most lucrative investment options. The key is to see the world withoutt national borders.

In and of itself, offshore investment is neither legal nor illegal. It becomes legal (or illegal) only by the way in which it is used. The great majority of offshore activities involve businessmen and investors such as those described in earlier chapters. Most offshore operators are simply seeking safe harbors for their money and/or legal ways to avoid taxes — trying to take advantage of profit-making opportunities that are unavailable onshore.

■EIGHT STEPS TO OFFSHORE SUCCESS

Since you are taking the time to read this book, you're obviously serious about an offshore financial involvement. Many of you may have already experienced the international arena; others are undoubtedly considering a "first venture."

In either case, I would like to offer you some simple advice: eight steps to success in the offshore marketplace. There is nothing particularly unusual about them. In fact, you may have heard similar advice from other consultants.

However, there is one big difference. I've been out

there. The following steps are based primarily on firsthand experience with real people. Working on the front lines has prepared me to offer you advice tempered by reality, not far-fetched academic theories.

Over the years, I've watched a lot of investors enter the world of offshore finance. Many of them have become tremendously successful in the process. I've seen some failures, too. In my view, each of those failures can be traced to an unwillingness or an inability to follow these basic steps.

STEP ONE: Decide If An Offshore Financial Move Is Right For You

Not everyone is cut out for international finance. There are people who simply don't want to do business in a foreign country. Even among those who do like the global market, there are decisive differences. Some are satisfied when they are "invisibly" involved in an off-shore investment. Others aren't happy until they get right in the middle of it: taking frequent trips abroad and juggling the challenges of offshore business relations for themselves.

So the first step to successfully entering the offshore market is careful self-assessment. Know your own level of interest and comfort. This book advocates an informed and assertive approach. In my view, the facts speak for themselves. Domestic investment cannot offer you the profit, tax protection or operational flexibility that you can enjoy abroad. Nevertheless, the booming offshore market dictates that you diversify your assets by moving some of them offshore and allowing them to work for you.

This may be the time to point out how strongly I disagree with those experts who urge U.S. investors to "learn" cross-cultural business skills in order to go international. The fact is, most successful U.S. businessmen have extensive cross-cultural experience. Anyone who lives in Manhattan and handles transactions in Los Angeles, New Orleans, Houston, or even Chicago understands that. The United States really consists of many different cultures functioning together as a single country. So the challenge, as I see it, is one of expanding professional skills that already exist.

More importantly, offshore investment no longer requires your physical departure from the United States. High technology, along with a well-developed international financial network, makes it possible for you to conduct virtually any transaction from your own office or even a home study — at any time of the day or night.

In short, going offshore is committing to an entirely new way of making money. It's expanding your investment perspective, and capitalizing on financial opportunities whenever and wherever they occur. Remember, before you get involved, be sure you're really attracted to this very contemporary approach to personal investment.

STEP TWO: Develop A Strategy

Once you've decided that offshore action is for you, you must begin to develop a feasible financial strategy. You can't hope to make money, save taxes or protect your privacy by merely stumbling around in the offshore marketplace. You must know what you're doing.

So take the time to ask yourself: what do you want from, say, a silent partnership in Tokyo? From your brass-plate bank in the Caribbean? From an import/export firm in the Pacific? Each of these offshore ventures can be extremely profitable and each one is a distinct business activity with very specific demands and benefits.

Developing a strategy involves serious consideration

of your needs, your goals and your future. Clearly, it's unwise to rely soley on the U.S. market. The global marketplace is too interdependent to place all your faith in one economy. Today, you can select your economy (or, better stated, economies). Unlike investors of the past, you can gather information to help you counterbalance international opportunities against domestic downturns.

Every successful businessman or investor that I've ever met has known the value of strategic thinking. It begins when you realize that it is essential to diversify in order to protect your holdings. Once that idea is firmly engrained in mind, it is time to lay out a well-designed plan of action.

Take the William Simon story I've already related. *He* has a strategy. It's true that he knows the value of financial flexibility, but Simon has mapped out a plan that's designed to direct his daily, weekly and monthly decisions for the next few years. His overall goal is to profit from the growing investment opportunities in the Pacific Rim. That goal allows him a wide market in which to conduct his activities, but it also builds parameters around his playing field. In my view, that makes for the most successful strategy.

Like Simon, you also need to devise specific tactics that will make it possible for you to carry out your stratregy. In order to meet his particular objective, he plans to buy specially situated financial institutions that can be be used to conduct particular types of transactions. If your overall aim is to use an offshore base to lessen your tax load, then you must think of appropriate ways in which to carry out that strategy. These will be your tactics.

My advice is that those tactics embody the golden rule of financial investment: diversify. Like even the best things in life, each individual offshore venture can satisfy only so many economic needs. I strongly discourage anyone from imagining that there is a single international investment, acquisition or new business concept that can legally address all your financial needs. That's why the best international investors have assets strategically working around the world, functioning in different ways in different places.

STEP THREE: Select An Experienced Offshore Advisor

Realizing the need for a practical strategy, you must now consider the services of a first-class financial expert. While shopping for an advisor, remember that a number of professional qualities characterize a really good consultant.

- *Superior Financial Skills*: You need someone who can develop an optimal strategy tailored especially to your needs. Don't accept a "one-size-fits-all" approach to offshore investment. Look for an advisor who is willing and able to help you design the plan that's right for you. Any reputable consultant will be well-versed in handling foreign exchange matters, preparing proper documentation and setting offshore operating parameters. Your consultant must also be someone who can help with the implementation of your business strategy, not just with the concept behind it.

- *Excellent Knowledge of Offshore International Investment Alternatives*: A qualified advisor will offer various investment vehicles, and will encourage you to compare them before making a final choice. Every investment has its own complexity and each requires careful consideration. You should be able to count on your consultant for help in balancing out the various accounting, tax and legal issues involved in all your options.

- *A Wide Network of International Contacts*: Avoid fly-by-night operations. By and large, international financial consultants are honest and reliable, but there are a few scam artists who make it their business to identify inexperienced investors. A good way to know if you've met a real professional is to ask about his international business network. You want to look for an advisor who is well-connected to people and institutions abroad. Those contacts are your insurance that an offshore venture will be implemented legally and on the best possible terms for you.

- *An In-depth Understanding of the Offshore Market and the Staff to Efficiently Execute All Transactions*: Establishing an offshore operation and conducting transactions in another country often involves close and regular interaction with government officials. You need to work with an advisor who understands the intricacies involved in your preferred offshore location. What's more, your advisor should offer you an experienced and efficient staff, capable of serving as back-up for your project. Also, be sure the advisor you select has the communication technology to quickly and accurately execute complicated transactions.

Once you have selected an offshore advisor who meets the criteria described above, it's time to reassess your strategy — this time with his input. By working through the plan you've designed for yourself, you can benefit from his feedback and guidance. Although you probably have a good sense for what's right for you, don't be bull-headed about taking your professional consultant's advice. After all, his advice is what you're paying for. Let him help you refine and hone your offshore game plan.

STEP FOUR: Put All The Proper Systems In Place

After you've clarified your priorities, mapped out your strategy and identified a good advisor, it's time to put your systems in place.

Before you attempt to negotiate your first deal, be sure you're prepared to do business the way it's done off- shore. That means setting up a sound organizational structure to manage your international investments and/or operations. You need good people and the right equipment. That may sound like an obvious step but you'd be surprised at how many new investors forget to take it.

You should now select your key people: an accountant, an attorney and a clerical assistant. Depending upon the nature and scope of your particular strategy, you may want to hire them on a per-hour (or freelance) basis, rather than as full-time employees. This is an area in which a professional consultant can offer some ex- perienced advice.

You will need the right equipment in place and opera- tional. With the proper assemblage of a personal com-

Four Steps to Profit

1. Offshore Bank Account
2. Investment Game Plan
3. Offshore Business
4. Your Own Offshore Bank

puter, modem, FAX machine and copier, you will be able to create a virtual electronic control center. From this ultra-modern financial headquarters, you can operate anytime, day or night. You can work out of your home, or from your office. You might even want to add a sperate work station to your business office that's dedicated strictly to offshore interests. It all depends on your plans, your bank account and your ambitions.

An integral part of proper systems management is written confirmation of *everything*. To help you in this area, here are three basic tips on written communications:

- *Keep your writing simple*. Experience has shown me that basic, straightforward letters and memos are the key to successful business writing.

- *Make sure professional titles translate correctly*. Since the same position may vary around the world, getting the right title is essential.

- *Clarify all written items having to do with money amounts*. Be sure that currency differences and rate exchanges are taken into account.

STEP FIVE: Create The Right Image

In my opinion, one of the most important factors in the successful consummation of offshore ventures is your business image. Because I work and live in Los Angeles, one of the media capitals of the world, I am repeatedly reminded of the value in projecting a strong, clear image and the benefits of keeping that image in front of those you want to favorablly impress.

For offshore investors the importance of image should direct everything from the design of your business cards to the wording of all printed media you use to outline your offerings, products or services. Anything you produce to advance your financial activities should reflect the image you want to ptoject.

This is precisely the reason why you must establish your image before you go offshore. For example, your new offshore financial entity may offer banking services. Therefore, your bank will require a name, a logo, stationery, services brochure and various types of banking forms. The image you want to project will direct all these specific choices.

You will create and promote a very serious, cautious, financially conservative image by working with basic muted colors (like grey and brown). By the same token, you will generate a more relaxed, contemporary, and slightly adventurous impression by using pastel colors (like sky blue and sand). It's up to you. Both have their benefits and drawbacks. Remember too that no choice will appeal to every prospective customer in every nation. So carefully think through your prime markets and direct your choices toward their concerns and priorities.

The key is careful coordination. Make sure all your printed media is coordinated in some way. This makes it easier for investors, depositors, shareholders and customers to identify your service or product. Consistency is a must in business because it conveys stability.

Finally, some ideas about advertising. This will prove to be a critical decision when it comes to image-making. Advertising is a direct approach to the people whose involvement you want. As such, it must send a message about your business image. This kind of intelligent advertising will help establish your offshore business, and over time, it will make it grow.

Let me quote from one of the masters of business advertising, Ted Nicholas. "It is not an oversimplification to say that nearly every ad, regardless of its degree of sophistication, follows the Attention-Interest-Desire-Action formula." That's exactly what you should keep in mind when you advertise. First, your ad must grab your potential client's attention. Then it must earn his interest. Finally, it must arouse in him a real desire to act and it must tell him how to take that action.

Check with your consultant about all advertising. Ask him about this attention-interest-desire-action formula. Does he agree that it will produce bring results? Does he know marketing experts who would be willing to review your materials and offer their professional criticism? You should be able to receive this kind of support and guidance from your advisor. Again, that's why you've commissioned his services. So, don't be shy about asking for help.

STEP SIX: Do Your Homework

Going offshore is not like taking a vacation. Even for the most adventurous at heart, it is not a time for playing things by ear. To be successful overseas — even if you never leave the United States — you need to learn something about the place where you're investing your money.

To be realistic, the extent of your "homework" should be tied to your level of personal contact with the foreign locale. If your entire plan is to purchase stock at a brokerage firm which handles foreign investments, your information needs are clearly minimal. If, on the other hand, you plan to conduct business with South Korean textile manufacturers, you'd be smart to spend a lot of time learning what is and isn't acceptable behavior in their part of the world.

According to Stanford University's Richard Pascale, too many people think that a cocktail conversation with a few world travelers will prepare them for even the most in-depth offshore involvement. As he points out, "real effort is more like thirty hours of intensive study."

When it comes to this "homework" phase, I'm a firm believer in the value of small books and regular magazines. Clients who have been to my office often remark on my personal business library. They are sometimes amazed by my encyclopedia collections on various international business subjects as well as the scores of volumes on everything from international marketing to the history of world economic growth.

It's your responsibility to know what your options are and to understand the perks and pitfalls that attach to each of them.

Of course, my work demands that I keep abreast of a wide range of international and global developments. You don't need to tackle that kind of reading load. Nevertheless, I do suggest that you consider building a basic collection that will help you understand the exciting changes that are constantly taking place in the offshore market.

Frankly, far too many books on the market are hype, and they do nothing more than feed existing fears and misconceptions. Don't be suckered into the belief that you must read everything that's published on the subject. Instead, take a fairly casual approach to building your library. After all, the offshore market will be around forever. You have time to become a master at it.

If you do decide to build a basic international investment bookshelf, the following tips may prove helpful:

1. *General Reference* - Every investor should have at least one book on general investment. It should cover some of the essentials, like the dos and don'ts of personal financial planning. Make sure that any general reference books you buy were written after the tax reform of 1986. Anything published before that is out of date. We now

operate by completely different rules. You may also want to buy an investment vocabulary guide, such as the *Dictionary of Finance and Investment Terms* published by Barron's.

2. *Books about Offshore Funds* - Offshore funds are investment funds based in tax havens or low tax areas. As *The Financial Times* notes, "they are able to invest in a broader range of instruments than onshore domestic investment companies. It is this flexibility...which is their main attraction for investors." Because they are a cornerstone to offshore investment, I recommend that you get a basic background text about how they work. *Donoghue's Mutual Funds Almanac* is good. I also recommend that, before you invest in any fund, you send for its prospectus and study it.

3. *Books about Hard Assets* - With inflation always lurking around the corner, you may want to have a couple of books on real estate and gold. One well-recommended guide is Nichols' *The Complete Book of Gold Investing*. Another is *Real Estate After Tax Reform*.

STEP SEVEN: Know The Rules And Practices

Before you finalize the design of any international business plan, check out the legal requirements of your host country concerning local participation. It's no longer possible to just set-up a business anywhere in the world, run it entirely with your own staff and earn its full profit for yourself.

Growing nationalism and economic protectionism abroad have changed the nature of offshore ventures. Today, many foreign governments have strict laws governing the percentage of required native workforce and mandatory contributions to various national development goals. Don't be caught off guard. Know the laws of any country before you move beyond the thinking phase.

In short, other countries are raising the stakes for entrance into their economy. If the potential profit is substantial, it may be worth the price. But, if foreign governments become too demanding, they can begin to extinguish the allure of any site.

Before getting involved in an offshore center, try to meet people who have done business in that country. If that's not possible, then try meeting people with other experiences in (and connections to) the area. If even that becomes difficult, I suggest that you keep trying until you find at least one person who's willing to offer limited social and professional support. Even if you dislike this sort of networking, you'll ultimately be glad to know someone you can call for advice on matters as minor as currency exchange or as major as government involvement in business operations.

These "mentors" can serve another essential purpose. They can provide you with names of real people in the foreign location who, in turn, will refer you to even others who will direct you to more contacts. And knowing real people is the name of the game in international finance. Everyone likes a personal touch. That is especially true in other countries, where social values tend to emphasize personal associations and reputation.

As a second phase in this networking strategy, I would urge you to hire a reliable representative in the foreign center where you plan to conduct business. In some countries, this is a legal requirement. Even where it is not, experts agree that you should pretend it is. The local representative should be native to the country. It is not enough that he be from a neighboring nation.

Some people think they can just go out and place an ad in a foreign newspaper and they'll be deluged with resumes. That's simply not the case. First of all, the cost of advertising is prohibitive. According to *East Asian Executive Reports*, "A small ad in a national Japanese-lan-

guage newspaper can cost upwards of $20,000 per inser-
tion...." Secondly, the demand for talent far exceeds the
supply.

Once you do locate an agent, keep two warnings in
mind. First, if you don't click with a prospective agent,
move on right away. It will only become more difficult to
make a change later on. If you do replace your representative, be careful not to offend him because his negative comments about you can have serious consequences. Second, don't count on your representative for
everything. Few offshore operations can be initiated and
successfully completed entirely by proxy. An agent can
help, but at some point, you will probably need to get
directly involved.

STEP EIGHT: Make Sure You Can Get Your Money Out

If you work with a professional financial consultant,
you are unlikely to face this nightmare. However, if you
try to handle an entire offshore venture alone, you can
run into terrible trouble when it comes time to cash-out
and return home. Some countries make it very easy to
invest in but very difficult to get out of their economy.

The best insurance against this problem is to know
ahead of time exactly what the conditions are for transferring your involvement back into U.S. currency. How
can your stocks be sold? How can your franchise or distributor agreement be signed-over to another investor?
Can you dissolve your local partnership at anytime with
the understanding that your share of the profits-to-date
be liquidated and made payable?

Have all conditions of transfer and dissolution formal-
ly agreed upon in writing. Keep one copy in your foreign
business site and another here in the United States. That
way, in the event of any problem, you will have a legally-

binding agreement to show the exact nature of your investment arrangement.

Know, too, that Uncle Sam will lay claim to his share of every dollar earned abroad and brought back to this country. So don't plan to repatriate funds unless you're willing to be taxed on them.

■PUTTING IT ALL TOGETHER

These eight basic steps are only a beginning. They can provide you with the minimum that you will need to know for even the simplest international investment venture.

Perhaps the most important of all the suggestions is the value of a professional consultant. If you connect with the right person, he will help guide you through all the rest. Particularly in the beginning, when you are justifiably overwhelmed by most aspects of any offshore project, this seasoned expert can offer help and reassurance. Then, as you become more experienced, you may be able to initiate and implement some business deals without commissioning further expert advice.

International investment and business is a financial grab bag. Most of it is exciting. Much of it is lucrative. Some of it is risky. There are benefits and disadvantages to every kind of offshore venture. So it's your responsibility to know what your options are and to understand the perks and pitfalls that attach to each of them. In the process, you will prepare yourself to reach for the offshore involvement that is best for you and your financial priorities.

CHAPTER NINE

Offshore Money Havens: Where To Go

"Never keep all your wealth in the country where you live because anything can happen — and usually does."

—Adam Smith

The secret numbered Swiss bank account is a remnant from the financial past. Using one in today's intensely competitive and highly unpredictable economy is like riding a bike on a superhighway. The vehicle we use always depends on need. While no one would take a bike on the freeway, too many investors rely on a Swiss Account when a much more versatile option exists: offshore money havens.

People often ask me if they can *really* protect their money, earn a profit and pay less taxes by using the offshore option. I always say yes — as long as they are careful in selecting their offshore business venue. International money havens havens actually do exist, and in light of the worsening U.S. economy, they are fast becoming the preferred choice for schrewd investors.

Several years ago, a study called *Service Banking* was prepared for the prestigious London-based Institute of Bankers. In reviewing it, I came across an insightful observation and jotted it down because it contained the essence of the offshore rationale:

Like water finding its own level, entrepreneurial business, when constrained in one place, will emerge in another. When restrictions in one place become too burdensome, too discouraging and perhaps too punitive, the businessman will look elsewhere. As one door closes, another opens.

Over the years I've seen the truth of this observation borne out time after time in life as well as in business. If you don't like a situation, change it. Whether its your spouse, your employees, your dwelling, change it if it isn't working out. There is no reason to tolerate the current situation in Switzerland. As it has become subject to international agreements and its famous secrecy laws dissolve under international political pressure, other places pick up the slack. Some people now go to Austria. Other find Luxembourg useful. Many prefer the

Bahamas. The point is: every investor can find what he needs, if he's just willing to look far enough.

One of the reasons I was compelled to write this book is that more and more of my clients have expressed alarm and concern over the tenuous economic situation in the United States. They've also correctly seen that in times of swift economic change, they require flexibility and liquidity. When you factor in the bureaucratic red-tape that has become part of all financial dealings within this country, as well as the low rates of return on investments, the heavy burden of taxation and a general negative social environment, the offshore option possesses an attraction that is hard to overlook.

█ HOW THE OFFSHORE HAVENS CAME ABOUT

It's important to keep in mind that these offshore financial centers were originally established by onshore banks and corporations. Why? Because they also felt hemmed-in by archaic laws, regulations and statutes. For example, Citicorp (the largest American-owned bank in the United States) was one of the first to set-up offshore operations. It wasn't too long before 64 percent of its net income was being generated by offshore sources.

Some of the pioneering centers have evolved into world-class financial and economic headquarters. Since the early 1970s, these centers have initiated policies deliberately designed to attract international trade by minimizing tax obligations and reducing (or entirely eliminating) other restrictions on business operations. The result is that economic activity within these centers is specifically geared to the special global needs of outside businesses and investors.

Typically, these centers are small states with tiny

populations. To date, 50 them exist throughout the world. Each one of them is a unique offshore haven deliberately intended to attract very particular investors with very specific needs.

For example, a center like Aruba was set up primarily for economic development. Formerly dependent on oil refineries for its revenue, it has now implemented an investment policy that gives it entree to the global economic system. Becoming an offshore money haven was the answer. By "renting" its laws regarding taxation, incorporation and other related legal matters, Aruba has begun a much needed process of economic development and diversification.

Singapore, on the other hand, was designed to serve the Asian dollar market. Today it's one of the most prosperous money havens in the world on a per capita basis. And Bahrain was developed to process the Middle East's offshore financial needs, especially Saudi Arabia's.

All these offshore havens were made possible by the electronic revolution in fund transfer mechanisms which occurred in the 1970s. That single technological development made it suddenly possible and affordable to establish banks, corporations and holding companies in relatively remote locations. It also made inter and intra time-zone business a viable alternative to home-based operations. In turn, this gave rise to the creation of international wholesale banking — where large deposits could be maintained in a variety of currencies, transferred via a worldwide network of corporations, banks, governments and individuals, and lent to interested borrowers. This, in turn, led to new transnational business practices and the development of the international subcontracting of loans and other financial transactions.

Basically, international havens have become an established part of the international intermediate economy. They stand as "brokers" of a sort for global business and finance. It's important to keep in mind that all of this was initiated by large banks, corporations and even government agencies from around the world. Keep in mind that every government from the Soviet Union to the United States needs to obtain money on the international market. They, too, use money havens as convenient transaction points. The Bahamas became one of the biggest offshore havens because it serves the purposes of various government entities from finance ministries to intelligence agencies.

These offshore financial centers were originally established by onshore banks and corporations because *they* felt hemmed-in by archaic laws, regulations and statutes.

Offshore havens are, today, an accepted financial fact. Even more important, they are seen as legitimate vehicles through which individual investors can take advantage of the offshore option. It's simply a matter of applying the basic financial principles of profit, tax protection and privacy. They were developed over the centuries by Florentine merchants, royal treasurers and brillant bankers. The mechanisms and strategies change continuously, but the goals always remain the same.

■THE OFFSHORE INVESTOR'S GUIDE

The following guide is meant to serve not as a complete list of all offshore havens but, rather, as a map through the foreign financial centers that I consider most important for today's U.S. investor. Again, I caution against using the list as an absolute measure of a location's desirability. It is always best to hire a professional consultant who can balance the benefits of a specific location against your very individual needs.

At minimum, you should look for an offshore center that offers the following:

- *Secrecy* - your personal and business accounts should be completely confidential. Nobody but you and those you specifically designate should be able to learn anything about your investments or business activities. o Easy Movement of Assets - you need to be able to transfer your investments and assets without incurring a tax liability. Be sure to investigate tax laws as they apply to profits earned within as well as outside the potential money haven.

- *Flexibility* - you want to be able to freely plan your inheritance for family members and others beneficiaries. Not all international centers are set up to help in this area. Don't get involved with one that isn't.

- *Privacy* - you need to shield your financial transactions from prying eyes. The eyes of Uncle Sam and his army of government bureaucrats seem to get keener instead of weaker with age. Make sure the laws of your chosen jurisdiction protect you from any economic disclosures.

In addition, you'll want to look for a haven that offers government concessions, little or no taxes, easy access, smooth entry, political stability, absence of currency restrictions or controls, banking secrecy, a common language, trained personnel, excellent telecommunications and a positive attitude toward Americans.

ARUBA

Aruba is a separate entity within the Kingdom of the Netherlands. It is located in the Dutch Caribbean, less than 20 from the Venezuelan coast. Aruba is a single island that is about 20 miles long and approximately 5 miles wide. It has a total population of 61,000 people and a delightful climate. Oranjestad is the capital. The island has an excellent educational system and four languages are spoken: Dutch, (the official language), English, Spanish and Papamiento, the island's common language. Telecommunications are first-rate. Automatic international communication provides access to any country anywhere in the world. And a satellite groundstation means that instant satellite communication as well as the latest data systems are operational.

The best way to utilize the features of Aruba is to establish a tax exempted company there. The reason is that Aruba does not require these companies to maintain bookkeeping or annual accounts. It allows companies to determine the value of shares upon the date of issue. Incorporators and shareholders need not be the same individuals or entities. Shareholders may meet anywhere in the world. Minutes are not mandatory. And no special licenses are needed.

The Aruban government is very flexible, and concerned since the early 1980s in developing alternative sources of revenue. For several decades, it survived and prospered due to the presence of one of the world's largest oil refineries. When that refinery closed in 1985, the government decided to concentrate on tourism and international financial services.

Due to its longtime status as a center for oil, Aruba has a highly developed infrastructure. This combined with government flexibility and willingness to attract investors, gives Aruba a clear thumbs-up for anyone interested in establishing an offshore corporation in a friendly and strategically located center.

THE BAHAMAS

The Bahamas has always been a classic offshore money haven. Besides extending across 100,000 square miles of heavenly blue waters, they are also located 60 miles east of Florida. That's less than an hour's plane ride.

An additional plus for the Bahamas is its no tax policy. Since 1717, not a single penny has been paid in income, corporation, capitals gains, remittance, estate or inheritance tax in the Bahamas. Besides these advantages, the government actively encourages foreign investment.

As important as these benefits are, it's the latest improvements that offer the best opportunities for potential international investors. One of the most significant has been the passage of three new laws which make it far easier to do business there.

In particular, the international Companies Act of 1989 makes it possible for non-residents to form an international business company— "an IBC." This entity is very interesting and has many uses, especially for an investor who wishes to own and operate an offshore bank.

To begin with, a minimum number of subscribers — just a single director, individual or corporation — can form an IBC. Capital can be in any currency and reduction of capital can be achieved by resolution of the directors without court sanction. Board meetings can be held anywhere and by phone. A special attribute of an IBC is that no public record as to the identity of shareholders or directors may be maintained in any electronic form.

According to the Act, an IBC can engage in any lawful activity. This gives investors an unlimited level of financial freedom. Assets can be transferred within or without The Bahamas for the sole benefit of the IBC. And the law also makes it virtually impossible for a foreign government to expropriate the assets of, or impose confiscatory taxes on, an IBC.

Perhaps the most innovative use of an IBC is to use such a company as the management arm for an offshore bank located in another jurisdiction. For example, an investor who owns a bank in the Netherlands Antilles or Aruba can have its administrative affairs managed from The Bahamas. In this way, the bank owner can enjoy the benefits of one of the most congenial environments in the world with all the latest telecommunications systems instantly at hand and still be less than an hour away from the United States. This way a bank owner can maintain business efficiency, pay no taxes and soak up the sun in one of the most flexible, legal systems in the world. You can't ask for much more than that.

BARBADOS

Political stability is a major benefit to anyone considering financial ventures in Barbados. Without racial friction, military rule, or serious labor problems, it operates as a parlimentary government located a few hundred miles off the northern coast of South America. It is 21 miles long, 14 miles wide, and as of 1988, had a quarter of a million residents. It is considered a wonderful vacation spot due to the balmy trade winds that blow year-round, and the sunshine that reigns supreme during every season.

Communication systems are top of the line throughout Barbados. For example, it has an earth satellite which allows for international data transfer. It also offers the Caribbean's best roads and highways. As an added plus, the official language for business documents and everyday practice is English.

If you consider this offshore haven, be forewarned that the quality of local banking regulation is considered below par by most analysts. Like the Bahamas, Barbados discourages financial investment by individual entrepeneurs as well as small consortiums. To limit the pool of eligible investors, local government now requires a hefty $1 million paid-in capital requirement before issuing a bank license.

Between this capital requirement and a deteriorating economy (due to falling exports and a rising trade deficit), I suggest that you avoid Barbados for business activity. I would, however, encourage anyone to vacation there. It's a beautiful place and very welcoming to American tourists.

BERMUDA

Bermuda is the oldest self-governing states in the British Commonwealth. Located less than 1,000 miles southeast of New York City and 600 miles away from North Carolina, it is a small country consisting of 150 islands with a total area of less than 25 square miles. Communication and air facilities are excellent.

Truly a tax haven, there is no income tax, corporation tax, capital gains tax or withholding tax imposed by the Bermuda government. This makes it a hot spot for investors whose main concern is tax protection.

Nothing, of course, is perfect. When it comes to this island cluster, the major drawback is local capital requirement laws. For anyone planning to establish a corporation or insurance company, these laws will amount to a major stumbling block. For instance, the minimum paid-in capital needed to form an insurance company is $125,000, and some Bermudian attorneys actually suggest a minimum of $250,000 to ensure incorporation. In addition, a proposal to introduce offshore banking was recently defeated by the Houses of government.

Politically, Bermuda has been plagued by periodic unrest — including the assassination of a newly-appointed Governor in the 1970s. Tourism has traditionally accounted for a good part of the island's economy, but since the mid-1980s, its popularity as a vacation spot has plummeted. The problem is primarily economic: the island's currency is pegged to the U.S. dollar and 85 percent of its tourists are U.S. citizens. Frankly, most

American vacationers opt for getaways that offer a better exchange rate.

From almost every perspective, Bermuda is not a place to establish an offshore presence. Bermuda is quite dependent upon the U.S. economy. So if you want to avoid the economic negatives that affect the United States, it's best to go somewhere less vulnerable to the ups and downs of this financial arena.

BRITISH VIRGIN ISLANDS (B.V.I.)

Christopher Columbus is credited with the discovery of the Virgin Islands. Swayed by how many he found — 60 in all — he tagged this Caribbean chain "Las Virgenes," in honor of St. Ursula and her 11,000 virgins-in-waiting. During the 16th and 17th centuries, the volcanic rock islands were used as a base of operation by such notable buccaneers as "Blackbeard" and Sir Francis Drake.

Today, a new breed of adventurer has established a beachhead on the Virgin Islands. I'm referring, of course, to offshore investors, particularly U.S. companies that have set up subsidiary operations in the region. To understand the scope of this corporate activity, consider the folling figures. In just the first four months of 1988, a total of 2,122 companies registered in Tortola (the main island and the B.V.I.'s business center). That's more than registered in all of 1987. The reason for the rush is that many offshore companies are leaving or avoiding Panama.

The only language used in the B.V.I. is English. That's certainly attractive to U.S. investors. What's more, communications are excellent — with good telephone, cable and telex service to the United States. On the down side, there are no direct international flights to Tortola. In order to reach the capital you first must fly to Puerto Rico, the U.S. Virgin Islands, or Antigua. From any of these three spots, you can catch a plane to the main island.

Many observers feel that the B.V.I. are shaping up into a prime tax haven. In my opinion, the final verdict is still out. The crush of companies has caused some problems with space, and longtime residents have started to complain about the growing influx of foreigners. That may lead to social and legal limitations down the road. For the moment, I suggest that you explore a few other havens, and keep a careful eye on what happens here. This may well become a great money haven for the late 1990s.

CAYMAN ISLANDS

The Caymans are a special place and an extremely popular money haven. Local government imposes no taxes of any kind on income or profits, capital, wealth, capital gains, property, sales, estate or inheritance. Located 500 miles south of Florida and about 200 miles northwest of Jamaica, the Caymans are composed of three isles — Grand Cayman, Cayman Brac and Little Cayman. The capital, George Town, is the area's financial and business center.

As you walk down George Town's main streets, you are immediately struck by the number of buildings which house banks, trusts, captive insurance companies and various other offshore firms. However, before you rush head first into a Cayman operation, you should know that nearly all those institutions are subsidiaries of the the world's largest banks and corporations. Offshore business in the Cayman Islands is a very big money game, and it's pretty much reserved for the globe's major players.

To give you an idea of what constitutes a "major player," let me take your through an abbreviated who's who of the 18,000 companies and 550 banks now doing business in the Caymans: The Detroit Edison Company, Marine Midland Banks, Inc., Mellon Bank Company, United Energy Resources, Inc., Conagra, Inc., Kansas City Power & Light Company, McDonnell Douglas Corporation, Archer Daniels Midland Company, Amerada Hess Corporation, Houston Natural Gas Corporation, Arizona Bancwest Corporation, First Interstate Bancorp, Republic Airlines, etc., etc., etc. As you can see, very large, public and well-known companies are conducting offshore business in this region.

As a result, the Caymans are a first-class offshore center. Their infrastructure is excellent. Communications are top of the line. Direct flights to and from the United States are available. The official and spoken language is English and their dollar is pegged to the U.S. dollar at CI$1.25 = US$1.00.

But there's one major obstacle, and it too is the result of the Cayman's special involvement with big business. Charters and licenses are available only to long-established companies and banks with a paid-in capital of at least $500,000. The small to medium investor is left out completely. If it were not for the government's closed-door policy toward individual investors, the Caymans would be a perfect offshore choice.

CHANNEL ISLANDS

The Channel Islands are composed of the isles of Jersey, Guernsey and Sark. The two main islands, Jersey and Guernsey, are longtime offshore centers with thriving economies. Situated in the Bay of St. Malo — closer to the French coast than to England and only 50 minutes from London — the Channel Islands are one of the world's busiest tax havens. All three centers cater mostly to British and European companies and individuals. Nevertheless, they can provide a world-class financial environment for U.S. investors as well.

Like the Caymans, the Channel Islands have developed into a base of operations for major international banks and corporations. Chase Manhattan, Credit Suisse, Rothschild Bank, Hong Kong & Shanghai Banking Corp. are among the leading financial institutions based in Jersey or Guernsey. For individual investors, there is one special lure: a booming offshore fund market. Jersey alone is home base for some 300 international funds. So if the fund market appeals to you, I'd recommend that you explore this option further with a professional consultant.

The official and spoken language is English. The transportation and communications services are top of the line. Unfortunately, the Channel Islands are too far away to really serve the needs of most potential offshore investors from the United States. It's also worth mentioning that recent revelations of money laundering in Jersey may hurt the reputation of anyone involved with the islands. That's something no discreet investor ever desires.

HONG KONG

Located on mainland China's Southeast coast, Hong Kong extends 404 miles. It is composed of Hong Kong Island, Kowloon Peninsula and the New Territories. Victoria harbor, one of the best and most beautiful natural harbors in the world, separates Hong Kong Island from the Kowloon Peninsula. With a population of more than 5 million people, the region is well-known for its international financial activities.

Actually, I would not label Hong Kong a tax haven in the truest sense. It's true that no tax is levied on income earned outside Hong Kong. But if you move money into this center and invest it wisely, you will be required to pay taxes on all the profits you earn. What's more, you will be taxed again by Uncle Sam when you repatriate the money back to the United States.

As you probably know, there is an air of anxiety concerning Hong Kong because the Peoples Republic of China will be assuming administrative control of the region in 1997. Although China has recently made great strides toward free enterprise, old habits are hard to break. For good reason, most experienced offshore enthusiasts are divesting from the area, and few new investors are making this their first offshore activity site.

On a comparative basis, Hong Kong is the best place to operate a bank but it is very hard to qualify for a license. I suggest that you secure a license from a jurisdiction with less red tape and lower paid-up capital requirements and have it managed by a Hong Kong-based management company.

LIECHTENSTEIN

This tiny little state, wedged in a visually stunning mountain valley between Switzerland and Austria, covers about 61 square miles. It's located about 75 miles from Zurich, and about 28,000 people currently live there. Due to its proximity to Switzerland, it has benefited from the strength of the Swiss Franc. It is also one of the world's oldest and best tax havens with extremely strict bank secrecy laws. In fact, one European financier told me that Liechtenstein is where the Swiss go when they want to protect their money. In fact, there are more "letterbox" corporations (40,000) than Liechtensteiners.

Unfortunately, for small to mid-sized U.S. investors, this charming but miniscule principality has little to offer. Like some of the other money havens I've already covered, its users tend to be very high net worth individuals, large international corporations and multinational banking institutions.

If you love forests or like to ski, and you have a lot of money to spend, this could be a viable option for you. As the *Washington Post* noted in a report, "Liechtenstein has everything a traveler needs for a European vacation — flowing rivers and dark forests, bustling capital city and quaint farms, castle on the hill, mountains and lush valleys, good food, one superb hotel, Old Masters paintings, vineyards galore, fine wines, a benign prince, famous Winter Olympics competitors, friendly natives — all this in an area the size of the District of Columbia."

To enjoy Liechtenstein, you need to like rubbing elbows with Europeans, though. Because Liechtenstein is located on the continent, it caters mostly to European business. One reflection of this orientation is the official language; it's German. So for most U.S. investors, the attractions are outweighed by practical drawbacks.

LUXEMBOURG

This Grand Duchy is rapidly evolving into an appealing alternative to Switzerland. Its secrecy laws are wonderful, and it offers a host of tax benefits. Located in Central Europe, it is bounded by France, Germany and Belgium. Covering approximately 1,000 square miles, it experienced an influx of foreign capital and investment in 1988 that far exceeded expectations. Most of this activity has resulted from a loss of confidence in Swiss secrecy laws. Germans, in particular, have been drawn by the financial discretion that is part and parcel of doing business in Luxembourg.

Europeans aren't the only ones being drawn to this little country. Crown Prince Henri himself flew into Japan recently with a large contingent of advisors and businessmen to "sell" Luxembourg's status as a financial center. The big selling point: they came up with a plan that allows certain tax deferments on specific types of income. Never ones to pass up a good thing, nearly 20 Japanese insurance companies and a dozen banks have opened offices in that small land.

United States Banker reported in a recent issue that Luxembourg's "flexible legal framework, its generous accounting attitudes related to loan loss provisions, and the overall relaxed banking and exchange regulations" have helped its recent popularity. It also noted that "tax evasion (as distinct from tax fraud) isn't viewed as a crime" as it is in other locales. For the moment, this little state can enjoy its advantages.

For the average private investor, Luxembourg is best utilized as a banking resource. With over 120 banks crowding the Boulevard Royal — the Duchy's version of Wall Street — the banking business is enjoying a boom. I should add, however, that for the individual investor who wants to operate his own business or financial entity, Luxembourg is inappropriate.

To begin with, in terms of licensing, clear preference goes to large international companies. The official language is French, with German as the second language. Additionally, in 1992 the European Economic Community is going to free all capital movements and exchange controls throughout Western Europe. The effect will be to increase competition for banking customers and to clamp down on tax avoidance strategies by requiring banks to divulge details about their customers' accounts. For all these reasons, I advise even my most privacy-concerned clients to stay closer to home, and to choose a money haven that operates in their own language.

NETHERLANDS ANTILLES

There's an interesting story I'd like to tell you about the Netherlands Antilles because it illustrates the growing power and prominence of offshore business centers.

Called "Treasury's Blunder in Paradise" by *The New York Times*, the whole episode began in mid-1987, when the U.S. Treasury decided to end a tax treaty that had prevailed for years between the United States and the Netherlands Antilles.

Keep in mind that a tax treaty between the United States and any other country usually ensures that certain profits, interest payments and other investment income will not be double-taxed (in two different jurisdictions) or that if a double tax should occur, it will be imposed at a reduced rate. With the U.S.-Netherlands treaty on the verge of dissolution, anyone heavily invested in the offshore center stood to suddenly incur a very heavy tax burden.

Well, once the White House made a formal announcement concerning its plan, a firestorm of angry criticism came from some of this nation's biggest corporations, wealthiest private investors and most influential financial institutions. It seems that, year in and year out, more foreign investment flows into the United States from the Netherlands Antilles than from Japan and West Germany put together. By the mid-1980s, nearly $50 billion in investments and Eurobonds was held in this tiny island chain just north of Venezuela.

And who do you think constitutes that "foreign" investment flow? James A. Baker III, who was then the U.S. Secretary of the Treasury, found out in short order. No less than 30 percent of those investments were held by powerful American interests. These investors included major pension funds and banks such as First Boston Corporation, Harris Trust of Chicago, and big insurance companies like Travelers, Aetna and Pacific Mutual of Newport Beach, California. You can bet that Secretary Baker heard from those folks! And their messsage to him must have been crystal clear: reverse plans. Now.

As you might expect, after days of angry phone calls and increasing political pressure, the Treasury Department announced that the treaty with the Netherlands Antilles would remain in effect — particularly the tax exmeption for interest on Eurobonds and other investment vehicles.

What interests me most about this story is what it says about the influence you can have when you make the kind of money that's there for the making in the offshore market. The fact is, this nation's highest tax policy makers were forced to retreat and to allow a money haven to remain intact, unencumbered by excessive government intrusion.

Do shop the various services and limitations that are associated with different foreign money havens. It's only when you compare your needs with the benefits of each site that you can select the haven that's right for you.

The Antilles, as they are commonly known, offer vacationer a virtual paradise. Located at the crossroads of key shipping and airline routes, these South American islands combine wonderful, top-of-the-line international communications with trained personnel and easy access.

For the mid-sized private investor, the Antilles offer little in the way of true tax relief, profit potential or financial privacy. The start-up required for companies, banks and insurance firms is around $500,000 and the government prefers to work with multinational entities. My recommendation is to exercise caution in regard to using the Antilles as a base of operations or as an investment center.

PANAMA

Once upon a time, before General Manuel Noriega brought the ire of the U.S. government down upon himself and his country, the Republic of Panama was considered to be among the world's best money havens.

This strategically located isthmus, known as the gateway to the Pacific and Atlantic Oceans, was then home to more than 35,000 holding companies and tax sanctuary operations. It did not assess tax on income produced outside the country, and so, it attracted intelligent investors from around the globe, including the United States.

The whole Noriega affair changed the situation, at least for the time being. *Southern Banker* published a startling story detailing the scale and nature of Noriega's drug connection. As head of the Panamanian Armed Forces, he allowed drug smugglers to land their aircraft complete with their payload of cocaine right on military airfields. Sometimes this happened with the sanctioned protection of the Army. In addition, he received regular monthly payments of three to five million dollars for his cooperation. The magazine also reported that many payments to Noriega were simply massive cash deliveries in suitcases taken to his office by couriers and bagmen.

The situation reached the point where Noriega's activities went so far that they finally preicipitated the U.S. indictments against him. Finally, the U.S. invade Panama just to capture Noriega and install a new government in his place. As financial analysts love to say, without political stability there can be no economic stability. Since the clash between Noriega and the United States, Panama has been losing much of its offshore business. Nearby centers — like the British Virgins Islands, Bermuda and various Caribbean havens — are happily picking up the slack and offering comparable if not improved services. Things are starting to return to its pre-Noreiga days but I would recommend careful monitoring of the situation for a couple more years.

My advice about a Panama venture? Avoid it. As things stand now, the nation has lost too much credibility. That could change over the next few years, but for the time being, this must be ranked one of the least desirable choices for any offshore involvement.

SWITZERLAND

Once considered the number one money haven in the world, Switzerland has now slipped to the second tier of offshore financial centers. Nearly 6.5 million people call the 16,000 square miles that comprise Switzerland their home. According to some estimates there is one bank for every 1,400 citizens in this visually stunning Alpine financial center.

Although its longtime reputation as a stable banking capital has helped it maintain a strong position in world finance, this country known as the "heart of Europe," is now more like the grand old dame of offshore finance. Her best days are behind her but she still has 250 years of earned dignity.

There are reasons that Switzerland has its reputation for banking expertise. For one, the Swiss have served as Europe's bankers as far back as the Middle Ages. More importantly, as one Swiss investor once told me at a conference in Geneva, "the single most important aspect that makes us different from other bankers is that we see the world without borders where money is concerned." In other words, as bankers and financiers, the Swiss were probably one of the first to see the value of the offshore concept.

Because Switzerland is bounded by so many large countries including France, Germany, Italy and Germany, it has been forced to see the world in a certain way. They've also been able to turn a geographic circumstance into a prized asset. Their famous neutrality has made it possible for them to attract money in search of protection and privacy.

Today's offshore market owes a lot to the Swiss. However, like so much else, all things must pass. I think that their days as the number offshore money haven have come and gone. Although they still play a key role in international finance, recent economic changes in the world and the emergence of new centers with stricter secrecy laws and an arms length relationship with the U.S. have made Switzerland a haven for those who are in no hurry to move their money.

You may want to put some small percentage of your assets into Swiss francs. Otherwise I recommend that you stay away from Switzerland as an offshore haven. Its ties to the U.S. government are too strong for anyone who wants to create a certain distance from Uncle Sam. Since so many of the big Swiss banks want to operate in the U.S., they must cooperate with American authorities. That effectively makes Switzerland an unsafe center.

VANUATU

Like Panama, the nearly 100 South Pacific islands collectively known as the nation of Vanuatu have recently lost their investment appeal. They were once considered a desirable money haven, but political instability has destroyed the confidence of investors throughout the world.

As Reuters News Service put it, "Normally sleepy Vanuatu, its islands fringed with coral and coconut palms, has no personal tax, no local exchange controls, no capital gains or profit tax, no company tax and offers complete secrecy. But rioting and political tension have sent shock waves through the financial community."

For 17 years, Vanuatu worked to build its status as a desirable tax and money haven. As one wire service reported, "Today over 1,200 companies, including major banks and law and accounting firms representing billions of dollars are incorporated in the small South Pacific island state. Most of these companies are primarily from Australia, New Zealand, Hong Kong, Taiwan, Singapore and Indonesia. Individual investors are a very small portion of the investment community.

Frankly, the loss is not a big one for U.S. investors. Located as it is, south of Australia, Vanuatu has always been too far out of the way to lure Americans or Europeans.

MAKING YOUR CHOICE

As you sit down to analyze your offshore options, it's important to clarify the financial benefits that mean most to you. It's just as essential to go about your research in a methodical way. If you're not the kind of person who wants to do that for himself, then hire a professional consultant to do it for you. But do shop the various services and limitations that are associated with different foreign money havens. It's only when you can compare your needs with the benefits of several offshore sites that you can confidently select the spot that's right for you.

Does it sound like too much to hope for? It's not. You've entered the international arena, remember, where entire governments are organized around policies aimed at attracting foreign investment. They want your business, and they'll do a lot to get it. So start asking!

CHAPTER TEN

Investors On File

"Every man, as long as he does not violate the laws of justice, is perfectly free to pursue his own interest in his own way...."

—Adam Smith
The Wealth of Nations

On the average, I talk with twelve prospective international investors a week. That adds up to six hundred potential clients every year. I've been a consultant for more than fifteen years. So, to date, I've talked with nearly ten thousand people who are seriously interested in the offshore banking option.

Some of them are extremely informed and swayed by the benefits associated with offshore banking even before we shake hands for the first time. In fact, I'm amazed by how aware many investors have become of international finance. Maybe their growing sophistication is still one more reflection of the dwindling profit opportunities available in the domestic marketplace.

Of course, many people contact me with only a hazy sense of what offshore involvements can offer. Occasionally, they tell me they've seen or skimmed through one of my books. Maybe they've heard about me from a friend or business associate. Usually, they talk about the prospect of internationalizing their assets with a combination of anxiety and hope — anxiety over a leap into the unknown and hope for some level of economic freedom.

Not all these conversations end with a signed agreement. But to date, my firm has put together enough offshore banks and companies for individuals, partnerships, small consortiums and mid-sized companies to know that a lot of people are making a lot of money in complete privacy.

Too often, I think, people imagine all international investors to be glamourous kingpins of the underworld, famous Greek tycoons, or crowned royalty from Europe. Certainly there are offshore facilities owned and operated by these movie-like characters. But the majority of my clients are much more down-to-earth.

They live and work in virtually every part of the

United States. Some come from wealthy families, from a financial support system in which creative investment is like second nature. Others are self-made businessmen and career professionals. There are doctors, politicians, university professors and ministers. There are also used car dealers, building contractors, real estate agents, and plumbers.

I want to help people carry out their dreams. I want to be the means toward their aspirations.

And, in every case, it's lifestyle and personality that ultimately determine the specific nature of their offshore plan. For example, a professional couple in their mid-30s may set very modest economic goals: a bigger home in a better part of the city, a guaranteed education for their two kids at one of the country's leading universities, and the assurance of a comfortable retirement. Offshore banking is tailor-made to meet those objectives.

Meanwhile, an aggressive and experienced businessman in his late-40s may approach the international market as the best means to a diversified investment program that earns mega-profits in Asia, Europe, Latin America and Canada — all at the same time. Private bank ownership can handle that assignment, too.

For me, the true enjoyment comes in knowing that I've helped someone enhance their life. That's my main motivation. I want to help people carry out their dreams. I want to be the means toward their aspirations. I understand that because I've been moving toward my own personal goals. Like everyone else, I have my own aspirations and dreams. And that's where the empathy I have for my clients comes from; out of my own life experiences.

So read through the following client profiles. Maybe you'll see a bit of yourself popping up between the lines. If not, call me. I'd like to hear from you because, just maybe, yours is the one offshore game plan that I still haven't heard!

▮THE BIG BONANZA

Imagine this: a man in his mid-40s — well-dressed in a navy blue suit, striped shirt buttoned all the way up and no tie, hair combed straight back and wearing dark glasses inside a hotel — walks up to me at one of my seminars with a check in his hand. He says a simple hello, and hands me the check. It's made out to my firm in the amount of $45,000. Clipped to it is a hand-written note. "I need an offshore company. You select the place. Call me when all the papers have been prepared." There was also a phone number on the note and the area code was 212. New York City.

This is a true story. The client's name is Donald Brenner, and in the two years since that initial encounter, I have become one his many admirers. Not, I might add, because of his personal charm. Don is not a charming guy. But he is a brillant guy. And he typifies a new breed of offshore investor. They're lean and a little mean and they waste no time in getting down to business. What they lack in conversational savoir faire they more than make up for in brains and gumption.

I was surprised to find out that Don was an attorney. He didn't have the air of a lawyer. He was fast-talking and a bit pushy. When I returned to my office after the seminar, I called him. I was not about to make the decisions he had asked me to make without knowing anything about his particular offshore concerns.

He did not seem happy to get the call. "I thought the note was clear enough," he said. "I don't know where to buy an offshore company. That's your business, isn't it? Pick the best spot and buy me one." I pursued the matter a bit further by asking, in general, why he wanted it. "To make deals," he said. "To make a killing. Isn't that why everybody wants one?"

And that rock-bottom explanation of the offshore investing motive still tops my list for hitting the nail right on the head.

I selected Aruba for Don's offshore center. Titled, simply, The Bank of Aruba it has become one of the fastest-growing facilitiies in the area. Naturally, it offers all the basic services you'd find in any offshore facility. But that's only the start. Don most avidly utilizes the bank as a kind of intermediary between himself and a wide array of international investors looking for U.S. financial involvements.

Don himself may not be all that knowledgeable about cross-cultural, transnational business negotiations, but he has put together a team of people who are. Together, they nurture close and ongoing associations primarily with Japanese and Arabian investors who want to start, acquire or merge with a U.S.-owned company.

Most of my clients use their offshore banks to get involved in foreign business opportunities. And they're well-rewarded for their effort. Don likes to work the other way around. He uses his bank to structure deals with foreigners who are trying to get in on the U.S. marketplace. He charges a hefty fee for making the proper introductions, handling the delicate stage of negotiations, and drawing up the final business contracts.

Even more important, though, The Bank of Aruba aims to create a role for itself in the ongoing international partnerships that result from the initial deals. In a sense, the bank brings major global players together and makes itself a third member of the profitable business triads that get established.

Not many investors could wheel and deal like Don Brenner. Not many would want to try. He spends all his time running a very diversified investment program, and his profits show it. Last year alone, the bottom line surpassed 25 million dollars. That means Don is playing a high-risk game, not to everyone's liking. But his enormous success bears out what I've been saying all along: when you're involved in offshore banking, the sky's your only limit.

■A SILICON VALLEY SUCCESS

William Roesser was already a very successful man when I met him in 1986. He was an established leader in high-technology research and industry development. He had worked for some of the biggest names in the Silicon Valley — sometimes as a staff executive and other times as an independent consultant. He told me quite matter-of-factly that he charged handsomely for his time and still never had any of it to spare. In fact, our first meeting was over lunch in San Francisco. Bill invited me up there because a flight down to Los Angeles involved more "down" time than he could afford.

As a private investor, Bill had also done quite well for himself. His computer savvy played a big role in that success. By feeding stock market information into his own software program design, he could predict with uncanny accuracy the companies that would do well over the coming months. His prerequisites for an attractive stock option were strict: a six-month forecast had to show at least a five to one profit advantage. And even then, he was skeptical. "But at that point," he said, "I will seriously consider it."

Halfway through that afternoon's appetizer, it became

clear that offshore banking was not a new concept for Bill. For some time, he had been researching it as an investment technique. First and foremost, he told me, he was drawn to its flexibility. A hardcore high-tech wiz, Bill wanted the freedom to control a truly diversified international investment plan from his comfortable home study in Palo Alto.

He also liked the privacy guarantees that come with careful offshore finance. Again, his computer background had taught him the extent to which personal information is gathered, stored and even exchanged between software data banks. His investments were entirely legitimate, but he liked the idea of circumventing what he considered excessive government and private industry investigation.

Five weeks to the day after our first meeting, Bill received formal title to Independent Commerce, his offshore bank in Vanuatu. In the beginning, he worked closely with an investment management firm that was based in Montreal. With their help, he diversified his portfolio to include investments in the Far and Middle East, Germany, Latin America and Australia. Technically, of course, all these investments were owned and managed by Independent. So Bill's privacy was guaranteed.

I saw Bill late last year at one of my two-day seminars. He had come, he said, to explore the idea of exanding his offshore business. More than satisfied with the results of his international investment program, he had earned a two-year profit of just over one million dollars. Now he was interested in attracting a wider spectrum of international depositors and borrowers.

My suggestion was that he keep Independent Commerce as his offshore investment arm and open a second foreign bank — perhaps in Aruba or the Netherland Antilles — to operate as a more active banking services facility. That way, he could keep faster track of where his profits were being generated. And he could spread out his financial independence, enjoying top-notch banking benefits at two foreign financial centers instead of just one.

What kind of profit could he expect on the second facility, he asked me. Immediately, I remembered our initial meeting and his strict rule about a five to one profit advantage. "Better than five to one," I smiled. "Well, then," he replied, "I'll seriously consider it."

■OFFSHORE MOUNTAIN MAN

One of the most intriguing clients I've had in a long time is Chuck Davis. My first contact with him came through the phone. He called me out of the blue and asked if he could come in to talk about a venture capital idea he had in the works. We settled on an appointment time for the next day.

When Chuck walked in, he looked like he had stepped right off a Marlboro Man billboard. He was tall and thin, and dressed top to bottom in faded denim. He wore boots and his beaded and bone wrist bands were some of the most beautiful Indian artwork I'd ever seen. In every way, Chuck radiated masculinity. He was confident but fairly soft-spoken. He knew what he wanted from our meeting but was totally at ease in working through his agenda.

As it turned it, Chuck was only in Los Angeles for a week. He lived and worked in Anchorage, Alaska. Originally trained as an engineer, he had been working for the past three years for a company owned and operated by the Inuit Indian tribe as a consultant on alternative energy development. Along with two other associates, he had been commissioned to design cost-effective solar-powered architectural plans for family residences and small business offices. Together, the three partners were now interested in forming their own company which would market very similar plans throughout the uppermost Northwest.

The problem was simple and common: insufficient venture capital. They just didn't have enough cash on hand to commission a marketing firm and follow through on a professional promotional campaign. Interestingly, Chuck had heard about offshore banking from one of the tribal officials who, himself, had purchased a facility through my firm a number of years ago. He suggested that Chuck use an offshore bank to generate part of the necessary money, and then use it to help borrow the rest from various international sources.

Although Chuck's long-term aim was quite unique, his basic offshore banking plan was rather basic. He wanted to own a bank as a way of funding his own onshore business projects. The profits earned from depositors, borrowers and assorted offshore business transactions would constitute the venture capital base that he needed to get them off the ground.

I suggested that, from the start, Vanuatu Citizens' Bank work with an experienced international advertising consultant who could help select appropriate publications for ads letting potential depositors know about the facility's attractive interest rates and specialized international banking services. In truth, there was nothing so amazing about Chuck's bank. It offered precisely the kind of customer-oriented amenities that have become closely associated with most offshore banks. But Chuck and his partners did something that most other banks don't do: they put some real time and effort and money into a really professional advertising campaign.

The results were impressive. When I last talked with Chuck, it was by phone. He had been shut-in by 12 feet of fresh snow, but he was as pleased as he could be.

Citizens' Bank had on account deposits of more than 6 million dollars, and his newly-titled design firm (Solar Homes Unlimited) had already marketed over a hundred residential and office floor plans.

I've made it my business to know my clients. They form the basis of my business. They are the pioneers, the global adventurers who are making tomorrow's world today.

With a little creativity and the confidence to try what other people might only dream about, he and his partners had made the first phase of their professional dream come true. Undoubtedly the profits they will continue to earn should help propel them into an exciting phase two.

■ A HIGHER CALLING

Can international investment and Christian virtue go together? They certainly can! Jack and Maggie Osborn taught me that, and in the process, developed a really innovative application of offshore bank operation and profit.

Actually, it was Maggie who first called me — representing a small group of Seventh Day Adventists in Springfield, Illinois. One of them had picked up a book of mine while on business in Chicago, and had slowly convinced the others that collective bank ownership might be a route to significant profit and tax protection. Of course, I agreed with that analysis and we quickly decided that a more in-depth personal meeting was in order.

When the Osborns arrived at my office, they went completely against the grain of all my personal preconceptions about religious zealots. They were good look-ing. They were both fashionably dressed, and they had an aura of unrepressed fun about them that was irresis-table. They teased me about working in Los Angeles, "the Sodom and Gomorrah of modern times," they said. In every possible way, they conveyed an utter lack of judgemental superiority.

Neither Jack nor Maggie knew a lot about offshore banking. They had each come from a traditional, religious family — middle-class people who worked hard, saved as best they could, and relied heavily on Social Security for a livable retirement. Nevertheless, both of them had managed to work their way through college. He was an accountant; she was a bookkeeper. And along with two other professional couples from their church, they hoped the international market could lead to something better than their parents had known.

Only minutes into the meeting, though, Jack presented me with an ultimatum of sorts: if the offshore option was going to work for the group, it had to do more than make them money. It had to benefit people less fortunate than they. "That's an absolute for all of us," he told me. "Naturally, we want to help ourselves, but we want to help others as well."

No other client had ever asked me to design an off-shore project quite like the one they were requesting. Frankly, the challenge fascinated me, and with a little creative thinking, we came up with a workable plan. A six-member consortium would purchase a private bank in Nauru. Their license would allow them to provide all the typical bank services — checking and savings ac-counts, credit card accounts, personal and business loans, as well as trustee authority. Like all foreign facilities, their bank would be able to offer far more at-tractive interest rates than anything available from a U.S.

bank. Best of all, the group would enjoy a built-in customer base: members of their congregation.

To satisfy their more altruistic objectives, I suggested that the consortium establish a philanthropic arm. It could be set-up to function much like a corporate foundation, receiving a predetermined percentage of all bank profits. Then, on a quarterly or twice-a-year basis, the bank's Board of Directors could meet to identify worthy charities and non-profit agencies that would be awarded funds for new or continuing services.

Jack and Maggie liked the basic parameters of the plan. They told me they would meet with the other members of the group and get back to me. Within a few weeks, I received an OK to proceed with the bank license purchase. The United Bank and Trust of Nauru opened about a month later.

Because this particular project was so unusual, I made it a point to stay in touch with the consortium. In a word, their program was a hit. Within two years, in fact, it had expanded its customer base to include Adventist congregations in four mid-Western cities. The six owners were receiving a better return on their initial investment than they had expected. Their customers were very satisfied, and in general, proud to be even a small part of a religious charity they could trust.

When I last talked with Maggie, she was making flight arrangements for a trip to Nauru. Along with the rest of the bank's Board, she and Jack were committed to a two-day meeting at which funding decisions would be made for the coming six months. "The gifts are still fairly small," she said. "We're awarding between five and ten thousand dollars to each recipient. But we hope to be giving larger awards within two years." At that time they had already ensured the temporary survival of a homeless shelter in Chicago, helped to open a nursery school for abused children in St. Louis, and funded six-months worth of hotline suicide prevention in their own city.

■THE INVENTOR'S APPROACH

Clayton Louis Young did not fall in love fast with the offshore option. Looking back, I think that's because it struck him as too clever a way around U.S. banking regulation. "You have to understand," he said, "Blacks have only just begun to gain financial entry into this country. Somehow, it doesn't feel right to walk out the back door of a banking system that funded my education for six years."

Basically, Clayton was an inventor. After receiving an MBA from Morehouse University in 1980, he had worked nearly three years for a New York-based import/export firm. The job never suited him, he told me, but it gave him the chance to monitor a steady flow of electronic imports. Fascinated by the idea of designing mimic products that could be produced less expensively right here in the United States, he eventually quit, and opened his own business.

It was initially a small operation. His girlfriend ran the front office, and a crew of five women worked in back, assembling parts for his electronics line. He developed and marketed his inventions — products like a portable ionizer (designed to clean the air and generate negative ions within a six foot radius), a hand-held hologram camera (capable of producing three dimensional images), and a digital thermometer.

When I met him, the business was four years old, and Clayton was doing well. Still, he had a major problem: aggressive competition. Almost everytime he developed a new item, his company ran into legal trouble. He had been sued three times by manufacturers who claimed unfair product duplication. Other times, he had initiated legal action against competitors.

Regardless of who sued who, Clayton said, he had been through one too many court battles in which access to his financial records were awarded to another manufacturer. "That means my entire business operation is laid bare," he explained, "for long and drawn-out legal review." Although most rulings had been in his favor, Clayton was tired of fighting the war. He wanted an escape from constant regulatory intrusion. And he knew he wasn't going to find it in the domestic banking scene.

We talked first about the benefits of maintaining bank accounts offshore — in someone else's private foreign bank. I assured him that simply by transferring his company's checking account to an overseas facility, he would gain significant protection. Nevertheless, I encouraged him to consider a private purchase.

One of the great allures to offshore banking is "intellectual product" protection. In other words, for inventors like Clayton, the international arena offers a way around copyright redtape and bureaucracy. Each time Clayton sought to copyright a new formula or product, he had to disclose it to the U.S. Copyright Office. In the process, his million-dollar concepts were made part of the public domain, and became vulnerable to reformulation and subsequent competition.

By owning his own offshore bank, Clayton could convert his product designs into "financial information." Technically, they might be called "exhibits to an agreement between scientist and formula owner." Of course, each forumla's owner would be the offshore bank, strategically located in a jurisdiction where bank secrecy laws prevent reporting to any foreign investigator including the U.S. court system.

It took almost three months, but Clay finally did call to

say he was ready to proceed with a purchase. I could hear a level of resignation in his voice. I tried to reassure him that a bank in the Mariana Islands would offer him a level of professional privacy and product protection that he deserved. Then, without much more conversation, we hung up.

Just a month ago, I had lunch with Clayton. He was in L.A. for a few days before starting a three-week research trip to Japan. I told him — as I have before — how different he seems from the man who made that phone call two years ago. In that sense, he is a lot like many of my clients. They start out unsure of what inter-nationalization can do, but they're willing to test the waters.

His bank, like theirs, has been the springboard to important introductions. In fact, his ionizer is now the rage in Germany — all because one of his bank's customers got to know him and decided to test market his electronic line in Berlin. "That should put an extra million in my pocket this year," he told me. And then he laughed, "Not bad for a kid from Harlem, is it?"

MR. ELEGANCE

My work introduces me to a lot of sophisticated people, but when it comes to sheer personal elegance, they all take a back seat to Carson Slater. With his chiseled features and deep voice, he is the picture of old California gentry. He's suave and he's charming, and no matter what the circumstances, he makes the right move. To my way of thinking, he is refinement personified.

Carson is not a self-made man. His family has been a respected part of L.A.'s high society for several generations. His grandfather amassed a literal fortune in agribusiness. His father was a doctor. His mother was actively involved in various cultural and charitable institutions throughout the city.

A graduate of of an Ivy League Architectural School, Carson had run his life just as you might expect. He had married a woman from an equally respected family. They had two sons and a daughter — all of them grown and involved in their own lives. Years before I met him, he had left his own thriving architectural firm in order to devote full time to his and his wife's assets management. He did, however, sit on the the Board of two major corporations.

Shortly after one of my firms' two-day seminars, Carson called the office to let me know that he had been there and had enjoyed the workshops. He was also interested in meeting privately about his own international options. Naturally, I invited him to my office, but he suggested instead that we have lunch at his club. "You might enjoy a quick steam before," he said, "and this way, we can feel comfortable about talking as long as we like." The invitation was casual, like everything about Carson Slater, but I suspect he does quite a lot of serious business over these "casual" lunches at the club.

I enjoyed that first meeting. I especially enjoyed watching the ease with which Carson talked about investment diversification. It was a familiar subject for him, I could tell. Off the cuff, he mentioned regular columns and specific articles from a wide array of financial publications. He obviously read all the right newspapers and made it his business to stay abreast of the newest trends and profit-making strategies.

It was also clear that Carson was extremely well-traveled. He talked about Japan as confidently as most people talk about their hometown. He was unshakably convinced that Asian markets would continue to surge ahead and, as a result, wanted to pursue investment opportunities throughout the Far East. He was intrigued by the role a private offshore bank might play in that pursuit.

Although his interests were specifically geared toward Asia, I urged him to consider Aruba as an appropriate foreign jurisdiction. I knew it would be eaasy to establish operations there. What's more, it is respected by U.S. bankers, and I thought that would be important to Carson given his extensive contact network. Finally, Aruba is an exceptionally beautiful vacation spot — perfect for someone who makes it a habit to mix business with pleasure.

Within a month, Fidelity International Bank and Trust had opened for business. At first, Carson ran the bank truly as a private institution. It handled only his financial transactions. His many checking and saving accounts were immediately transferred. And a number of stocks — domestic and international — were quickly purchased in the bank's name.

Unlike most of my clients, Carson decided to roll up his sleeves and hand-pick his own island representative. He ran a classified ad in one international publication, and got enough qualified responses to schedule six interviews. After meeting all the applicants, he chose a Dutch gentleman who had been a stock broker for 18 years. His knowledge of offshore banking was extensive. He himself now lived in Aruba and knew local officials on a first-name basis. He had replied to Carson's ad because he liked the idea of a low-key involvement in a diversified investment plan. The match was perfect.

Occasionally, I get a call from Carson. Always the gentleman, he typically mentions having read about me in this magazine or that. Usually, he's calling for a referral. That's one of Carson's many strong points: he likes to keep up on who's who in every aspect of financial planning.

He never boasts about the success of his offshore venture. In fact, I almost have to drag information out of him. At last report, his portfolio had expanded to include a number of Asian market involvements. He had also added several friends, associates and social connections to his client roster. A few of them were utilizing the bank for just checking and savings accounts. Most were taking advantage of the attractively low interest rates Fidelity can offer on business loans.

It's also interesting that Carson's interest has shifted somewhat away from Asian. It's Australia that seems to intrigue him most these days. In fact, he has recently used the bank to purchase a hefty percentage of two mineral resource plants deep in the outback. Maybe it's time for another bank purchase...

▮DRS. LASMAN & LASMAN

When Judith Lasman graduated from orthodontic school in 1983, she could have joined any number of prestigious practices in Miami Beach. Instead, she joined her father in the small family dentistry practice he had established many years before.

From the way Dr. Bernard Lasman described his office, it was hardly the high-tech environment we now associate with medical care. It had two exam rooms, a waiting area, and the same receptionist he hired 37 years ago. "But it's comfortable and it's familiar," he told me. "You have to remember, a lot of my patients have been coming to me since they were kids."

Judith had read my first book, she said, while she was still in school. By the time we met in my L.A. office, she had been in practice wih her dad for two years. She had saved some money and had convinced him to save some, too. She was interested in talking about a bank purchase partnership. Essentially, she wanted two things from the venture. First, to liberate her own finances from excessive taxation. Like most medical and dental professionals in this country, she was in the 30 percent tax bracket, and needed relief. "My other concern is Dad's retirement," she said.

It seems Bernie had taken care of just about everyone but himself. He had spent a good deal of his career time treating low-income families for very low fees. He had also been offering volunteer services through the same synagogue for more than twenty years. His accounts were a mess. In fact, some of his patients had owed him money for untold lengths of time. In short, he had ignored the realities of financial planning and now found himself over sixty without the security he wanted. "I don't want a luxurious old age, mind you," he kept insisting, "but I think Judy's right. I need to take some action."

What intrigued me most about this client team was the fact that they had such different offshore objectives. Judith obviously planned on a lucrative career and wanted to protect a substantial income from the long reach of the IRS. Bernie just wanted to retire in a comfortable fashion. I remember thinking, after we concluded that first meeting, how ironic it was that they should need to move assets offshore in order to achieve those objectives. But, then, that is the economic reality of our time.

Before we shook hands goodbye, I suggested that they attend an upcoming seminar that I had scheduled for Miami. They did, and shortly afterward, contacted me with a firm OK on the bank charter and license purchase. They chose Nauru as their offshore base. I helped locate a management firm to handle the operational end of the business. They did purchase a telefax machine for their office. That way, they could rapidly send and receive pertinent information. The entire package cost them less than $35,000 and it formed the basis for a banking and investment plan that changed both their lives.

As this book goes to press, Drs. Lasman and Lasman have operated the International Bank of Nauru for a little more than three years. Judith tells me that through a series of investments, she has already earned close to $100,000 — tax-free. She has focused most of her attention on commodities: gold bullion, silver, and various gems. When we last spoke, she was still instructing her management firm to handle most acquisitions and sales. But she had begun to dabble a bit in diamonds. In fact, she had taken a trip to South Africa just to meet a dealer who was offering a number of unusual cuts.

And how's Bernie? He's great! He's changed a lot, though. Like a lot of people who walk in the offshore door, he's glimpsed a different world on the other side. He's still in practice with his daughter, but their office has been transformed. They moved last year to a new building in downtown Miami. It's larger and equipped with more state-of-the-art equipment. Bernie has cut his patient load almost in half. He sees only the people who've been coming to him for years. All new patients are referred to Judith — or to a third partner who joined their practice in 1987.

Bernie's offshore involvements have stayed fairly conservative. He has investments in Canada and Australia. He also joined Judith in the purchase of a Miami mini-mall — through the bank's name, of course. In short, Bernie's retirement is secure. What's more, it will be a lot more "comfortable" than he ever imagined. And what about his volunteer work? "Oh, I still do that," he chuckles. "We rich guys have to do what we can, you know."

■THE TRIUMPHANT TRIAD

For some of my clients, offshore savvy is almost instinctive. Nelson Scopp is a perfect example. Generally, he's a soft-spoken person, but when it comes to the international option, Nelson gets animated. He can race through various strategies and profit-making possibilities at a speed that hovers around Mach-1. It's more than a rational understanding of the subject with Nelson. He has an intuitive feel for the global marketplace, and he's allowed it to make him a very wealthy man.

I was in my office one day in the Spring of 1990 when Nelson just showed up unannounced. Actually, he didn't have to wait too long before we were sitting in the conference room, getting to know one another. It turned out that he was from South Dakota. So we spent a few minutes comparing notes, covering the finer points of Southern California summers and South Dakota winters.

It also turned out that Nelson held three professional degrees. He is a lawyer, a CPA and an engineer. Perhaps that triple achievement should have tipped me off to Nelson's ultimate aim. But, initially, I was too busy watching him watch me. He took a good measure of everything I said. I must have passed his test because within the week he had fashioned a financial plan that now serves as a model for 1990s-style investors. I call it the triad approach.

"I want to build a triple threat," he said. "I want to use my marketing corporation based in Florida, establish a trust in the Bahamas, and buy an offshore bank."

Spoken like a true manufacturing, design and mechanical engineer, Nelson's description was of something unique and tight. As he explained it, these three entities would work hand-in-hand to help him fashion a hard-driving, high-earning financial machine.

He said he would use his marketing corporation as security for funds deposited in the bank. He would then offer this security through the trust. He planned to hire a

Canadian management firm to manage to bank, and had already found one of the country's best international tax attorneys to help advise on tax matters. To shore up his triad project even further, he decided that the bank would be owned by an offshore holding company and would open accounts in various money havens throughout the world.

Frankly, as I listened to Nelson explain his financial game plan, I sat back in awe. This guy had really done his homework!

"To make deals. To make a killing. Isn't that why everybody want one?"

It wasn't too long after the charter and license had been finalized that I started to see advertisements for the bank in several international publications. And it wasn't too long after that when I got a call from Nelson who said the bank was receiving an unexpected (but welcomed) flood of deposits and inquiries. You see, Nelson's timing had been perfect: as the U.S. market got worse and worse, his offshore financial oasis looked better and better to disgruntled Americans who sought a viable economic option.

Another one of Nelson's inspired strokes was to limit his bank's services to only International Certificates of Deposit (ICDs) and pass-through money market funds. Nelson decided he would offer the ICDs through his offshore bank, but the pass-through money market funds would be available through a number of major international financial institutions. This plan had two major benefits. First, it allowed him to attract a lot of profitable business without putting undue operational stress on the private bank. Second, the association with these long-established firms offered him a tremendous amount of worldwide credibility.

To his credit, Nelson offered a highly competitive interest rate for his bank's ICDs. At the same time, he offered the money market fund at the market rate, and added to it the kind of tax advantage that is available only though an offshore bank.

At last report, Nelson Scopp was still enjoying a boom in his bank's business. Properly engineered, the triad concept had proved to be a winner. I also predict that as economic times continue their downward spiral here in the United States, he will remain positioned to profit from an increasing number of American investor "dropouts," people abandoning our domestic banking system because it has virtually nothing to offer them.

■THE POWER OF EXPERIENCE

I can tell story after story about my clients, people who have caught sight of an economic opening and walked right through it. I can describe all their idiosyncracies, the personal traits and tendencies that motivated them toward assertive international investment. I can do that because I've made it my business to know my clients. They form the basis of my business, and I admire almost all of them. For me, they are the pioneers, the global adventures who are making tomorrow's world a reality today. They are the people who will be interviewed and profiled in economic journals twenty years from now for having taken a daring plunge at the right time.

There is only one thing that distinguishes these people from you: the first move toward protecting assets, avoiding unncessary taxes and securing privacy. As you've learned, it wasn't easy for all of them to make that move. It may not easy for you. But I truly believe that unless you do it, you'll never know what it is to be financially free. Only experience bring you the exhilaration of joinging a world economy outside the stifling constraints of the U.S. government.

CHAPTER ELEVEN

Getting Started The Easy Way

"Even the longest journey begins with a single step."

—Ancient Chinese Proverb

I would like to repeat once again that only decisive action stands between you and lucrative offshore opportunity. If you've taken the time to read this book, then you must be fairly serious about entering the international market. If you're like most readers, you've probably moved from one chapter to the next, calculating the investment profits you could earn outside the United States. You're undoubtedly attracted to the idea of genuine financial privacy. Like everyone, you'd like to reduce your tax burden.

Still, there's a decisive difference between admiring the concept of offshore financial activity and actually taking part in it. Don't get me wrong: offshore "fans" have their place. In fact, over the past several years, they have become a major force in the growth of global investing and business. They buy books, subscribe to newsletters, attend workshops, and in general, contribute to the popularity of a burgeoning offshore market.

It's the offshore "participants," however, who transform enthusiasm into profit. There's nothing magical about making money offshore. You simply need to take the proper steps. As you've already learned, that means you must separate yourself from your assets and then strategically place funds into the foreign markets most likely to generate sizeable income. Then, as international financial dynamics change, you can move your money around, always making sure that it works for you in the most profitable places.

My major aim in writing this book is to help you decide what's right for you. Will you be happiest pledging your allegiance to the offshore fan club? Or would you prefer to take the plunge into an actual international involvement. I've tried to give you the facts you'll need to make that decision. I've also tried to acknowledge the psychological considerations that come into play when you consider a personal role in global finance.

Ultimately, though, it is up to you. Taking into account all that I've said, and tossing in whatever you may have picked up from other reliable sources along the way, you must decide for yourself on the next move. If you think it through and decide that foreign money-making doesn't suit you, I hope you'll consider this book a worthwhile investment in your financial education.

If, however, you feel that you're ready to get started, then the rest of this chapter is meant to point you in the right direction.

▌REVIEWING YOUR OPTIONS

In presenting my argument for offshore investment, I've covered a number of different foreign financial possibilities. There are lots of ways to make and save money within the domestic economy. Well, that goes double when you're operating internationally. In fact, it's hard to conceive of a profit-making venture that could not be legal and feasibly implemented somewhere in the world.

The point is, there are various ways to enter the global economy. I suggest that you learn a bit about the ones that really interest you. I would not encourage you to become an expert on every conceivable offshore investment option. You'll only exhaust yourself by trying, and still not get the job done.

Ultimately, it is up to you. You must decide for yourself on the next move.

To help you outline some of your choices, let's review the six most popular ways in which Americans get financially involved offshore. Consider the benefits as well as the drawbacks associated with each of these investment strategies, and then begin developing a game plan that complements you and your portfolio objectives.

OPTION NUMBER ONE: FOREIGN TRUSTS

Until the late 1970s, foreign trusts were an extremely popular form of offshore financial investment. Before the federal government implemented the Tax Reform Act of 1976, they offered a creative form of tax avoidance and simultaneously allowed people to take long-term care of their heirs.

The key to a successful foreign trust, something I touched upon earlier in the book, is the selection of a friendly host country. You want a place that has extremely tight secrecy laws. To reiterate, you also don't want your center to have anything that's equivalent to the U.S. "statute of frauds." I suggest you review Chapter Seven for my arguments on behalf of the foreign trust. Basically, this is one very positive way of protecting your assets especially during hard economic times. The bottom line with foreign trusts, expecially those designed to protect your assets, is that they are available and highly effective.

OPTION NUMBER TWO: FOREIGN ANNUITIES & ENDOWMENTS

Annuities and endowment policies are most easily understood as special types of savings deposits with some specific features guaranteed by the issuing insurance compnay.

Foreign Annuities can be either lump-sum or periodic savings deposits, and they guarantee an income for the rest of the depositor's (or named beneficiary's) lifetime. The income level will vary based on the owner's age, deposit size and frequency, and when the income payments begin. They're a fairly common approach to offshore investment. And for good reason. If the international currency exchange rate is in your favor, they can allow you to make a handsome profit.

Swiss banks have become particularly well-known for handling these foreign annuities, and during times when the Swiss franc exchanges favorablly with the U.S. dollar, a guarantee-level franc annuity income can produce increasing dollar income. For example, if you had purchased a a single payment, immediate-income Swiss franc annuity worth $10,000 in 1970, it would have been worth more than $17,000 by 1976. Endowment policies add life insurance protection and dividends to annuities, and are also available in single deposit, periodic deposit, and increasing deposit forms. An example of the single deposit form might go like this. For a 45-year-old man making a single 100,000 Swiss franc deposit payment, the cash account value would grow to 252, 107 francs by age 65. The immediate death benefit to his beneficiary would be 159,058 francs at age 45 and would rise to equal the cash value by the time he reached age 65.

The drawbacks to foreign annuities and endowments are, I think, obvious. First, their appeal is inseparably tied to international currency exchange rates. So long as the dollar compares negatively with the currency in which you happen to hold your annuity, you're safe. But as the exchange balance fluctuates, you are vulnerable to profit loss and, perhaps, even capital devaluation.

Another problem that I see with annuities is that they make their profit so slowly. In the case illustrated above, it took six years for $10,000 to grow to $17,000! That's very sluggish activity when you begin looking at the international market. This same criticism applies to endowments. Again, the example above shows a 4.75 percent annual rate of dividend compounding. Most other offshore ventures offer much more impressive profit potential.

If you know what you're doing, have a good consultant to work with you, and take the time to monitor the market for impending adjustments in the international currency exchange rates, I think that annuities and endowments can be reliable investments. They're a conservative choice, and as such, they don't involve a great deal of risk. Neither do they promise impressive profit. My advice would be to eliminate them from your offshore strategy, or to see them as a minor element of your overall game plan.

OPTION NUMBER THREE: A FOREIGN BANK ACCOUNT

You can move toward faster and larger profits by opening a checking or savings account with a foreign bank.

For starters, an offshore account allows you to rest assured that your money is being held by a financially stronger and better managed institution than you could ever find here in the United States. In part, that's because your offshore bank must maintain a higher ratio of liquid assets to accumulated debts.

An offshore account will also let you avoid the high service costs that have become part and parcel of domestic banking. And you'll benefit from the international banking environment, where regulations are kept to a minimum and customer service is made the top priority.

We have already covered the specific benefits that come with an offshore bank account. Just for review, here they are again.

- Foreign banks offer a very attractive interest rate — typically several points above what you could find onshore. Remember, too, that the longer you keep the money on deposit, the more interest you earn.

- Checks written from a foreign account allow you to

enjoy "float time," usually three or four weeks between the writing of a check and its arrival at the offshore bank for clearing. During that period, you will continue to earn interest on the money in your account.

- "Twin accounts" let you combine the benefits of a current checking account with the profits of a high-interest deposit account. You keep most of your money in the bank for high interest earnings, but maintain a small balance for everyday withdrawal.

- Offshore banks also offer fiduciary accounts which allow you to direct the bank to make proxy investments for you. The record shows that your bank acted on its own behalf, but all profits earned on the investment are paid to you. They're tax-free, too, because they were earned outside the United States.

Are there problems with having one (or more) of these offshore accounts? No, but there are limitations to what they can do for you. That's because an offshore bank is usually established and operated for the profit and investment convenience of the person who owns it. Part of that owner's profit comes from having you as a customer with his bank. As such, you are a more valued and pampered client than you would be at any U.S.-based bank.

Still, your needs and investment priorities are never going to be as important to the bank as the concerns of its owner. So, when you enter into such an arrangement, be aware that the profits and perks are great, as far as they go. There's a clear line that's drawn, however, between you and the bank owner. When all is said and done, he will always have it his way because that's the nature of offshore banking.

OPTION NUMBER FOUR: PRIVATE
INTERNATIONAL CORPORATIONS

If you like the idea of actually running a foreign business, you might want to own your own private international corporation. Maybe you'd want to establish a manufacturing business, and make your million-dollar invention concept a reality. Believe me, it's been done by people no more experienced at international business than you.

If you're less confident about what you'd like to do with your business, you can finalize the purchase and allow the corporation to function simply as your broker in the international marketplace. It can invest in stocks, commodities, CDs, real estate and foreign currencies. It can import and export, and serve as a holding compnay to protect patents and trademarks.

You can also choose a professional offshore management firm to operate your new corporation. If you don't know how to identify such a firm, talk with any reputable offshore consultant. He's likely to refer you to a number of Hong Kong and Bahamas firms — any one of which will impress you with a wide range of investment and administrative services.

There's not a lot to be said against the private international corporation concept. Particularly if you can manage to buy a company that's already been licensed and approved for operation, it can be an affordable way to enter the offshore market. These pre-packaged, "turnkey," situations are not easy to find, but they're worth pursuing. Again, talk with some financial consultants. A good one can sometimes help you locate a business that's named and ready to go.

OPTION NUMBER FIVE: PRIVATE OFFSHORE BANK OWNERSHIP

If you want the benefits associated with all four options outlined above, and several more, then consider the purchase of your own offshore bank. In my opinion, it is the single most complete and profitable move you can make into the international arena.

For starters, your own offshore bank will provide all the advantages of a foreign checking and savings account. And at no charge, because you'll be your own customer. All your transactions can be handled in the bank's name, so, your financial privacy is assured. You will also manage to legally escape financial eavesdropping because your assets will be technically alienated from you. Officially, they will belong to your bank — which functions outside the jurisdictional authority of U.S. laws. Nevertheless, you will have complete control over how and where your money is used.

Like all businesses, your offshore bank will aim to make an impressive profit. So, it will probably advertise in various international publications for deposits. As the deposits come in, they will figuratively pass through a revolving door and become money with which your bank offers loans to international borrowers. Within a matter of months, the interest generated by those loans will form the basis of a handsome bottom line.

Your bank can increase its profit by expanding services. For example, once you get enough depositors, you can begin issuing letters of credit and financial guarantees. You can offer back-to-back loans. You can also provide venture capital loans at whatever interest rate the free market will allow — sometimes as much as 10 percentage points above the comparable domestic rate.

A private offshore bank protects your exposure to financial attacks. When you put your assets into the bank, they become bank property. Whatever profit they generate belongs, at least on paper, to the bank. Third parties cannot obtain information about those profits because foreign banks are not required to devulge facts or figures. You gain the upper hand. You make the decisions about what others should know and what they shouldn't know. Best of all, your new-found power is entirely legal.

Offshore banks offer you as much investment flexibility as you desire. If you tend to be cautious in your portfolio management, you can use your bank as a discrete international broker. Essentially, it can be a one-person operation. Using its name rather than your own, you can purchase low-risk stocks and commodities from around the world and watch your profits gradually build without an excessive tax penalty. If you're a more adventurous investor, you can use the bank to structure high-stakes business partnerships and ventures in virtually every continent. You can turn your bank into a full-scale operation, with an experienced staff of employees to monitor your numerous international involvements.

OPTION NUMBER SIX: OFFSHORE INVESTMENT FUND

At its most basic, an offshore investment fund is any pool of investment capital. It can be either a fund (often called a mutual fund) that invests in various investment vehicles, or it can be a special-purpose fund that targets its capital in one or a handful of related businesses.

The sponsor of the investment fund can use the capital in the pool to lend funds, make investments of a private nature or invest in real estate or in companies either in the United States or in other countries. One of the great things about an offshore investment fund is that you can invest your capital anywhere in the world including in your own home country.

An offshore investment fund is simply an investment company that combines the assets of many smaller investors (the shareholders) into a single large pool of capital — that is, the fund — for the purpose of investing in a variety of instruments including securities, commodities, development projects and real estate that would otherwise be out of the reach of the individual investor. Simply put, it is a mutual fund. It can also be a money market fund if it invests in a money market investment, that is, any vehicle that matures under a year. You can create your own money market fund by owning a bank. The fund's money can be held in the bank.

When such a fund is domiciled offshore, it offers additional advantages that are unavailable to funds based within the borders of the United States.

Offshore investment funds are based in money havens such as those I discussed in Chapter 9. As I write, the most popular centers for offshore funds are in the British Virgin Islands, the Netherlands Antilles, the Cayman Islands, The Bahamas and Singapore.

■ OFFSHORE INVESTMENT FUND OR ■ OFFSHORE BANK?

There are seven key benefits to sponsoring your own offshore investment fund or owning your own offshore bank.

1. *Raising Capital* - The number one option is being able to raise capital to fund your various investment endeavors. In this way you can build the capital for almost any type of project or vehicle. Raising capital is the key first step toward generating profit.

2. *Tax Benefits* - By virtue of the fact that they are incorporated in tax haven centers, they usually pay no capital gains taxes or other excessive fees. In addition, most in-

come generated by the fund is subject to minimal or no taxation.

3. *Little Regulation* - There is very little regulation involved because an offshore-based fund is not subject to the stiff rules found in a domestic fund. The organizer of the fund does not have to present a string of investment credentials. Usually, investors can utilize the services of a professional fund management firm to assist them in the operation of the fund.

4. *Flexibility* - The lack of governmental regulation means that offshore funds have a far greater range of options than those based in onshore locales. This allows organizers a level of flexibility that results in higher returns and portfolio diversification.

5. *Asset Protection* - An investment fund has the added benefit of being used as a means to protect your assets from liability judgments and court seizures by U.S.-based courts.

6. *Financial Privacy* - Those countries that allow you to set up an offshore investment fund also have very strict secrecy laws regarding intrusion into the fund's activities. These funds provide a level of privacy insurance unavailable onshore.

7. *Profit Potential* - Because a fund can operate without undue regulation, it allows its organizer the flexibility and freedom to build higher profits than more restricted and regulated investment vehicles.

Many of the operators of offshore banks and funds include major corporation such as Dow Chemical, Merrill Lynch, Bank of America, Security Pacific Bank, American Express and numerous others. In addition, every major mutual fund operating onshore in the United States also has an offshore arm. You name it: Templeton, Fidelity, Scudder, etc. Their leadership sin this field is a clear signal to individual investors, consortiums and investment groups that offshore banks and investment funds are sound and profitable investment vehicles.

■DOING IT YOURSELF

If you decide that either offshore bank ownership or offshore investment fund ownership is for you, then you immediately face a critically important choice. Do you want to try to handle the entire transaction on your own? Or would you prefer to work with a company that can manage the process for you?

Frankly, most people are intimidated by the prospect of so much research and so many international business maneuvers. I think they're wise to feel that intimidation. There's nothing more foolish than biting off more than you can chew, especially when there are qualified professional teams that can help you.

Nevertheless, over the course of my career, I have known a few investors who have successfully established their own banks or funds without professional assistance. Typically, the people who opt to go it alone are secrecy zealots, so concerned about financial privacy that they resist sharing information even with their own consultant. If you fall into this category, let me offer a few simple pointers and words of caution.

First, be aware that there are two kinds of offshore funds and two types of offshore banks: new ones and already-established ones. Both types have their own appeal, but new ones take a lot longer to option. So ask yourself how much time you're willing to spend on setting up your operation. If you want to do the work yourself, you must set-up your operation from scratch. That means months just to research the various offshore jurisdictions and their particular strengths as well as weaknesses. Even if you feel certain that you've identified the right place, several overseas visits will also be required in order to meet with island officials and process the necessary paperwork.

As you consider all this, remember that if you spend a lot of time establishing your offshore bank or setting up your offshore fund, you will pay a price in lost investment opportunity. They say that time is money, and I certainly agree. When you're looking at offshore profit strategies, every minute counts.

One of the great things about an offshore investment fund or offshore bank is that you can invest your capital anywhere in the world including your own home country.

Second, to ensure that your bank's or fund's legal framework is well-conceived, I would suggest that you work with a reputable attorney based in your preferred offshore center.

If you don't know anyone who can refer you to a good lawyer in the area, resign yourself to still another phase of meticulous research. I suggest that you thoroughly check professional references because, upon occasion U.S. investors find themselves faced with a costly legal bill and no offshore charter or license to show for it. The legal acquisition of an offshore bank or fund is not an extremely complicated matter, but it does require specific knowledge and skill.

Third, be prepared for a lengthy application process. For example, under your guidance, the attorney can begin drafting your bank or fund charter. That process alone is likely to take several weeks. After all, these articles of incorporation and fund by-laws constitute the backbone of your private international bank or international fund. The charter should literally spell out the reasons why you have decided to establish the bank or fund, and it must specify all the financial activities that you intend to conduct.

Since you're establishing a new fund, you lawyer will also need to run a check on the bank's or fund's proposed name. Far more often than you might think, investors choose a name only to discover that someone else is operating under the same title. In that case, the entire procedure must begin again, but with another name.

Usually, the host government approves a well-drafted charter, but you must submit it for official review. This, too, takes time. If your foreign attorney is well-connected within his jurisdiction, you can expect legal authorization within several weeks. If not, the process could take several months.

It is not uncommon for an independent investor to be sent back to the drawing board. In other words, a foreign government may demand that you recast your entire charter. It's possible, in fact, that you may be denied an operating license altogether. At that point, you're back to square one, and you must look for another offshore jurisdiction.

Fourth, if your license is approved, plan to spend both time and money on initial operation set-up. At the very least, you will need a personal computer, a fax, phone systems and the services of a small clerical staff. With luck, your offshore attorney will be able to help with this. If not, you should plan another trip to the island to personally oversee the process.

You'll also need to print necessary forms: stock certificates and other corporate documents. Personal associates may be able to suggest a printer. If not, you face still another research phase.

I don't want all this to seem overly negative or unfairly pessimistic. At the same time, I want to be honest. If you establish a brand new offshore bank or fund, you will end up with a vehicle that's been made entirely to your personal specifications. That's very appealing. Still, this approach involves a lot of time, usually six to eight months. What's more, it can be riddled with false starts, dead ends and U-turns. You need to determine whether or not the benefits are worth the price you pay for them. And if you do decide to go this route, you must be prepared to mold nearly one year of your life around long-distance phone calls, certified letters and government red tape.

■ MY APPROACH

Whether you are interested in setting up a bank or a fund, I suggest that you consider my firm, WFI Corporation, for the job. WFI is one of the few companies in the United States that offers a low-cost program through which investors can acquire their own offshore banks or offshore funds within a matter of days. As a result, we are able to help our clients enter the international market faster and for less money than any financial consulting firm. We also offer over 17 years specialized experience in the offshore investment market. We are familiar with all the banking jurisdictions. We have a well-developed network of government and banking contacts within each of these offshore centers. That means we can ensure a level of offshore efficiency that cannot be guaranteed to those who pursue a bank charter and license or a fund charter and license on their own.

For example, as one of our service components, we can help you organize your offshore fund on a convenient and simplified basis. The fund charter has been issued. The license has been granted. The agreement has been negotiated with the relevant foreign government and all documents have been printed. In short, the months of legwork have been completed. Following a background check to confirm your acceptability to the foreign government, you will be free to immediately begin using your fund for profit, privacy and tax protection.

WFI also pre-arranges for an international fund management firm to handle the specific operations of your foreign operation. Frankly, we put a strong emphasis on the availability of such international management because few things can have a greater impact on the ultimate success of a bank or an investment fund than a quality management service. That's because most of our clients have little or no firsthand international fund experience. As a result, they should have a top-notch management team upon whom they can rely for key administrative functions and skilled investment advice.

For example, for a surprisingly low annual fee, WFI can help you solidify a contract with an international management firm which guarantees that your mail, telephone and fax communications will be handled. In addition, the firm will process investments and keep accurate track of all receipts. It will help you administrate your fund, provide typing and photocopying service and keep up all required fund files. It will draft key documents or deposit agreements, send out bills and statements, handle funds, transfers to and from the United States and act as custodian of your confidential records, documents, minutes, books and ledgers. Most important, your management company can give you foreign exchange privileges.

WFI has also eliminated the risk of an offshore operation in disadvantageous jurisdictions. From the numerous international offshore centers, we have secured private funds only in island environments supportive of private fund operation. Our clients can select from jurisdictions that:

- impose no income tax, no capital-gains tax, no death tax, no stamp duty, no estate duty and no gift duty;

- charge an extremely low annual license renewal fee;

- maintain excellent investment legislation.

Every offshore investment fund (as well as every offshore bank) that is purchased through WFI comes with specific assets and property. These include:

- The Memorandum and Articles of Associations which are signed by an incorporator and which outline the rules governing the internal operations and organization of the fund.

- The Certificate of Incorporation which is given by the Registrar of Companies and states that the Memorandum and Articles of Association have been duly filed and found to be in accordance with the laws of the relevant island jurisdiction. This document provides conclusive proof that the fund has been duly incorporated and legally formed. It also states that the fund is duly licensed to conduct and engage in the investment business.

- Stock Certificates which are representative of the total number of initial authorized shares in the fund for transfer to the eventual purchasers of the investment fund's shares.

- Corporate Supplies which include the Corporate Seal and Pouch; Corporate Minute Book, minute paper, dividers for the Minute Books and other necessary forms and documentation.

Another important benefit that comes with WFI's offering is our prearranged provision for the registered office, resident agent, corporate secretary and one director in your preferred offshore investment fund or offshore bank jurisdiction. All individuals selected for these positions possess in-depth experience in international finance. In this way, WFI can promise you the kind of expert support that guarantees appropriate handling of your fund's international transactions.

Finally, WFI makes it a point to offer post-purchase support to all our clients. The purchase of an offshore investment fund is a brand new venture for most people. As America's pioneer in private offshore investment and banking, WFI has assisted in the establishment of more private international banks for more individuals and corporations than any other firm int he world. After more than a decade of proven experience, we are acknowledged as the number one source for counsel and guidance in the establishment and operation of an international investment fund. Part of our reputation is based on the long-term support we offer our clients. On a continuing basis, we provide:

- access to books, articles, and newsletters dealing with the latest trends and developments in international investing, international tax planning and tax havens:

- current information and recommendations on new business ideas that can have a positive influence on business growth, tax savings and the attainment of maximum privacy;

- periodic invitations to attend WFI's seminars and conferences, which feature demonstrations of the most profitable and cost-effective ways to operate a private investment fund.

In exactly the same way that we are committed to the use of offshore investment funds, we are committed to the continued purchase and operation of offshore banks.

Just as every offshore fund purchased through WFI comes with its own specific assets and property, every international bank acquired through our offices incudes all necessary incorporation materials.

WFI is the master company of private international banking. Not only have we been committed longer than anyone else to offshore banking we also have acquired extensive knowledge and expertise regarding the intricacies of international banking practices. WFI and offshore banking are synonymous. The expansion of our services into offshore funds has only enhanced our ability to serve our clients.

■SHALL WE MEET?

This has been a book about the profit, privacy and tax protection that is available to you through offshore investing. In these pages, I've reviewed the current state of the U.S. economy and offered a bit of insight into the global economy — those mysterious dynamics by which even countries with opposing political orientations rely on one another financially and face a future of escalating interdependence.

I hope I've managed to convince you that the financial outlook within the domestic economy is not promising. Our national debt keeps growing, while those who owe us money find themselves increasingly unable to meet their commitments. Inflation looms over us as a constant threat. Even our biggest corporations are often unable to compete effectively with their foreign counterparts. In short, the future is bleak for U.S. investors who confine their financial activity to domestic ventures.

By contrast, I've tried to show you that the offshore market is booming. There's more money to be made today than there has ever been. And it's there for a song. But you have to know the tune. Offshore investing is the reflection of tomorrow's most successful investment strategy. It's the vision of a bright economic future. Best of all, its legally and affordably available to you today.

So think about it, but don't think too long. Every day the federal government closes a few more doors to international profit potential. My advice is to get out there and get started while the laws still allow you to discreetly make a lot of untaxable money. And when you're ready to get started, let me hear from you. I'd like to be involved in developing your offshore game plan. I think my experience would allow me to offer some worthwhile pointers. I know I could learn from you, by watching you create the international investment package that best reflects your priorities.

When you're ready, give me a call. Let's get together because, who knows, it could be the start of a great friendship.

Appendix

How To Open A Foreign Bank Account

■INTRODUCTION

Suggest to the average American that he or she might benefit by owning a foreign bank account and you'll more than likely get a questioning look and a response such as, "Why on Earth would I want to do that?"

Americans, you see, tend to have an extremely parochial attitude when it comes to their money — and they also tend to have an almost unnatural suspicion of foreign banking activities. After all, the media have exposed them to an unending series of foreign banking tales involving political shenanigans, financial fiascoes and criminal capers.

Yet, the simple fact is, most Americans *could* benefit by owning a foreign bank account. Already, foreign banking — or, as it is more popularly known today, "offshore banking" — has become an important tool for thousands of legitimate and highly successful businesses and individuals.

In practice, a foreign bank account gives the prudent investor the opportunity to synchronize the benefits of various banking activities and blend them into a unique profit-making and tax-saving financial strategy. For the careful and conscientious investor, it is one of the most pragmatic ways of expanding the realm of financial opportunity, because it is one of the most creative ways of diversifying assets.

Since offshore banks don't operate within the United States (hence their name), accounts held in them are rarely subject to our state and federal laws and regulations. Offshore banks can also offer a wide range of services well beyond the legal ability of domestic banks. Through aggressive use of these services, investors can increase their profits, reduce their tax burdens and raise capital at lower interest rates — all without the restrictive maze of red tap often encountered in the United States.

SECTION 1: WHY OPEN A FOREIGN BANK ACCOUNT?

There are a number of legitimate reasons for opening a personal bank account in a foreign country, foremost among them the fact that maintaining a foreign bank account carries a greater degree of freedom, security and opportunity than would be possible in the United States. Depending on the depth of one's portfolio, a penchant for adventurous investing or strategic financial needs, a foreign bank account can provide a varying degree of advantages and conveniences.

Following are some of the principal reasons why an ever-increasing number of savvy U.S. investors are opening one or more foreign bank accounts for themselves (these are by no means all the reasons, and you may well find additional personal motivations for banking off-shore):

1. Privacy

Americans who have accumulated any kind of retained wealth are finding it more and more difficult to hold on to their assets. Other people, as well as the federal and state governments, are becoming increasingly nosy about the financial affairs of individual Americans — and the courts are helping them.

The best solution to this ever-increasing assault on your financial well-being is to do your banking in a country safe from the prying eyes of government agents, creditors, competitors, relatives, ex-spouses and others who might want to appropriate your wealth. In a hyper-litigious society — where anyone will sue at the drop of a hat — it's nice to know that your money is in a country where your enemies can't touch it.

Many countries specialize in guaranteeing bank secrecy. Some offshore havens have bank secrecy laws so strict that it is a crime for a bank employee to disclose *any* information about a bank account to any person other than the owner of the account.

Unfortunately, as some countries have strengthened their secrecy laws, the U.S. has virtually eliminated bank secrecy. Any transaction involving more than $10,000 must be reported to the Treasury. Records of transactions involving less than this amount can be subpoenaed by the IRS, litigants in a lawsuit or anyone else with a real or imagined need to pierce your secrecy.

Thus, if want to maintain real financial privacy, you have little choice but to look offshore, where your bank accounts are protected, rather than opened by the governments and the courts.

2. Currency Controls

Despite the fact that more than 80 percent of the nations of the world impose some form of currency control, few U.S. citizens have actually experienced the discomfort of living in a country that severely restricts their ability to move their money across their own borders. However, with annual budget deficits running at $200 billion and with trade imbalances growing steadily larger, the U.S. may be the next country to clamp a lid on the outward movement of dollars. In fact, we may have already seen the beginning of a trend — under current law, you must complete a customs declaration when you take more than $10,000 overseas.

Thus, it only makes good financial sense to move at least a portion of your assets into a foreign country while you still can. Such a move also protects you against the possibility that the U.S. government, at some point in the future, may confiscate a portion of the wealth of its citizens — most likely under the guise of combatting drug trafficking or dealing with the underground economy. Citizens living under totalitarian regimes in Latin America and the Middle East have already experienced the trauma such actions can bring — and they would be the first to advise you to move at least a portion of your assets offshore.

3. Higher Return on Investment

If a foreign bank will give you a better interest rate on your invested money than a U.S. bank, there is little reason to keep your money here. Many foreign banks can offer better rates because they're unregulated and can make more lucrative investments with their depositors' funds. In addition, many foreign banks operate in countries that don't place a premium on lavish offices, high rents and excessive executive salaries. Thus, they are able to pass these savings on to you in the former of higher deposit rates.

Taxes are often an important consideration as well. By maintaining assets in an offshore jurisdiction, the prudent American investor gains tremendous opportunities to realize capital gains — and, by keeping those gains offshore, he can also avoid paying taxes on the profits. Many foreign financial centers have earned an international reputation as legal tax havens — and many investors find that the tax benefits of offshore investment activity greatly enhance their financial performance.

4. Diversification

You would never put all your assets into one investment — it's inherently too risky. Yet, most people do all their banking in one country. No one knows what the future will bring. Thus, if you hope to hedge your financial security against the unforeseen, it's best to hold your assets in bank accounts in more than one nation.

5. Have Fun While You Earn

Wouldn't it be nice to vacation in a tropical paradise while doing your banking? Many Americans do. Many of the world's offshore banking centers are also located in the world's best vacation spots.

SECTION 2: DIFFERENT TYPES OF FOREIGN BANK ACCOUNTS

There can be no doubt as to the advantages arising from banking in a foreign country — advantages such as privacy, freedom, diversification and an enhanced investment opportunity set. In addition, the American who banks in an offshore locale also enjoys added flexibility in the selection of accounts that can be maintained. Here are just a few of the types of accounts that are offered by most foreign banks:

1. A Current Account

This is the most common type of foreign bank account — and the one that gives you the most flexibility in managing your funds. It allows you to withdraw all or part of your account balance at any time. Most current accounts pay interest on your balance, though some do not. Many current accounts can be maintained in U.S. dollars, or they can be held in a host of foreign currencies — and some offer "multi-currency" privileges, meaning you can deposit or withdraw funds in your choice of currencies.

Most current accounts provide you with checking privileges, and some foreign banks will provide you with a check card (the most popular of which is the "Eurocard"), which will permit you to write checks anywhere up to a certain amount. You will probably receive a statement of your account's activity semiannually.

Regardless of the complexity of your international business, you should have at least one current account.

2. Deposit Accounts

A deposit account is a savings account in a foreign country. The account will pay you interest, but the rate of interest will vary according to the currency in which the account is denominated and the length of time for which the money is deposited. Generally, the longer the money is deposited, the higher the interest rate. Most deposit accounts require a minimum deposit of $5,000 or more.

Deposit accounts are not as liquid as current accounts, and you may be prevented from withdrawing your money for a periodof time. As with a current account, you will receive a semiannual statement of the account's activity.

3. Numbered Accounts

Switzerland, Belgium, Luxembourg and Mexico all provide for numbered accounts. A numbered account is an account identified by a number, rather than by a name. To that extent, it provides a certain amount of protection and privacy, especially if bank records or passbooks are lost, stolen or obtained under duress.

It's important to remember what a numbered account is *not*: A numbered account doesn't mean that no one at the bank knows who the real owner of the account is. It just means that the junior people at the bank, who handle the transactions, don't know your identity.

4. Safekeeping Accounts

A safekeeping account is one in which you deposit such things as bonds, stocks and other valuables. The bank will clip the coupons, redeem the bonds and do whatever needs to be done with the valuables entrusted to them. The bank will charge you for the service, something in the range of 0.015 percent of the market value of the securities or other assets they are safekeeping.

5. Commodities Accounts

Some of the larger foreign banks have geared themselves up to trade in commodities on your behalf. (This a prime example of the freedom foreign banks have to operate, as contrasted to the restrictions imposed on U.S. banks.) They're set up to give you the latest commodities prices, and to let you buy and sell commodities over the phone.

6. Managed Accounts

Many of the larger foreign banks also offer a variety of managed accounts, wherein you entrust your money to the bank's investment advisors and they choose the types of investments to make, based on your objectives and investment goals. Managed accounts are offered for stocks, currencies, debt instruments, commodities or combinations. Again, the bank charges for this service, with fees usually based on a percentage of the funds under management.

The foregoing list represents only the tip of the iceberg. There are countless types of accounts and services — including such familiar American-style amenities as automated tellers, Visa and MasterCard accounts — that foreign banks can provide for you. And, the number of such services is growing annually.

SECTION 3: HOW TO OPEN A FOREIGN BANK ACCOUNT

Before you can actually open one of the accounts we've just discussed, you must take some time to select both a foreign country and a foreign bank for your account. (An evaluation of some of the major offshore financial centers is featured in Section 6, and a list of many of the leading overseas banks is provided as an appendix to this report.)

If you plan to visit the country in which you'll be banking, you should check out a number of banks. Insist on meeting with a director of each bank you visit. If they won't meet with you, don't give them your business. Whether you visit or can only correspond by mail, here are some of the criteria you should consider when selecting a bank:* Does it provide the banking services you require? For example, if you need to earn interest on your current account, and also require a check card, keep searching until you find a bank that will provide both services. One of the best sources of leads is the *Rand McNally International Banker's Directory*.

- How large is the bank? There are trade-offs here. A larger, more established bank may offer greater security than a smaller bank, but at a price — the larger bank may pay a lower interest rate and charge you higher fees for its services.

- How secure is your investment? Deposit insurance is not nearly as prevalent overseas as it is in the United States. If you require that your account be insured, you should inquire specifically as to the types of accounts that are insured and the investment limitations. Local insurance regulations can be confusing. For example, most Swiss banks do not provide insurance, but some Swiss cantonal (i.e., regional) banks do. Be aware, too, that the absence of deposit insurance can actually be an advantage since banks must employ prudent investment and business practices in order to successfully compete and remain in business. In the United States, banks can be inefficient, poorly managed and follow imprudent investment strategies because they know their mistakes will be rectified by the government.

- How easily will you be able to communicate with your bank? There's no problem here if you plan on doing all your overseas banking in person. However, if you'll need to communicate with bank officials by mail, it's important to establish whether the officials will communicate with you in English. Even if they do, some offshore banking centers are so remote that mail, courier and even telephone communications are tenuous. There's nothing more frustrating than needing to conduct a banking transaction and not being able to get through to your bank.

Once you've narrowed down the possibilities, the next step (assuming you won't be visiting the bank) is to send each bank a *short, typed letter*. The letter should state that you are interested in opening a certain type of account. You should inquire as to the following:

- The fees that the bank charges — both to open and to maintain to the account.

- The minimum balance you will be required to maintain.

- The currencies in which you will be able to maintain the account, and the ease or difficulty you will have in switching from one currency to another.

- The extent to which the account will be insured, and who will insure it.

Ask about how the bank will communicate with you, and you with it. Some banks will provide you with a telex code, which will allow you to give the bank instructions and conduct normal banking business without revealing your identity. The use of the code also assures the bank that it is dealing with you and not someone who wants your money.

You also may wish to ask about any other services the bank provides, such as a check card, credit cards, safe deposit boxes, etc.

The first thing you'll receive from most banks in response to your letter is an account application form (similar to the sample shown following Section 6) and signature cards, similar to the forms needed to open an account in the United States. Some banks may also require letters of reference. Be wary of this — the more information you have to reveal, the lower your level of confidentiality.

If you plan on opening a *corporate* account — i.e., one whose owner is a corporation — you may have to provide proof that the corporation is in existence, and minutes of resolutions from the Board of Directors authorizing the account.

You may wish to consider keeping an account in a fictitious name. Before you do, you should inquire into the laws of the country in which you'll be banking. Many countries prohibit accounts with fictitious names, even those countries with strong bank secrecy laws.

You may also wish to open an account for a minor. Before you do, check with the bank to determine their local rules regarding an adult's maintaining an account for a minor.

Since almost every bank requires a minimum deposit to open an account, you'll have to send money with the application form and the signature cards. The guidance for the initial deposit is the same for any subsequent transmittal of funds. Wire transfer is the best way to do it — they are more secure than sending checks or money orders through the mail, and there is a minimal loss of interest (your local bank will, however, charge you for the wire). The overseas bank should provide you with wire transfer instructions.

If you use the mail to send checks, have the checks made out to you, endorsed: "For deposit only at _____ Bank for the account of _____ ." Whenever you mail funds, the mail should be preceded by a fax transmission, alerting the bank that a deposit is in the mail, and stating the amount of the deposit and any further instructions you deem helpful to the bank's personnel. (NOTE: If you send more than $10,000 overseas, your bank is required under the Bank Secrecy Act to report the transaction to the U.S. Treasury. Under current law, they are not required to report a wire transfer, regardless of the amount.)

If you are opening a managed account of any kind, the bank may also require you to grant it a power of attorney over the assets in the account. If so, make sure the power of attorney is specific and offers protections for both you and the bank (a sample power of attorney form is included following Section 6).

SECTION 4: SOME SUGGESTIONS ON HANDLING YOUR ACCOUNT

There are as many different particular investment needs as there are investors, so it is impossible to tell you exactly how to handle your foreign bank account. However, here are some general tips that should apply in almost every instance:

- Start Conservative. If you've never owned an over-seas bank account, start out by being a conservative investor. We suggest starting out with an account denominated in U.S. dollars. Place only a fraction of the amount you have available for savings in an overseas account until you ascertain you are com-fortable with the concept, the country and the bank. If, after six months or so, you're comfortable, you can add to the account or open a different account. We advise against such activities as commodities accounts until you have your feet on the ground and are comfortable with your overseas banker.

- Diversify. Once you're comfortable overseas, you should consider diversifying your overseas hold-ings. This may result in your spreading out the countries in which you do your banking, or at least diversifying the currencies in which you invest. There is one downside to diversification — the more you have in any account, the higher the rate of inter-est you'll usually earn, and diversifying obviously reduces your account size. Thus, it's important to diversify in such a way that your effective rate of interest is reduced as little as possible.

- Consider a Managed Account. If you are unfamiliar with the foreign investment markets and unaccus-tomed to dealing in foreign currencies, you may want to consider opening a managed, or *discre-tionary* account — i.e., one where your banker is given the authority to invest your funds on your behalf. Of course, your banker will charge you for the service, but you will get the benefit of his exper-tise.

You should never open a discretionary account by mail. It is essential that you get to know your funds manager and that he get to know you. Only after you're comfortable with his investment philosophy and background should you entrust any funds to him.

If your investment philosophy is conservative in nature, a Swiss managed account may be for you. The Swiss reputation for conservatism is well-earned (though recent changes in Swiss attitudes toward secrecy have diminished the appeal of Swiss bank accounts).

■ SECTION 5: REPORTING REQUIREMENTS

You may have noticed on your Form 1040 personal income tax return the following question: "Did you have at any time during the taxable year a financial interest in or signature authority over a bank, securities or other financial account in a foreign country?"

If the answer is yes, and you have more than $5,000 in a foreign account, you must file Form 90-22.1 by June 30 of the year following any year in which you had the account (a copy of the form is attached). There is a stiff fine — and the possibility of criminal prosecution — for failure to file this form. The form cannot be obtained from the IRS by your creditors or by opponents in a lawsuit.

If you physically transport more than $10,000 outside of the country, you'll have to fill out an appropriate customs declaration. There is nothing, in and of itself, illegal about moving money outside of the United States — you violate the law only if you fail to declare it. The declaration requirement applies if you mail, ship or carry bearer securities, traveler's checks or cash. You don't need to report wire transfers, cashier's checks or personal checks that are made out to an identifiable party over whom you have no control.

SECTION 6: A BRIEF REVIEW OF OVERSEAS BANKING CENTERS

Here is a checklist of some countries that want to do business with foreigners. Each of these countries has done something to make itself attractive to overseas investors. The list is by no means complete, and changes rapidly.

- *Anguilla.* Anguilla is a small British colony located at the northernmost end of the Leeward Islands in the Caribbean. It has a very stable government, and no taxes are imposed on the profits of foreign bank account holders or foreign bank profits — which can improve your investment performance. Though the financial industry here is fairly young, there are a number of stubbiest banks with proven track records — though you should still exercise extra care in choosing a bank for your account. Strict bank secrecy laws are in place, and the island features a good communications system, an adequate mail service and the island has the advantage of close proximity to the United States. It is also a pleasant, if somewhat quiet vacation spot.

- *Austria.* Located in central Europe, Austria has a reputation as one of the most politically and financially stable countries in Europe. Austrian bank accounts are freely convertible from one currency to another, which makes them attractive. Austrian bankers also have a strong commitment to privacy, yet Austrian bank accounts are seldom viewed with the same suspicion that might be engendered by an account in other jurisdictions. Austria's bank secrecy law is very strict in that it is a crime for any Austrian bank official to reveal information on an account without authority. However, they will reveal information to a foreign government in the context of a criminal investigation or an investigation regarding tax evasion.

- *The Bahamas.* Now an independent nation in the northern Caribbean, the Bahamas has made itself into one of the premier offshore banking centers of the world. Bahamian banks are modern and efficient, and communications with the U.S. and the rest of the world are excellent. The country is also a tax haven, and attracts all aspects of international business as well as banking. Adjuncts of all kinds are available, in any currency. There are no foreign-exchange controls. The Bahamas has a strong bank secrecy law. However, it is newly independent and has a vocal left-wing minority, and cannot be considered as politically stable as other countries.

- *Bermuda.* Of all the tax and banking havens in close proximity to the United States, Bermuda is the oldest and has the best reputation. Located 570 miles southeast of Cape Hatters, it is conveniently located for most U.S. investors, and boasts excellent banking and communications facilities. Bermuda has no exchange controls, accounts may be kept in any currency and no taxes are imposed on interest earned by non-residents.

- *Cayman Islands.* Located due south of Cuba, these three little islands have one major industry — international banking. This is no fluke; the government does everything it can to nurture the industry. Funds may be transported out of Caymans free of any reporting requirement, and accounts can be maintained in any currency. Travel, hotel and communications services are excellent. The Caymans also have what may be the strongest bank secrecy law in the world. However, even the Caymans have recently had to knuckle under to pressure from the

U.S. government, and local banks will cooperate with U.S. criminal and tax investigations.

It is relatively easy for a non-resident to form a bankin the Caymans. Consequently, you should exercise extra caution when choosing a bank located in the Caymans.

- *The Channel Islands.* The Channel Islands consists of eight small islands in the English Channel — the most important of which are Jersey and Guernsey. Except for defense and foreign policy, the Channel Islands are independent from Great Britain. Over the years, Channel Islands banks have developed an excellent reputation for secrecy and probity in the handling of offshore investors' business. As a result, it is the principal offshore financial center for British citizens. There is no taxation of interest paid to foreigners, no exchange controls and accounts may be maintained in any currency.

- *Hong Kong.* Hong Kong has, for many years, been the world's leading international banking center. However, its future is clouded since the colony will revert to the People's Republic of China in 1997. For now, however, it continues to flourish. Hong Kong takes bank secrecy seriously, but its bankers will cooperate with foreign criminal investigations. Unlike many offshore centers, Hong Kong imposes a 15 percent tax on foreign bank account earnings.

- *Singapore.* Singapore is an island nation on the eastern edge of the Mealy Peninsula in the Indian Ocean. It has been independent since 1965, and is politically and economically stable, being one of the busiest ports in the Pacific. The government has worked to make Singapore an international banking center. Communications are excellent. There are no taxes on interest earned by non-residents, and it is relatively easy to open an account in any currency.

There are approximately 45 other jurisdictions around the world that bill themselves as offshore financial centers or banking havens. However, many of these centers are remote, lack adequate support facilities or have flaws in their banking or tax laws that could affect your privacy or your rate of investment return. That does not necessarily mean you should avoid banks in these jurisdictions when shopping for a location for your foreign bank account. However, it does mean that you should exercise additional caution, making sure the bank is well managed and offers the services, experience and security you are seeking.

Application for Opening of Account

I/We request you to open an account with the following specifications (mark if applicable):

☐ Individual Account   ☐ Current Account   ☐ In Swiss Francs (Sfr)
☐ Joint Account   ☐ Deposit Account   ☐ In U.S. Dollars (U.S.$)
☐ Corporate Account   ☐ Managed Portfolio,   ☐ In German Marks (DM)
                            Type _____   ☐ Other _____

Personal Information (Please Print or Type):

Family Name(s)
or Company Name   _____

First Name(s)   _____

Street and No.   _____

City, State, Zip Code   _____

Country _____

Nationality   _____

Occupation
or Type of Business   _____

Date of Birth
or Company Formation   _____

Telephone No.:_____   Telex No.: _____

Correspondence Is To Be:
☐ Retained at the bank and forwarded only on special request
☐ Forwarded regularly to the following address (If different from above): _____

_____

Initial Deposit in the Amount of   _____
☐ Is Enclosed   ☐ Will be Mailed Separately
☐ Will be Wire Transferred Through (Bank Name): _____

Place: _____   _____
                                              (Signature)

Date: _____   _____
                                              (Signature)

POWER OF ATTORNEY

I/We the undersigned (please print) _____

residing at _____

_____

hereby grant _____ (hereinafter called "the Bank")
full powers with a view to represent me/us validly within the limitations of the following
provisions:

1. The Bank is authorized to dispose, on behalf of the principal(s), of the securities and assets whatsoever of the undersigned principal(s), lodged with the bank, insofar as these deposits and assets may be increased or reduced as a result of purchases, sales or conversions of securities, and for this purpose any possible subscription rights may be exercised or sold at best.

2. The Bank is furthermore authorized, in a general manner, to do everything it will deem necessary or appropriate for the management of the assets lodged with the Bank.

3. However, the Bank is not authorized to carry out, in any way whatsoever, any withdrawals of all or part of the funds and securities deposited or to pledge the assets and securities in question; nor is it empowered to order bonuses, except when these are destined for taking over securities of an equivalent amount.

4. The principal(s) expressly approve(s), and they/he do(es) so in advance, all acts of management or abstentions of the Bank and recognize(s) that the bank does not assume any responsibility whatsoever for the consequences of the transactions which the Bank, acting in good faith, will have made or will have abstained from making. In addition, the principal(s) undertake(s) to compensate the Bank for any expenses or damages it might have incurred on account of this power of attorney.

5. The power of attorney will remain valid until and unless revoked in writing.

6. It is expressly agreed that this power of attorney will not become void upon the death or loss of exercise of the civil rights of the principal(s), but will continue in full effect.

7. The parties agree that the constitution and validity of this power of attorney are governed by the laws of the jurisdiction in which the Bank is domiciled and that transactions carried out by virtue of said power of attorney will be judged in accordance with such laws. Any litigations between the parties will be brought before the competent courts of said jurisdiction. The Bank, however, is authorized to assert its claims at the legal domicile of the principal(s).

Signed at this place: _____

And on this date: _____

By the principal(s): _____
(Signature)

_____
(Signature)

Account No.: _____

Department of the Treasury	REPORT OF FOREIGN BANK AND FINANCIAL ACCOUNTS	Form Approved: OMB No. 1505-0021
TD F 90-22.1 (9-86)	For the calendar year 19___	Expiration Date: 8/89
SUPERSEDES ALL PREVIOUS EDITIONS	Do not file this form with your Federal Tax Return	

This form should be used to report financial interest in or signature authority or other authority over one or more bank accounts, securities accounts, or other financial accounts in foreign countries as required by Department of the Treasury Regulations (31 CFR 103). You are not required to file a report if the aggregate value of the accounts did not exceed $10,000. Check all appropriate boxes SEE INSTRUCTIONS ON BACK FOR DEFINITIONS. File this form with Dept. of the Treasury, P.O. Box 32621, Detroit, MI 48232.

1. Name (Last, First, Middle)	2. Social security number or employer identification number if other than individual	3. Name in item 1 refers to
		☐ Individual
4. Address (Street, City, State, Country, ZIP)		☐ Partnership
		☐ Corporation
		☐ Fiduciary

5. ☐ I had signature authority or other authority over one or more foreign accounts, but I had no "financial interest" in such accounts (see instruction J). Indicate for these accounts:

(a) Name and social security number or taxpayer identification number of each owner _____

_____

(b) Address of each owner _____

_____

(Do not complete item 9 for these accounts)

6. ☐ I had a "financial interest" in one or more foreign accounts owned by a domestic corporation, partnership or trust which is required to file TD F 90-22.1. (See instruction L). Indicate for these accounts:

(a) Name and taxpayer identification number of each such corporation, partnership or trust _____

_____

(b) Address of each such corporation, partnership or trust _____

_____

(Do not complete item 9 for these accounts)

7. ☐ I had a "financial interest" in one or more foreign accounts, but the total maximum value of these accounts (see instruction I) did not exceed $10,000 at any time during the year. (If you checked this box, do not complete item 9).

8. ☐ I had a "financial interest" in 25 or more foreign accounts. (If you checked this box, do not complete item 9.)

9. If you had a "financial interest" in one or more but fewer than 25 foreign accounts which are required to be reported, and the total maximum value of the accounts exceeded $10,000 during the year (see instruction I), write the total number of those accounts in the box below: Complete items (a) through (f) below for one of the accounts and attach a separate TD F 90-22.1 for each of the others. Items 1, 2, 3, 9, and 10 must be completed for each account.

Check here if this is an attachment. ☐

(a) Name in which account is maintained	(b) Name of bank or other person with whom account is maintained
(c) Number and other account designation, if any	(d) Address of office or branch where account is maintained

(e) Type of account. (If not certain of English name for the type of account, give the foreign language name and describe the nature of the account. Attach additional sheets if necessary.)

☐ Bank Account   ☐ Securities Account   ☐ Other (specify)

(f) Maximum value of account (see instruction I)

☐ Under $10,000   ☐ $10,000 to $50,000   ☐ $50,000 to $100,000   ☐ Over $100,000

10. Signature	11. Title (Not necessary if reporting personal account)	12. Date

■AUSTRIA

1. **BANK FUR ARBEIT UND WIRTSCHAFT AKTIENGESELLSCHAFT**
    Joint Stock & Commercial Bank
    Seitzergasse 2-4 (A-1010)
    P.O. Box 171 (A-1011)
    Estb: 1947 Member: Verband osterreichischer
    Banken und Bankiers, Vienna
    Ownership: Austrian Federation of Trade Unions
    (61.1%); Konsum Osterreich (30.7%), Others (3.2%)
    Management Chairman: Walter Flottl
    Principal Correspondents: Frankfurt Am Main,
    Bank Fur Gemeinwirtschaft Ag; London, Barclays
    Bank Pic; New York, Chase Manhattan Bank NA
    Phone: (43-222) 53 4 53 0 Telex: 115311
    Fax: (43-222) 53 4 53/2840
    (Genl) 53 4 53/2202 Cable: BAWAGBANK WIEN
    S.W.I.F.T: BAWA AT WW

2. **THE BANK OF TOKYO, LTD.**
    Rep Office of Tokyo, Japan
    Opernringhof, Stiege 3, Elisabethstrabe
    6 (A-1010)
    Phone: (43-222) Telex: 112902

3. **CENTRO INTERNATIONALE HANDELSBANK AKTIENGESELLSCHAFT**
    Commercial & Merchant Bank
    Tegetthoffstrabe 1 (A-1015); P.O. Box 272 (A-1015)
    Estb: 1973 Member: Austrian Bankers Association, Vienna
    Ownership: Banco di Sicilia, Palermo, Italy (25%)
    Bank Handlowy W. Warszawie S.A.
    Management Executive: Dr. Gerhard Vogt
    Phone: (43-222) 515200 Fax: (43-222) 525861
    Telex: 13 69 90 CENT A Cable: CENTROBANK VIENNA
    S.W.I.F.T.: CENB AP WW

4. **CHASE MANHATTAN BANK (AUSTRIA) AKTIENGESELLSCHAFT**
Parkring 12a (A-1010), P.O. Box 582 (A-1011)
Estb: 1973 Member: Verband osterreichischer Banken und Bankiers, Vienna
Holding Company: Chase Manhattan Bank Overseas Banking Corporation
General Manager: Andreas Treichl
Principal Correspondents: Frankfurt am Main, Chase Manhattan Bank
Phone: (43-222) 51589-0 Telex: 12570
Fax: (43-222) 51589-27 Cable: CMBA
S.W.I.F.T.: CHAS AT WW

5. **CITIBANK (AUSTRIA) AG**
Commercial Bank
Lothringerstrabe 7 (A-1015)
P.O. Box 90 (A-1015
Estb: 1959 Member: Verband osterreichischer Banken und Bankiers, Vienna
Holding Company: Citibank Overseas Investment Corporation, Wilmington, DE, USA (100%)
Management Chairman: Christoph Kraus
Principal Correspondents: Frankfurt am Main, Citibank NA; Johannesburg; Citibank, NA
Phone: (43-222) 75 65 34-0 Telex: 112105
Fax: (43Q222) 73 92 06 Cable: CITIBANK VIENNA
S.W.I.F.T.: CITI AT WW

6. **DIE ERSTE OSTERREICHISCHE SPAR-CASSE BANK**
FIRST AUSTRIAN BANK
Commercial Bank
Graben 21 (A-1011); P.O. Box 162 (A-1011)
Estb: 1819 Member: Hauptverband der Osterreichischen Sparkassen, Vienna
Management Chairman: Konrad Fuchs
Phone: (43-222) 53100-0 Telex: 114012 ESPKW
Fax: (43-222) 53100-377 Cable: GRABEN SPAR VIENNA
S.W.I.F.T.: ESPK AT WW

7. **OSTERREICHISCHE LANDERBANK**
Commercial Bank
Am Hof 2 (A-1010); P.O. Box 271 (A-1011)
Estb: 1880 Member: Verband osterreichischer
Banken und Bankiers, Vienna; ABECOR
Ownership: Republic of Austria (53%)
Private Shareholders (47%)
Management Chairman: Gerhard Wagner
Phone: (43-222) 531 24-0 Telex: 11 5561
Fax: (43-222) 531 24 55 Cable: LAENDERBANK
S.W.I.F.T.: OELB AT WW

8. **OVAG OSTERREICHISCHE VOLKSBANKEN-**
AKTIENGESELLSCHAFT
Commercial Bank
Peregringasse 3 (A-1090)
P.O. Box 95 (A-1011)
Estb: 1922 Member: Osterreichischer
Genossenchaftsverband, Vienna
Management Chairman: Robert Madl
Phone: (43-222) 3134-0 Telex: 134206
Fax: (43-222) 31340 3103/3589
Cable: VOLKSBANKENAG WIEN
S.W.I.F.T.: VBOE AT WW

9. **ROYAL TRUST BANK (AUSTRIA)**
Joint Stock Bank
Rathausstrasse 20 (A-1011);
P.O. Box 306 (A-1011)
Estb: 1890 Member: Austrian Bankers Association
Forex Club, Austria, Vienna Stock Exchange, Vienna
Ownership: Royal Trust Co. Ltd, Toronto, Ontario
Canada (100%)
Management Chairman: Martin A. Murbach
Phone: (43-222) 42 61 61 Telex: 114911 RTB A
Fax: (43-222) 42 81 42

10. BANK OF VIENNA
ZENTRALSPARKASSE UND KOMMERZIABANK-WIEN
Commercial & Savings Bank
Vordere Zollamtsstrabe 13 (A-1030)
P.O. Box 35 (A-1011)
Estb: 1905 Member: Hauptverband der osterreichischen
Sparkassen, Vienna
Ownership: Guaranteed by the city of Vienna
Management Chairman: Dr. Karl Vak
Phone: (43-222) 711 91 Telex: 131251 (Genl),
133167 (Intl), Fax: (43-222) 713 46 84
Cable: SPARZENTRALE WIEN
S.W.I.F.T.: ZSPK AT WW

■BAHAMAS

1. BANCA SERFIN
Sociedad Nacional De Credito
Bank of Mexico City, Mexico
P.O. Box N-4723
Branch: MGR Ronald C. Kern
Head Office: Intl & Corp Banking
Ing Miguel Alvarez Del Rio, Dpty Pres.
Phone (1-809) 322-81-34

2. BANKAMERICA TRUST AND BANKING CORPORATION (BAHAMAS)
Trust and Banking Company
Subsidiary of BankAmerica Corporation
San Francisco, CA, USA
BankAmerica House, East Bay St. P.O. Box N-9100
Estb: NR Member: NR Chairman: Tom Quigg
VP/Mng Dir: Trevor D.A. Sunderland Mgr: Robin A.C. Smith
Phone 809) 393-7411 Fax 809) 393-3030
Telex: 20-159 Cable: BATNASL

3. BANKERS TRUST COMPANY
Branch of New York (Manhattan) NY, USA
Claughton House
P.O. Box N-3234
Holding Company: Bankers Trust New York Corporation
New York City (Manhattan) NY, USA
Branch: MGR NR:
Head Office Chairman: Charles S. Sanford, Jr. Ceo
Phone: (809) 325-4107/8 Telex: 20262

4. BANK OF LONDON & MONTREAL
Bank of London & Montreal Limited, Joint Stock Bank
Bolam House, King & George Sts: P.O. Box N-1262
Ownership: Lloyds Bk Plc, London, United Kingdom
Management
Chairman: T.E.S. Hodgson
Senior Management: Mng. Dir. N.T. Simpson
Directors: T.E.S. Hodgson, Chmn; J.B. Galbraith
D.H. Drewery; N.T. Simpson
Principal Correspondents:
London Lloyds Bk Plc; New York Irving Trust Company
Phone: (809) 322-8711 Telex: NS 107 Cable: BOLAM
Estb: 1958 Member: NR

5. CHEMICAL BANK
Branch of New York City (Manhattan) NY, USA
Claughton House, Shirley St.
P.O. Box N-4944
Holding Company: Chemical New York Corporation
New York City (Manhattan) NY, USA
Head Office: Chairman Walter V. Shipley
Branch Manager: H. Peter Hensel, Agt.
Phone: (809) 322-1291 Telex: 20156
Cable: PROBANK

6. CITI TRUST BAHAMAS
Cititrust (Bahamas) Ltd.
Joint Stock Bank
President: Peter H. Page
Subsidiary of Citibank N.A. New York City
(Manhattan) NY, USA
Thompson Blvd at Oakes Field: P.O. Box N-1576
Phone: (809) 322-4240 Telex: 20153 Citibank
Cable: Cititrust Estb: NR Memb: NR

7. **FIRST INTERSTATE BANK**
   First Interstate Bank of California
   Branch of Los Angeles, CA, USA
   c/o P.O. 54191
   Los Angeles, CA, USA (90054)
   Holding Company: First Interstate Bancorp
   Los Angeles, CA, USA
   Manager: David F. Loretta, Svp.
   Phone: (800) 421-0163 Telex: 674886
   Cable: FICALBANK

8. **BANK OF BOSTON**
   First National Bank of Boston
   Branch of Boston, MA, USA
   Charlotte House, P.O. Box N-3930
   Holding Company: Bank of Boston Corporation
   Boston, MA, USA
   Head Office Chairman: William L. Brown
   President: Ira Stepanian, CEO
   Branch Manager: W. Bruce Fairchild, Pres.
   Phone: (809) 328-2750 Telex: 20189 BOS TRUST T

9. **LLOYDS BANK INTERNATIONAL (BAHAMAS)**
   Joint Stock Bank
   Bolam House, King & George Sts.
   P.O. Box N-1292
   Member: NR Estb.: NR
   Ownership: Lloyds Bank Pic., London, United Kingdom
   Management, Chairman: J.B. Galbraith
   Senior Management Dir/Prin Mgr.: N.T. Simpson
   Administration: J.R. Funes, Asst. Mgr.
   Directors: J.B. Galbraith, T.E.S. Hodgson
   D.H. Drewery, and N.T. Simpson
   Principal Correspondents: London Lloyds Bank Pic
   New York Irving Trust Company
   Phone: (809) 322-8711 Telex: 20107 BOLAM
   Cable: BOLAM

10. UNITED STATES TRUST COMPANY OF NEW YORK
Branch of New York City (Manhattan), NY USA
First Fl, Harrison Bldg., Marlboraugh Street
P.O. Box N-8327
Holding Company: U.S. Trust Corp. of New York City
(Manhattan), NY, USA
Head Office Chairman: Daniel P. Davison, CEO
President: H. Marshall Schwarz
Branch Mgr: NR
Phone: (809) 322-7461 Telex: 20-172

■BARBADOS

1. **BARCLAYS BANK PIC**
   Branch of London, United Kingdom
   Broad Street, P.O. Box 301
   Manager: K.L. Lewis
   Phone: (809) 429-5151 Telex: 2348 BARCLADOM WB
   Fax Phone: (809) 436-7957 Cable: BARCLADOM

2. **THE CHASE MANHATTAN BANK, N.A.**
   Branch of New York (Manhattan), NY, USA
   Neil and Broad Streets, P.O. Box 699
   Manager: David Da Costa
   Phone: (6) 1100 Telex: WB269 CHASEBANK BARBADOS
   Cable: CHAMANBANK BARBADOS

3. **THE ROYAL BANK OF CANADA (BARBADOS) LIMITED**
   Off-Shore Bank
   Subsidiary of RBC Bahamas Limited, Nassau, Bahamas
   Royal Bank House, Bush Hill, The Garrison
   P.O. Bag Service 1022, St. Michael
   Estb: 1981 Member: NR
   Ownership: The Royal Bank of Canada
   Montreal, Quebec, Canada
   Mng Dir: J. Ian Murray Dpty Mng Dir: R.L. Carter
   Prin Corr Montreal: Royal Bank of Canada; New York
   Manufacturers Hanover Trust Company
   Phone: (809) 429-5252 Fax: (809) 436-9675
   Telex: (386) 2459/2460 ROYSHORE ROYALOBU

4. **SCOTIABANK**
   The Bank of Nova Scotia
   Branch of Toronto, Ontario, Canada
   P.O. Box 202
   Manager: A.C. Allen, Area Mgr.
   Phone: (809) 426-0230 Fax: (809) 426-0969
   Telex: 2223

■BERMUDA

1.   THE BANK OF BERMUNDA LIMITED
Commercial Bank
6 Front Street, Hamilton HM II
Estb: 1860 Member: American Bankers Association
Wire Networks: S.W.I.F.T. BBDBMHM
Management Chairman: Eldon H. Trimingham
Head Office: The Bank of Bermuda Building
(same address as above) Mgr. Patricia M. Thorne
Phone: (809) (29) 5-4000 Telex: BA3212
Cable: BANCO BERMUDA

2.   THE BANK OF N.T. BUTTERFIELD & SON LTD.
Commercial Bank
65 Front Street, Hamilton, Bermuda
P.O. Box HM 195, Hamilton HM AX, Bermuda
Estb: 1858 Member: American Bankers Association
Washington, DC, USA
Bank Marketing Association, Chicago, IL, USA
Wire Networks: S.W.I.F.T. BNTB BMHM
Ownership: NA
Management Chairman: The Hon Sir David Gibbons, Kbe, Jp.
Phone: (809) 295-1111 (Genl), (809) 295-4880 (Forex)
Telex: 3211 FIELD BA (Genl), 3606 NTBFX (Forex)
Fax: (809) 292-4365 Cable: FIELD BERMUDA

3.   STANDARD CHARTERED TRUST COMPANY, LTD
Trust Company
P.O. Box HM 1735 (HM GX)
Estb: NR Member: NR
Ownership: Bank of NT Butterfield & Sons, Ltd. (60%)
Standard Chartered Trust Group Holdings Limited (40%)
General Management: Joint Mng Dirs: Stephen W. Kempe, VP
Michael P. Brogan; Off.: Kenneth W. Morgan, Trst. Off.
Intl Dept: NR Prin Corr: NR
Phone: (809-29) 5-1111 Fax: (809) 292-1258
Telex: BERMUDA 3211 Cable: FEILD BERMUDA

CAYMAN ISLANDS

1. **ALGEMENE BANK NEDERLAND, N.V.**
   Branch of Amsterdam, Netherlands
   c/o 335 Madison Ave., 16th and 17th Floor
   New York, NY, USA (10017)
   Branch Manager: NR
   Head Office Chairman: R. Hazelhoff
   Intl Dept: J.J. Oyevaar, Ch Genl Mgr.
   Telex: RCA 232445

2. **BFG: CAYMAN ISLANDS**
   BFG: Bank - Bank Fur Gemeinwirtschaft Aktiengesellschaft
   Branch of Frankfurt am Main, West Germany
   c/o BIG: New York, 400 Park Ave
   New York, NY, USA (IOp22)
   Branch Mgrs: Donald E. Culkin, SVP
   Heinrich P. Schmitz, SVP
   Head Office Chairman: Thomas Wegscheider
   Intl Dept: Wolfgang Muller, Genl Mgr.
   Phone: (212) 546-9000 Telex: 126250 BFG NY
   Cable: BANKWIRT NEWYORK

3. **CAYMAN INTERNATIONAL TRUST COMPANY, LTD.**
   Joint Stock and Trust Company
   Cayman International Trust Bldg.
   Albert Panton Street, P.O. Box 500
   Estb: 1973 Member: NR
   Ownership: Cayman National Corporation, Ltd.
   Management Chairman: Benson O. Ebanks
   President: Peter A Tomkins
   Directors: John C. Beirley
   Phone: (809) 949-4277 Fax: (809) 949-7506
   Telex: CP 4313 Cable: CAYNATBNK

4. **FIRST FIDELITY BANK**
   National Association, New Jersey
   Branch of Newark, NJ, USA
   Holding Company: First Fidelity Bancorporation
   Newark, NJ, USA
   Manager: NR

5. **FIRST INTERSTATE BANK**
First Interstate Bank of Oregon, N.A.
Branch of Portland, Oregon, USA
c/o 1300 S. W. Fifth Avenue
P.O. Box 3131, Portland, OR, USA (97208)
Manager: C. Acheson, SVP
S.W.I.F.T.: FIOR US 66
Phone: (503) 225-2512 Fax: (503) 225-2163
Telex: 160580 FIORE PTI Cable: MULTNOHAH

6. **MANUFACTURERS HANOVER BANK (DELAWARE)**
Branch of Wilmington, DE, USA
Bank of Nova Scotia Bldg, Cardinal Avenue
Holding Company: MHC Holding (Delaware), Inc.
Wilmington, DE, USA
Management: Paul Koehrsen, VP
Phone: (302) 428-3300 Telex: RCA 244984

7. **SCOTIABANK**
The Bank of Nova Scotia
Branch of Toronto, Ontario, Canada
P.O. Box 689
Management: W. Boyko
Phone: (809) 949-7666 Fax: (809) 949-7097
Telex: 4330

8. **UNITED STATES TRUST COMPANY OF NEW YORK**
Branch of New York City, NY, USA
P.O. Box 694
Branch Management: Douglas B. Gearhart
Holding Company: US Trust Corporation, New York City
(Manhattan), NY, USA
Head Of f ice Chairman: Daniel P . Davison, CEO
President: H. Marshall Schwarz
Phone: (809) 949-2126/7 Telex: CP254

9. **Washington INTERNATIONAL BANK AND TRUST, LTD.**
   Commercial Bank
   Wholly owned Subsidiary of the Bank of N . T .
   Butterfield & Son Limited, Hamilton, Bermuda
   Washington International Bank Bldg.
   Edward Street. P.O. Box 609
   Estb: 1967 Member: NA
   Management Chairman: Hon Sir David Gibbons, K.B.E., JP
   President: Nicholas J. Duggan VP: Grahame S.O. Howells
   Principal Correspondents: Frankfurt Am Main Citbank, NA
   London Barclays Bank Pic; Miami Southeast Bank, NA
   New York Irving Trust Company; Toronto, Toronto-Dominion
   Tokyo Irving Trust Company
   Phone: (809) 949-8144 Fax: (809) 949-7761
   Telex: CP 4214 Cable: WINBANK

■CHANNEL ISLANDS

1. **BANKAMERICA TRUST COMPANY (JERSEY) LIMITED**
Joint Stock Bank
Subsidiary of Bank of America National
Trust & Savings Association, San Francisco,
California, USA
Union House, Union street, P.O. Box 120
S.W.I.F.T.: BOFA GB 2U JER
Management Director: Anthony M. Robinson
Phone: (44-534) 74431 Fax: (44-534) 78546
Telex: 4192017 Cable: BAMTRUST

2. **BANKERS TRUST COMPANY**
Branch of New York City (Manhattan), NY, USA
West House, Peter Street
Holding Company: Bankers Trust New York Corporation
New York City (Manhattan), NY, USA
Branch Management: Michael J. Harmon, VP
Head Office Chairman: Charles S. Sanford, Jr., CEO
Phone: (0534) 79077 Telex: 4192364 BTCJER G
Cable: BTCOJER

3. **CHASE BANK & TRUST COMPANY (C.I.) LIMITED**
Joint Stock Bank
Chase House, Grenville Street
P.O. Box 127
Estb: 1966 Member: Jersey Bankers Association, St. Helier
S.W.I.F.T. CITI GB 2J
Holding Company: Chase Manhattan Overseas Banking Corp.
New York City, NY, USA (100%)
Management Chairman: David Gibson-Moore
Phone: (44-534) 25561 Fax: (44-534)35301
Telex: 4192209 Cable: CHASJY

4. CITIBANK (CHANNEL ISLANDS), LTD
Joint Stock Bank
Channel House, Green Street, P.O. Box 104
Estb.: 1968 Member: NR
Holding Company: Citibank NA, New York City
(Manhattan), NY, USA
S.W.I.F.T.: CITI GB 2J
Management Director: R.L. Mitchell
Phone: (44-534) 70707 Fax: (44-534) 72721
Telex: 4192313 Cable: CITI JERSEY

5. LLOYDS BANK TRUST COMPANY (CHANNEL ISLANDS),LTD
Joint Stock Bank
Subsidiary of Lloyds Bank Pic, London, United Kingdom
Waterloo House, Don Street, P.O. Box 195
Estb: 1947 Member: NR
Management Chairman: W.P. Plummer
General Management: M.G. Foster
Principal Corr.: London: Lloyds Bank Pic
Phone: (44-534) 27561 Fax: (44-534) 78986
Telex: 4192283

6. MIDLAND BANK TRUST CORPORATION (JERSEY) LIMITED
Trust Company, Commercial & Merchant Bank
28/34 Hill Street, P.O. Box 26
Ownership: Midland Bank Pic, London, United Kingdom
Management Chairman: S. Toker
General Manager: R.J. Moseley, Bnkg & City Mgr.
Phone: (0534) 37788 Fax: (0534) 74966
Telex: 4192098

7. MORGAN GUARANTY TRUST COMPANY OF NEW YORK
Branch of New York City (Manhattan), NY, USA
Queensway House, Queen Street
Holding Company: J.P. Morgan and Company, Inc.
New York City (Matthattan), NY, USA
Management: Edwin J. Perry
Phone: (44-534) 71566 Telex: 4192358/9
Cable: MORGANBANK

8. ANZ WORLDWIDE
Australia and New Zealand Banking Group (Channel Islands)
Joint Stock Bank
St. Julian's Ave; P.O. Box 153
Estb: NR
Member: Association of Guernsey Banks, International
Bankers' Association of Guernsey, St. Peter Port
Ownership: Australia and New Zealand Banking
Group Limited, Melbourne, Victoria, Australia
Management Chairman: D.G. Creasey
Management Director: K.P. Hazel
Phone: (0481) 26771 Telex: 4191663
Cable: ANZBANK

9. BARCLAYS FINANCE COMPANY (GUERNSEY) LIMITED
Wholly owned Subsidiary of Barclays Bank Pic.
London, United Kingdom
Cambria House, New Street; P.O. Box 269
Member: Association of Guernsey Banks,
St. Peter Port
Management: W. Allan & P.L. Griffiths
Phone: (44-481) 23223 Fax: (44-481) 712368
Telex: 4191629 BARFIN G
Cable: BARFINCO GUERNESY

10. MANUFACTURERS HANOVER TRUST COMPANY
Branch of New York City (Manhattan), NY, USA
Le Truchot; P.O. Box 230
Holding Company: Manufacturers Hanover Corporation
New York City (Manhattan), NY, USA
Head Office Chairman: John F. McGillicuddy, CEO
Branch Manager Keith W. Pamplin, VP
S.W.I.F.T. MAHA GG SP
Phone: (44-481) 23961 Fax: (44-481) 26734
Cable: MHTGSY G

▪HONG KONG

1. **AUSTRALIA AND NEW ZEALAND BANKING GROUP LIMITED**
   Branch of Melbourne, Victoria, Australia
   27th Floor, One Exchange Square,
   8 Connaught Pl Central
   Head Office Chairman: W.J. Bailey
   Branch Manager: N.J. Warnest,
   Phone: (5) 215511 Telex: 86019

2. **BANK OF CHINA**
   Branch of Beijing, China
   2 A, Des Voeux Road, Central: GPO Box 19
   Management: Zhang Xueyao, Genl Mgr
   C.T. Dong, Sr. Dpty Genl Mgr.
   Phone: (852Q5) 212626 Telex: 73772 BKCHI HX
   S.W.I.F.T.: BKCH HK HH Cable: CHUNGKUO HONGKONG

3. **THE BANK OF EAST ASIA, LIMITED**
   Commercial Bank
   10 Des Voeux Road Central: GPO Box 31
   Member: The Hong Kong Association of Banks, Hong Kong
   Ownership: Joint Stock Company
   Estb: 1918 S.W.I.F.T.: BEAS HK HH
   Management Chairman: Li Fook-Wo
   Phone: (852-5) 8423200 Fax: (852-5) 8459333
   Telex: 73017 BEASHI HX Cable: BANKASIA

4. **CHEKIANG FIRST BANK, LIMITED**
   Commercial Bank
   60 Gloucester Road, Wanchai & 5 Queen's Road
   Central: GPO Box 691
   Estb: 1950 Member: Hong Kong Association of Banks,
   Hong Kong Ownership: The Dai-Ichi Kangyo Bank, Ltd.
   Tokyo, Japan (95%), Goodwood Investment, Inc.(5%).
   Management Chairman: James Z.M. Kung, CEO
   S.W.I.F.T. CFHK HK HH
   Phone: (852-5) 8236400 Fax: (852-5) 8236456
   Telex: 73686 HX FIRST Cable: HONFIRST

5. **CITICORP INTERNATIONAL LIMITED**
    Merchant Bank & Licensed Deposit-Taking Company
    Subsidiary of Citicorp International Group-Delaware, USA
    26th Floor, Citicorp Crt, 18 Whiefield Road
    Causeway Bay; P.O. Box 38089
    Member: Association of International Bond Dealers
    Management: Group Executive: Philip B. Lassiter
    Phone: (852-5) 8305111 Telex: HX 74132
    Cable: CAPCORP

6. **FIRST INTERSTATE BANK OF ASIA LIMITED**
    Wholly owned Subsidiary of First Interstate Bank
    of California, Los Angeles, CA USA
    29th Floor One Exchange Sq. 8 Connaught Pl.
    Central: GPO Box 35
    Estb: 1973 Member: NR
    Management Director: John D. Harris
    Association Director: David Brennan
    Phone: (852-5) 8443500 Telex: 73052 FICAL HX
    Cable: FICAL BANK

7. **THE HONG KONG CHINESE BANK LIMITED**
    Commercial Bank
    61-65 Des Voeux Road, Central:
    P.O. Box 194
    Estb: 1954 Member: The Hong Kong Association of Banks,
    Hong Kong
    Ownership: Worthen Holdings (H.K.), Limited (99.73%)
    S.W.I.F.T.: HKCB HK HH
    Management Chairman: Mochtar Riady
    General Manager: Chack-Seung Au Yeung
    Principal Correspondents: Tokyo Irving Trust Company
    Hong Kong; Hongkong & Shanghi Banking Corporation
    Phone: (852-5) 8448833 Fax: (852-5) 8459221
    Telex: 73749 HONCH HX Cable: HONCHIBANK

8. HONG KONG AND SHANGHAI BANKING CORPORATION
Commercial Bank
1 Queen's Road Central: GPO Box 64
Estb: 1865 Member: Hong Kong Association of Banks,
Hong Kong; British Bankers Association, London
United Kingdom
Ownership: Numerous shareholders (less than 1% each)
Main City Branch: 1 Queen's Road Central:
GPO Box 64
Management Executive Directors: W. Purves, CBE,
DSO, Chmn
General Manager: P.E. Selway-Swift
Phone: (852-5) 8221111 Fax: (852-5) 8101112
Telex: 73201 HKBG HX Cable: HONGBANK

9. MITSUI BANK, LIMITED
Branch of Tokyo, Japan
41st Floor, Far East Finance Ctr.
16 Harcourt Road
Management: Yoshio Abe, General Mgr.
Phone: (5) 299611 Telex: 83413 MITBK HX

10. SECURITY PACIFIC ASIAN BANK, LIMITED
Commercial Bank
41-42 Fl. Jardine House, 1 Connaught Pl,
Central GPO Box 133
Estb: 1912 Member: Hong Kong Association of Banks
Chinese Banks Association, Hong Kong
Ownership: Security Pacific National Bank,
Los Angeles, CA, USA (99.9%)
Management Chairman: Ressel Fok
Subsidiaries: Hong Kong Canton Pacific Finance Ltd
Security Pacific Private Capital (Asia) Ltd.
Phone: (852-5) 8411811 Fax: (852-5) 8100027
Telex: 73471 SPABLHK Cable: SPABLHK

█LIECHTENSTEIN

1. BANK IN LIECHTENSTEIN AG
Commercial and Merchant Bank
Herrengasse 12 (9490); P.O. Box 85 (9490)
Estb: 1920 Member: Liechtenstein Bankers Association
and Swiss Bankers Association
Ownership: Prince of Liechtenstein Foundation (99.7%)
Management Chairman: Christian Norgren, Pres.
General Manager: Dr. Egmond Frommelt
Phone: (075)5 11 22 Fax: (075) 5 15 22
Telex: 88 92 22 S.W.I.F.T.: BLFL LI 22
Cable: BANK VADUZ

2. LIECHTENSTEINISCHE LANDESBANK
Universal Bank
Stadtle 44 (9490); P.O. 384 (9490)
Estb: 1861 Member: Swiss Bankers Association
Liechtenstein Bankers Association
Ownership: Liechtenstein Government
Management Chairman: Andreas Vogt
General Manager: Karlheinz Heeb
Phone: (075) 6 88 11 Fax: (075) 6 83 58
Telex: 88 94 00 S.W.I.F.T.: LILA LI 22
Cable: LANDESBANK

3. VERWALTUNGS - UND PRIVAT-BANK AKTIENGESELLSCHAFT
Commercial and Merchant Bank
P.O. Box 885 (FL-9490) (075) 5 66 55
Estb: 1956 Member: Liechtenstein Bankers Association
Swiss Bankers Association, Association of Swiss Stock
Exchanges
Ownership: More than 700 shareholders, mainly in
Liechtenstein
Management Chairman: Dr. Erich Seeger
General Manager: Dr. H. Heinz Batliner
Phone: (075) 26697 Fax: (075) 26697
Telex: 889200 S.W.I.F.T.: VPBV LI 22
Cable: PRIVATBANK

■LUXEMBOURG

1. **BANK OF AMERICA INTERNATIONAL S.A.**
   Commercial Bank
   35, Blvd Royal (L-2449)
   P.O. Box 435 (L-2014)
   Estb: 1971 Member: Association des Banques et Banquiers,
   Luxembourg; Association of International Bond Dealers
   Ownership: Bank of America National Trust and Savings
   Association, San Francisco, CA, USA (100%)
   Management Chairman: Glen Smith
   Management Director: Odon De Vienne
   Prin Corr: Johannesburg; Standard Bank of South Africa;
   London; Bank of America NT&SA; Montreal; Tokyo Fiji Bank
   Phone: (352) 20841 Fax: (352) 40785
   Telex: 2290 Cable: BNKAMERICA

2. **BANQUE DE LUXEMBOURG**
   Private Stock Bank
   80 Pl de la Gare; P.O. Box 2221 (1022)
   Estb: 1937 Member: Association des Banques et
   Banquiers, Luxembourg
   Ownership: Credit Industriel d'Alsace et de Lorraine,
   Deutsche Bank Compagnie Financiere, Deutsche Bk
   Saar AG
   Management Chairman: Gaston Zerr
   General Manager: Marc Weinand
   Phone: (352) 499241 Fax: (352) 494820
   Telex: 2449 BLLUXLU S.W.I.F.T.: BLUX LU LL
   Cable: BLUXLULL

3. **BANQUE GENERALE DU LUXEMBOURG**
   Commercial Bank
   14 rue Aldringen/27, Ave Monterey (L-2951)
   Estb: 1919 Member: Association des Banques et Banquiers,
   Association des Banques et Banquiers Luxembourgeois,
   Luxembourg
   Ownership: Generale Bank N.V. Brussels (44%)
   Luxembourg Public Ownership
   Phone: (352) 47991 Fax: (352) 47994388
   Telex: 3401 BGL LU S.W.I.F.T.: BGLL LU LL
   Cable: GENERALBANK LUXEMBURG

4. **BANQUE INTERNATIONALE A LUXEMBOURG**
    Commercial Bank
    2, Blvd Royal (L-2953); P.O. Box 2205 (L-2953)
    Estb: 1856 Member: Association des Banques et Banquiers
    Luxembourg (ABBL), Associated Banks of Europe
    (ABECOR), Brussels, Belgium
    Ownership: Groupe Bruxelles Lambert SA (20%)
    Pargesa SA (20%)
    Management Chairman: Gaston Thorn, Supv Bd
    Principal Correspondents: Boston; First National Bank
    of Boston: Brussels; BBL-BK Brussels Lambert SA
    Phone: (352) 4590-1 Fax: (352) 4590-2625
    Telex: 3626 BIL LU S.W.I.F.T.: BILL LU LL
    Cable: INTERNATIONALBANK

5. **BANQUE PARIBAS (LUXEMBOURG) S.A.**
    Commercial Bank
    IOA, Blvd Royal (2449): P.O. Box 51 (2010)
    Estb: 1964 Member: Association des Banques et
    Banquiers, Luxembourg
    Ownership: Group Paribas, Paris, France
    Management Chairman: Georges Bettermann
    Principal Correspondents: Brussels; Bque Paribas Belgium
    New York; Manufacturers Hanover Trust Company
    London; Manufacturers Hanover Trust Company
    Phone: (352) 4771911 Fax: (352) 470331
    Telex: 2332 PARIB LU Cable: PARIBAS LUX

6. **BFG: LUXEMBOURG, S.A.**
    Commercial Bank
    2 rue, Jean Bertholet (1011)
    P.O. Box 1123 (1233)
    Estb: 1973 Member: Association des Banques et
    Banquiers, Luxembourg
    Ownership: Bank fur Gemeinwirtschaft AG.
    Frankfurt am Main, West Germany (100%)
    President: Dr. Ralph Kruger
    Executive Mgr.: Dieter Feustel
    Phone: (352) 4522551 Fax: (352) 309
    Telex: 1415 BFG LU Cable: BANKWIRT

7. **CHASE MANHATTAN BANK LUXEMBOURG S.A.**
Joint Stock Bank
47, Blvd Royal (2449)
P.O. Box 240 (2012)
Estb: 1973 Member: Association des Banques et Banquiers
International Bankers Club, American Bankers Club,
Luxembourg
Ownership: Chase Manhattan Overseas Corporation (100%)
Management Chairman: David Gibson-Moore
Principal Correspondents: Brussels; Chase Manhattan Bank
Phone: (352) 4626581 Fax: (352) 35224590
Telex: 1233 LU Cable: CHAMANBANK

8. **THE FIRST NATIONAL BANK OF BOSTON**
Branch of Boston, MA, USA
41 Blvd, Royal
P.O. Box 209
Branch Management: Peter W. Gerrard
Head Office Chairman: Ira Stepanian, CEO
Holding Company: Bank of Boston Corporation
Boston, MA, USA
Phone: (352) 4779251 Telex: 2597 FNBBOSLU
Cable: THE FIRST BOSTON

9. **INTERNATIONAL TRADE AND INVESTMENT BANK S.A.**
Commercial Bank
22-24 Blvd Royal (2449)
P.O. Box 320 (2013)
Estb: 1973 Member: Association des Banques et
Banquiers, Luxembourg
Ownership: Middle East Financial Group Holding
S.A. (100%)
Management Chairman: Khalid Salim bin Mahfooz
Phone: (352) 26004 Fax: (352) 462829
Telex: 1350 Cable: ITIBLU

10. UNION BANK OF FINLAND INTERNATIONAL S.A.
Merchant Bank
189, Ave de la Faiencerie (L-1511)
P.O. Box 569 (L-2015)
Estb: 1976 Member: Association des Banques et
Banquiers, Luxembourg
Ownership: Union Bank of Finland, Ltd.,
Helsinki, Finland (100%)
Management Chairman: Kari Kangas
Director Chairman: Ahti Hirvonen
Phone: (352) 4776111 Fax: (352) 477611251
Telex: 1575 UBFIN LU S.W.I.F.T.: UBFI LU LL
Cable: UBFINLUX

PANAMA

1. **ALGEMENE BANK NEDERLAND, N.V.**
Branch of Amsterdam, Netherlands
Calle Manuel Maria Lcaza (4);
Apartado Postal 10147 (4 RP)
Branch Manager: P.H. Scharringa
Head Office: Chairman, R. Hazelhoff;
Intl Dept, J.J. Oyevaar, General Mgr.
Phone: (507) 63 -62 00 Telex: 2 644
Cable: BANCOLANDA

2. **BANCO DE SANTA CRUZ DE LA SIERRA (PANAMA) SA**
Commercial Bank
Avda Samuel Lewis, Edif Torre Bco Union, 11 Floor
Apartado Postal 6-4416, (El Dorado)
Estb: 1980 Member: Panama Banking Association
Panama City
Ownership: Sociedad de Inversiones Santa Cruz
de la Sierra, S.A. Panama City; Banco de
Santa Cruz de la Sierra, S.A. Santa Cruz, Bolivia
President: Juan Manuel Parada
General Manager: Luis Saavedra B.
Principal Correspondents: Buenos Aires, Bco de la
Provincia de Buenos Aires; New York, American Express
International, Chemical Bank, National Westminster Bank
Phone: (305) 63-8177 Fax: (305) 63-8401
Telex: 2613 BSCSAPG Cable: BANCRUZ

3. **BANCO POPULAR DEL ECUADOR (PANAMA), S.A.**
Commercial Bank
Calle 51 Bella Vista;
Apartado Postal 6-1061 (El Dorado)
Estb: 1981 Member: Associacion Bancaria de
Panama, Panama City
Ownership: Banco Popular del Ecuador, Quito,
Ecuador
Management Chairman: Francisco Rosales Ramos
General Manager: incolas Landes
Principal Correspondents: New York, Chase Manhlttan
Bank, N.A.; Quito, Bco Popular del Ecuador
Phone: (507) 69-1084 Telex: 2872 BANPOPAN PG

4. **BANK OF AMERICA NATIONAL TRUST & SAVINGS ASSOCIATION**
    Branch of San Francisco, CA, USA
    Edificio Bank of America, Calle 50 y Calle 53
    Apartado Aero 7282 (5)
    Manager: Roberto Anguizola, VP
    Phone: (507) 63-5500 Telex: 362756
    Cable: BNKAMERICA

5. **CHASE MANHATTAN BANK, N.A.**
    Branch of New York City (Manhattan) NY, USA
    120 Via Espana; Apartado Postal 9A-76
    Manager: Luis H. Moreno, Jr.

6. **THE FIRST NATIONAL BANK OF BOSTON**
    Branch of Boston, MA, USA
    Edif Bco de Boston, Via Espana
    Apartado Postal 5368 (5)
    Branch Manager: Luiz Navarro
    Head Office: Chairman, Ira Stepanian, Ceo
    President, Charles K. Gifford
    Holding Company: Bank of Boston Corporation,
    Boston, MA, USA
    Phone: (507) 64-2244/25 Telex: 328-3232
    Cable: BOSTON BANK

7. **MITSUI BANK, LIMITED**
    Branch of Tokyo, Japan
    Avda Ricardo Arango y Calle 53E, Urb Obarrio
    Apartado Postal 8-028 (8)
    General Manager: Yutaka Funazaki
    Phone: (507) 23-8802/6 Telex: TRT 2025

8. **BANK OF NOVA SCOTIA**
    Branch of Toronto, Ontario, Canada
    Edif Bonanza, Calle Manuel Maria Icaza
    Campo Alegre; Apartado Postal 7327 (5 R.P.)
    Manager: M.J. Gonzalez-Delgado
    Phone: (507) 63-6255 Fax: (507) 63-8636
    Telex: 207/3266

9. **UNION BANK OF SWITZERLAND (PANAMA), INC.**
   Commercial Bank
   Edif UBS, Calles 50 y 56;
   Apartado Postal 6792 (5)
   Estb: 1975 Member: Asociacion Bancaria de Panama,
   Panama City
   Ownership: Union Bank of Switzerland, Zurich,
   Switzerland
   General Management: Werner P. Luthi
   Principal Correspondents: Miami, Northern Trust Intl;
   New York, Irving Trust Company
   Phone: (507) 63-9766 Telex: 2645 UBSPG
   Cable: UBSPAN-BANKUNION

■SINGAPORE

1. ALGEMENE BANK NEDERLAND, N.V.
Branch of Amsterdam, Netherlands
18 Church Street (0104)
(Corr Address) 1 Maxwell Road;
P.O. Box 493 (9009)
Branch Managers: J. Slotema, H.J. Buss
Head Office Chairman: R. Hazelhoff
General Management: J.J. Oyevaar
Phone: (65) 5322664 Telex: RS 22081
Fax: (65) 5323108 Cable: BANCOLANDA

2. ASIA COMMERCIAL BANK LIMITED
Commercial Bank
60, Robinson Road (0106);
P.O. Box 1921 (9038)
Estb: 1959 Member: Association of Banks
in Singapore, Singapore
Ownership: Goh Cheng Liang Group (26.08%)
Overseas Union Bank Group (24.43%)
Management Chairman: Lee Hee Seng
Principal Correspondents: Hong Kong, Citibank
New York, Citibank; Tokyo, Overseas Ltd.
Phone: (65) 2228222 Telex: RS 21911
Fax: (65) 2253493 Cable: ASIABANKCO
S.W.I.F.T.: ACBK SG SG

3. FIRST INTERSTATE BANK OF CALIFORNIA
Branch of Los Angeles, CA, USA
5 Shenton Way, #23-00 UIC Bldg (0106)
Holding Company: First Interstate Bankcorp,
Los Angeles, CA, USA
Manager: George A. Khouri, VP
Phone: 255-6998 Telex: 21798 FICAL RS
Fax: 255-2850 Cable: FICALBANK
S.W.I.F.T.: FICAL SG SG

4. FIRST NATIONAL BANK OF BOSTON
Branch of Boston, MA, USA
20 Collyer Quay #16-oO
P.O. Box 2900 (9048)
Holding Company: Bank of Boston Corporation
Boston, MA, USA
Branch Manager: James F. Martin
Head Office Chairman: Ira Stepanian, Ceo
President: Charles K. Gifford
Phone: (65) 225-6088 Telex: BOSTNBK RS 23689
Cable: BOSTON BANK

5. MITSUI BANK, LIMITED
Branch of Tokyo, Japan
Hong Leong Bldg, 16 Raffles Quay,
#01-04 (0104)
General Management: Takefumi Abe
Phone: 2209761 Telex: RS 21319
Cable: MITSUBANK

6. OVERSEA-CHINESE BANKING CORPORATION LIMITED
Commercial Bank
65 Chulia Street, #08-00, OCBC Centre (0104)
P.O. Box 548 (9010)
Estb: 1932 Member: The Association of Banks
in Singapore, Singapore
Ownership: Selat (Pte) Ltd (9.25%)
The Great Eastern Life Assurance Company
Ltd (5.19%)
Management Chairman: Teo Cheng Guan, Ceo
Directors: Choi Siew Hong
Principal Correspondents: London, Midland
Bank Pic; New York, Chase Manhattan Bank
Tokyo, The Fuji Bank Ltd, Mitsubishi Bank
Sanwa Bank Ltd.
Phone: 535-7222 Telex: RS 21209 OVERSEA
Fax: 535-6007 Cable: OVERSEA SINGAPORE
S.W.I.F.T.: OCBC SG SG

7. **OVERSEAS UNION BANK LTD**
   Commercial Bank
   1 Raffles Place, OUB Center (0104)
   Estb: 1947 Member: The Association
   of Banks in Singapore, Singapore
   Ownership: Wah Hin & Co. (Pte), Ltd.
   (24.95%); Overseas Union Enterprise
   Limited, (12.82%); Overseas Union
   Bank Nominees Pte Ltd, (9.45%);
   Oversea-Chinese Bank Nominees Private
   Ltd. (5.22%)
   Management Chairman: Lien Ying Chow
   Directors: Lee Hee Seng
   Principal Correspondents: Hong Kong,
   Hongkong & Shanghai Banking Corp.
   Tokyo, Dai-Ichi Kangyo Bank Ltd
   Phone: 5338686 Telex: RS24475 OVERSBK
   Fax: 5332293 Cable: OVERUNION
   S.W.I.F.T.: OUBK SG SG

8. **THE BANK OF NOVA SCOTIA**
   Branch of Toronto, Ontario, Canada
   10 Collyer Quay, #15-01, Ocean Bldg (0104)
   Branch Manager: A Von Hahn
   Head Office Chairman: C.E. Ritchie, Ceo
   Phone: (65) 5358688 Telex: RS 22177 SCOSING
   Fax: (65) 5322440

9. **SECURITY PACIFIC ASIAN BANK, LIMITED**
   Branch of Hong Kong, Hong Kong
   6 Raffles Quay, #ol-lo Denmark House (0104)
   Phone: (65) 2243363 Fax: (65) 2256316

10. TAT LEE BANK LIMITED
Commercial Bank
63 Market Street, Tat Lee Bank Bldg (0104)
P.O. Box 5099, Robinson Road Post Office
Estb: 1973 Member: Association of Banks
in Singapore, Singapore
Ownership: Publicly owned
Management Chairman: Goh Tjoei Kok
Principal Correspondents: Hong Kong,
Standard Chartered Bank; Tokyo,
Baiwa Bank Ltd
Phone: (65) 5339292 Fax: (65) 5342821
Telex: RS 22248 TLBBIL (Genl)
Cable: TATLEEBANK S.W.I.F.T.: TLBS SG SG

■SWITZERLAND

1. **ALGEMENE BANK NEDERLAND (SUISSE)**
   Branch of Zurich
   12 quai General-Guisan; P.O. Box 39 (CH-1211/3)
   Ownership: Algemene Bank Nederland N.V.
   Amsterdam, Netherlands (86.4%); Bank Mees &
   Hope N.V., Amsterdam, Netherlands (10%);
   De Neuflize, Schlumberger, Mallet S.A., Paris
   France (3.6%)
   Management: Dr. Eugene M. Besnard, Dpty Genl Mgr.
   Phone: (022) 21 66 44 Fax: (022) 21 72 09
   Telex: 42 2662 ABNG CH Cable: GARDONA GENF

2. **CHASE MANHATTAN BANK (SWITZERLAND) S.A.**
   Commercial Bank
   63 rue du Rhone (CH-1204)
   P.O. Box 257 (CH-1211/3)
   Estb: 1969 Member: Swiss Bankers' Association,
   Basel; Association of Foreign Banks in Switzerland,
   Zurich
   Holding Company: Chase Manhattan Overseas Banking Corp.
   Management Chairman: Robert D. Hunter
   General Manager: William M. Rowan
   Phone: (022) 35 35 55 Fax: (022) 36 24 30
   Telex: 28121 Cable: CHAMANBANK GENEVA

3. **CITIBANK, N.A.**
   Branch of New York City, (Manhattan), NY, USA
   16 quai General Guisan (CH-1211)
   P.O. Box 162 (CH-1204)
   Phone: (022) 20 55 16 Telex: 27479
   Cable: CITIBANK

4. KREDIETBANK (SUISSE) S.A.
Commercial Bank
7, Blvd georges-Favon (CH-1204)
P.O. Box 334 (CH-121/1)
Estb: 1970 Member: Swiss Bankers' Association
Basel; Association of Foreign Banks in
Switzerland, Zurich
Ownership: Kredietbank SA Luxembourgeoise,
Luxembourg
Management Chairman: Jean L. Blondeel
General Manager: Robert Iselin
Phone: (41 22) 21 36 22 Fax: (41 22) 21 54 43
Telex: 427303 KBS CH Cable: KREDIETGEN

5. MANUFACTURERS HANOVER (SUISSE) S.A.
Merchant Bank
6, rue d'italie (CH-1204)
P.O. Box 723 (CH-1211/3)
Estb: 1982 Member: Association Suisse des Banquiers,
Basel
Holding Company: Manufacturers Hanover International
Holdings Corporation (100%)
Management Chairman: Michael J. Neilson
Phone: (41 22) 21 00 44 Fax: (41 22) 21 01 48
Telex: 421 239 MHS CH Cable: MH SUISSE

6. BANCO BILBAO VIZCAYA (SUISSE) S.A.
Commercial & Investment Bank
Todistrabe 60 (CH-8039)
P.O. Box 1024
Estb: 1984 Ownership: Banco Bilbao, Spain (100%)
Management Chairman: Emilo De Ybarra
Phone: (41 1) 202 65 00 Fax: (41 1) 201 30 08
Telex: 817615

7. BANK HOFMANN AG ZURICH
Commercial & Stock Exchange Bank
Talstrabe 27 (CH-8001)
Estb: 1897 Member: Zurich Stock Exchange,
Zurich, Swiss Bankers' Association, Basel
Ownership: Credit Suisse, Zurich,
Switzerland, (100%)
Management Chairman: Dr. William Wirth
General Manager: Arthur Pfenninger
Principal Correspondents: London, Barclays
Bank Plc; New York, Chase Manhattan Bank;
Chemical Bank, Citibank, Cr. Suisse, Irving
Trust Company, Morgan Guaranty Trust Co.
Phone: (01) 211 57 60 Fax: (01) 211 73 68
Telex: 813485 Cable: HOFMANNBANK ZURICH

8. HABIB BANK A G ZURICH
Commercial Bank
Bergstrabe 21 (CH-8044)
P.O. Box 4931 (CH-8022)
Estb: 1967 Member: Association of Foreign
Banks in Switzerland, Zurich; Swiss Bankers'
Association, Basel
Management Chairman: Richard Schait
General Management: Hyder M. Habib
Principal Correspondents: Amsterdam,
Amsterdam-Rotterdam Bank NV
London, Habbib Bank AG Zurich
Phone: (01) 252 43 75 Fax: (01) 252 43 75
Telex: 815151 Cable: HABIBBANK ZURICH

9. **ROYAL TRUST BANK (SWITZERLAND)**
   Investment & Merchant Bank
   Limmatquai 8 (CH-8024)
   Estb: 1965 Member: Association of Foreign
   Banks in Switzerland, Zurich, Swiss Bankers'
   Association, Basel
   Ownership: Royal Trust Company Limited,
   Toronto, Ontario, Canada (86%);
   Publicly owned (14%)
   Management Chairman: Hartland M Macdougall
   General Manager: Martin a Murbach
   Phone: (01) 250 91 11 Fax: (01) 252 79 40
   Telex: 816 069 RTB CH S.W.I.F.T.: RTBS CH
   Cable: ROYALTRUST ZURICH

10. **ZURCHER KANTONALBANK**
   State-owned Universal Bank
   Bahnhofstrabe 9 (CH-8022)
   P.O. Box 4039 (CH-8022)
   Estb: 1869 Member: Swiss Bankers' Association
   Association of Assis Cantonal Banks
   Ownership: Canton of Zurich (100%)
   Management Chairman: B. Schurch
   Phone: (41 1) 220 11 11 Fax: (41 1) 211 65 39
   Telex: 812 140 ZKB CH Cable: KANTONALBANK
   S.W.I.F.T.: ZKBK CH ZZ 80A

Index

A

Accumulated Earnings Tax 148
Advertising
   image 193
   recruitment 198
Advisors
   important qualities 189
Mohamed Al-Fayed 40
American Express 92
Annuities and endowments 255
Arbitrage 104
Art
   investment in 41
Aruba 205, 207
Assets
   police confiscation of 162
AT&T
   international 800 service 63
Attorneys
   selecting 265
Australia 75

B

Bahamas 208
James Baker 219
Bank of Boston 27
Bank Secrecy Act 116
Banking
   acquiring your own bank 99
   benefits of offshore banks 90
   cash management 104
   commercial 30
   computerized 181
   confidentiality policies 121
   deposits in international private banks 38
   investment portfolios 90
   Japanese laws 48
   lending rates 101
   letters of credit 79, 101
   protecting records 125
   required services 90
   secret numbered accounts 103
   wholesale 205
Barbados 210

Ravi Batra 11
Bear Stearns 76
Bermuda 211
Bonds
    bought by Japanese 20
    junk 21
    municipal 139
Boston
    economic condition 26
    tax collections 26
British Virgin Islands 52, 170, 212
Harry Browne 81
George Bush 17
Businesses
    international acquisitions of 71

C

Canada
    stock market 74
Jimmy Carter 15
Cayman Islands 213
Channel Islands 51, 214
Chase Manhattan 19, 152
China 216
Citicorp 52, 204
Coca-Cola 54
Commodities brokerage 103
Controlled Foreign Corporation Tax 147
Currency exchange 103

D

Debt
    foreign 17
Donoghue's Mutual Funds Almanac 195
Dow Jones Industrial Average 85
Dresdner Bank AG 53

E

Equifax 111
European Community
    size of 75

F

Fair Credit Reporting Act 123
Family income 16
FBI

accuracy of records 114
Federal Reserve 23
Financial centers
  use in Japan 45
Financial consultants 190
Financial Privacy Act 118
Howard S. Fisher 155
Float time 93
Foreign Asset Protection Trust 170
Foreign Investment Company Tax 149
Foreign Personal Holding Company Tax 147

G

David Glasner 179
Global diversification 86
GNP 62
Alan Greenspan 23
Aldo Gucci 150

H

Haiti
  divorce laws 44
Mitsuyo Hanada 46
Hong Kong 215

I

Institute of Bankers 203
Insurance
  captive insurance companies 49, 98
Investment
  in art 41
Iran-Contra scandal 183
Ireland 54
IRS
  audit flags 114
  auditors hired 140
  files maintained 111
  paper corporation claims 98

J

Japan
  bond dumping 20
  economic miracle 44
  involvement in Panama 47
  stock market 85, 95

Arthur Johnson 74
Joint relationships 163

L

Latin America 76
Lawsuits
    personal injury 159
Liechtenstein 216
Living trusts 168
Luxembourg 217

M

Malta 43, 44
Ferdinand Marcos 184
Metromedia 65
George D. Moffett III 35, 48
Monaco 53, 54
Money Laundering and Drug Control Act 118
Moscom Inc. 112
Municipal bonds 139
Rupert Murdoch 65
Mutual funds 106

N

Netherlands Antilles 218
New Zealand 75
Ted Nicolas 194
Manuel Noriega 48, 184, 221

O

Offshore banks
    benefits of owning 102
    float time 93
    interest rates 92
    opening an account 90, 257
    purchasing 260
Offshore corporation
    advantages of 97
Offshore investment
    benefits to local governments 42
    by pension funds 67
    development of 39
    information on 78
    legal requirements 196
    money havens 37
    myths about 182

    potential customers 39
    privacy benefits 124
    proliferation of opportunities 39
    selecting an advisor 189
Orient Leasing Co. 49

P

Pacific Rim 96
Panama 184, 220
    Japanese involvement 47
Richard Pascale 195
Passive Foreign Investment Company 149
Passive income 137
Pension funds 67
Pepsi-Cola 54
Personal Holding Company Tax 149
Privacy
    fourth-amendment protections 109
    government files 111
    informational privacy 116
    telephone monitoring 112
Private International Corporations 259
Private international investment company 73

R

Ronald Reagan 15, 17, 22
Real estate
    controlled by rich 25
Reference books
    on offshore investment 195
Regulation
    banking 91
Robert Reich 20
R.M. Rodnick 71

S

S&L bailout 20
Safety deposit companies 97
Secrecy 207
William Simon 66
Singapore 205
Adam Smith 201, 225
Stocks 94
    Canadian 74
    crash of 1987 24
    U.S. share of world market 60
Switzerland 222

T

Tax shelters 144
Taxes
    avoidance vs. evasion 143
    capital gain 137
    federal rate 16
    in Monaco 53
    in New Zealand 75
    rates 136
    tax reform 134
    top rate 22
    withholding on interest 142
Donald Trump 21
Trusts 104, 166
    foreign 255
    irrevocable 173
    living·168
TRW 111
Twin accounts 93, 258

U

United States
    Commerce Department 61
    Congress 23
    Constitution 109
    debtor status 16
    GNP vs. rest of world 62
    recession 21, 32

V

Vanuatu 223

W

WFI Corporation
    approach 267
    services 268
Written communications
    tips on 192

Keep Abreast of the Latest In Offshore Banking News!

The world of international banking, investment and finance is constantly changing -- and those changes can greatly affect your interests as the holder of a foreign bank account. Fortunately, there's a **really simple** way to keep abreast of the latest in offshore banking news. All you have to do is become a subscriber to *Jerome Schneider's Offshore Moneyletter* -- America's most-respected monthly publication on the subjects of international banking, offshore investment, privacy and tax protection.

Now, you can save almost 60%...

A regular subscription to this exciting and informative publication normally costs $94 per year. However, as a special offer being made only to purchasers of *Jerome Schneider's Complete Guide To Offshore Money Havens*, you can now receive a full year of the *Offshore Moneyletter* for just $47 -- **50% off the normal subscription price**. And, if you sign up for two years, you'll receive an even better deal -- 24 full issues for just $80. *That's a savings of almost 60% over the regular subscription price!*

To take advantage of this special offer, just fill out the coupon below and send it, along with your check for either $47 (one year) or $80 (two years), to:

> *Jerome Schneider's Offshore Moneyletter,*
> WFI Corporation
> 357 S. Robertson Blvd.
> Beverly Hills, CA 90211

Or, if you want to ensure that you get the very next monthly issue of this valuable newsletter, call **1-800-421-4177** toll-free and order your subscription using your Visa, MasterCard, American Express or Discover card. *Don't delay! The information you get today could save you money tomorrow!*

YES! I want to receive my own personal copy of *Jerome Schneider's Offshore Moneyletter* each month for:

☐ One Year at $47   ☐ Two Years at $80

Name: _____

Street: _____

City: _____ State: _____ ZIP: _____

Phone: _____

☐ My check is enclosed
☐ Please bill my: ☐ Visa ☐ M.C. ☐ Am. Express ☐ Discover

Acct. No.: _____ Exp. Date: _____

Signature: _____